AF598437

SLOW LEARNERS

Woburn Educational Series

General Editor:
Peter Gordon, Institute of Education, University of London

Games and Simulations in Action
Alec Davison & Peter Gordon

The Education of the Gifted Child
David Hopkinson

Slow Learners: A Break in the Circle
Diane Griffin

The Middle School – High Road or Dead End?
John Burrows

Music in Education
Malcolm Carlton

SLOW LEARNERS
A Break in the Circle

A Practical Guide for Teachers

DIANE GRIFFIN

THE WOBURN PRESS

First published 1978 in Great Britain by
THE WOBURN PRESS
Gainsborough House, Gainsborough Road
London, E11 1RS, England

and in the United States of America by
THE WOBURN PRESS
c/o Biblio Distribution Centre,
81 Adams Drive, P.O. Box 327, Totowa, N.J. 07511

ISBN 0 7130 0137 2 (Cased)
ISBN 0 7130 4003 3 (Paper)

Printed in Great Britain by
Chapel River Press, Andover, Hampshire

ACKNOWLEDGMENTS

I should like to thank the following people for their contributions.

All of them were at the time of writing practising teachers, putting into operation the suggestions and ideas made in this book.

Carole Goodwin, Sheffield L.E.A. Schools Psychology Service – Diagnosis; Barry Chisholm, University of Sheffield, Psychology Course, Sylvia Burns, Countesthorpe College, Research Department – Mathematics; Keith Milner, Liverpool College – Drama; Bill Brindamour, University of Connecticut – Social Services; Peter Hendra, Bowthorpe Comprehensive School – School Organisation.

FURTHER ACKNOWLEDGMENTS

'Lazlo At Parents' Night' reprinted from Kenneth J. Weber: *Yes They Can*, by permission of Methuen Publications, a division of the Carowell Company Ltd., 2330 Midland Avenue, Agincourt, Ontario, Canada. Routledge and Kegan Paul (and Humanities Press, U.S.A.) for permission to quote from A. E. Tansley: *Reading and Remedial Reading*, and E. J. Arnold & Son for permission to quote from A. E. Tansley's Sound Sense Books.

Treehouse Associates, Great Barrington, Mass. for permission to use an abridged version of the list of books and materials from Weiss: *A Survival Manual – Case Studies and Suggestions for the Learning Disabled Teenager*.

Centre for the Teaching of Reading, University of Reading, for permission to quote from Elizabeth Goodacre: *Different Types of Reading Methods* and Colin Macpherson: *Teaching Non-Readers*. Also Centre for Teaching of Reading.

And the following pupils for their enthusiasm and cooperation: Jenny Bowles – *Diary of Edith*; Jenny Wooley – *People That Matter*; Debby Smalley and Judith Jones – *Children's Xmas Party*.

Many thanks to Dorothy Clark for all her help and advice and for typing the manuscript.

'I'd be surprisingly good for you'

CONTENTS

GLOSSARY

Newsom – A government commission report entitled *Half our Future*. The Chairman was Sir John Newsom and this report on the non-academic child, commonly known as The Newsom Report, was published in 1963 by Her Majesty's Stationery Office.
Plowden – A government commission report into primary education published in 1966 by Her Majesty's Stationery Office. The commission was chaired by Lady Plowden and is commonly known as The Plowden Report.
Underwood Report – A government commission report on maladjusted children first published in 1955, available from Her Majesty's Stationery Office.
11+ or Eleven Plus – The age at which children, at the end of their primary school education, are selected (usually by examination) for various types of secondary school.
'O' level – Ordinary Level General Certificate of Education – a series of examinations taken at the end of the 5th year of secondary school education. Necessary for entry into most further and higher educational institutions.
'A' level – Advanced level of the General Certificate of Education. Taken at eighteen years or over. The normal means of entry into University.
C.S.E. – Certificate of Secondary Education, originally intended for children for whom 'O' level was deemed unsuitable. Edges have become blurred since then. A grade 1 C.S.E. normally is considered to be equal to the lowest grade of 'O' level pass.
I.Q. – Intelligence quotient.
R.A. – Reading age.
I.A. – Interest age.
Thickies, Dummies, Backwards – Slang terms used to describe children in the bottom stream.
R.O.S.L.A. – Raising of the school leaving age from 15-years-old to 16-years-old, from 1973.
E.W.O. – Education Welfare Officer. Employed by the local education authority. Their job used to be primarily to bring absentees or truants into schools – much changed recently, with a greater emphasis on welfare.
L.E.A. – Local education authority.
L.D. – 'Learning Disabled'. In the U.S.A. some slow learners are called 'L.D. kids'.

INTRODUCTION

The expression, 'slow learners' is one which I have, over the past few years, tried to persuade teachers to disregard. I believe that it is a misleading name. There is a great need to look at what and how children learn rather than how they can be made to conform to the teacher's expectations. I have been persuaded, however, that the subtitle on its own would be meaningless. To those many teachers with whom I have discussed this point, my apologies.

In the case of slow learners the first and most critical thing to do is to recognise that children are individuals and then to break the circle of failure they expect to tread. All the ideas and suggestions in this book, therefore, are governed by this belief.

Each chapter is self-contained in so far as it can be read by itself and as a reference if a teacher or parent is meeting a particular difficulty in that field. Some chapters are pertinent to both primary and secondary school teachers, some, more to one age group than another, but all are related. The appendices are itemised separately so that their information may be used on its own.

All the materials, ideas and suggestions, are from practising teachers and have been, or are being at the present time, used in schools. They have all been used with some degree of success and the opinions of the pupils who have worked from them have been taken into consideration. It is not intended to imply that success is possible all the time. Failure is a fact of life that we all have to come to terms with. The book does try to show, however, that some success can be achieved by everyone and that everyone has a chance. School so often fails the present generation, most especially those who do not meet with academic success. If we are to prevent the overwhelming feeling of helplessness and failure which many youngsters feel on leaving school, then we must change our attitudes and our curriculum. Some of the ideas outlined in this book attempt to do that.

CHAPTER 1

THE NEEDS OF SLOW LEARNERS AS INDIVIDUALS

What is a slow learner?

Any book about slow learners must first try to define what a 'slow learner' is. The term 'slow learner' is generally regarded in a derogatory sense. Slow to learn what? In most cases the slow learner is so described because he fails to learn at the same rate as the majority of other pupils learn. He fails to learn, in an academic setting, what teachers feel he should learn. He is not slow at covering up a depressing home situation, or a particular learning difficulty, or the fact that his father is in prison. It is usually the reverse. He is very adept at covering up things of that nature.

Most teachers have had experience of slow learners at some time or another, and the new teachers are warned before they begin of the terrible problems that they will encounter with 'slow learners', or 'Newsom Children' or 'Rosla Children' or the 'Backward Class'. This group of pupils, rarely seen as individuals, but lumped together in uncomplimentary terms as though some particular breed, are of course individuals. They are individuals who need even greater care and understanding than most. They should not be thought of or treated as third-class citizens to be tolerated and occupied, or even worse, 'to be held in check and tightly controlled'.

The only thing they have in common is that by the time they reach secondary school they are all seen, by themselves, by their parents, by teachers and by other students as *failures*. The cause of their failure may be due to many reasons; an apparent or non-apparent physical handicap; a congenital defect; a disruptive and stressful home situation; material or emotional deprivation; a serious conflict with school or a teacher early in their school career; or intellectual lethargy. Whatever the cause, the slow learner has become accustomed to failure. Indeed he expects to fail.

Breaking the circle of failure

The expectation of failure is a vicious circle. Most slow learners, because they see themselves as failures, don't really try hard. After all, whatever they do will be of no use, so why bother to do anything? The most important problem to solve when dealing with slow learners is to find a way to overcome their negative attitude to themselves and their feelings of lack of self-worth. The only way to do this is to foster individual relationships and to cater for the needs of each student as an individual: to know and to care – to recognise the problems – to encourage and persuade – to find a way towards a solution, and mutually rejoice at success.

What are the objectives? Where do we start?

> The most we can hope to do is to help every individual to realise all his potentialities and become completely himself. (Aldous Huxley)

Before the teacher can begin to do anything to help the slow learners he must analyse their needs in an honest and realistic way – the needs that they have now, and those they will have in the future. Is it desirable, or necessary, for them to cover the same, or a watered-down version of the syllabus of the rest of the school? Will an end-result of a grade 5 C.S.E. be worth the effort? Will that kind of learning give them the ability to work at a problem and be able to solve it? The future is uncertain for all of us. Attitudes and demand are changing rapidly. But we do know that whatever is in store, the slow learners, in common with everyone else, will have to *think*. They will have to understand, make judgments, make decisions. They will have to *feel*, cope with emotions, upheavals, love and hate. They will need a positive attitude to life. To accept these as their needs, means that we, as teachers, must be prepared to direct our teaching towards the needs of the individual pupil and the development of that pupil. "Help them to feel confident and they will become socially competent; help them to think and they will solve their problems; help them to understand and they will understand themselves." (Kenneth J. Weber)

Motivation – a prime factor

One thing is certain. By the time the slow learner reaches secondary school, a prime factor in his learning will be 'motivation'. The desire to learn to read or paint or sing or do experiments in science will depend very much on the pupil's own wish to take part in an activity. This, in turn, wll depend on the degree of success he expects to achieve, and the relevance to his own life that he feels the task offers. Very often the only way of reversing the pattern of reluctance to attempt a task depends on the strength of a relationship. It is not possible for a teacher to go into a class and immediately establish a meaningful relationship. It is possible, however, to approach a class of slow learners without fear or prejudice. Some 'bottom stream' classes wait for the new teacher to indicate that he knows they are the 'thickies'. They accept this as true themselves, so why shouldn't the new teacher? It should not be surprising, therefore, if they act 'thick' either by passively showing no interest in anything or by behaving disruptively and noisily. Quite often they work hard to bring about what they feel is the normal state, the state of conflict!

What does a new teacher do when confronted with this situation? The only viable thing to do is to be honest, to say, 'Look, I believe you are all individuals, all different and all important. I want to get to know you, to find out what you are good at and to learn with you.' It is my experience that most pupils instinctively recognise a sincere teacher and do respond to that kind of approach.

Mutual trust

It is important, of course, for the teacher to then start proving that he genuinely cares and to begin to build an atmosphere of mutual trust. How can this be done?

a) By being well organised, i.e., having planned and prepared a variety of suitable material whereby each pupil is certain of success.
b) By showing a willingness to take the pupil's own interests as a starting point.
c) By acknowledging the cultural difference as present and important and welcoming whatever the pupil contributes.
d) By taking careful notice of what the pupil produces and clearly indicating in some way, such as a fairly long written comment, or verbal discussion, that you have read and appreciated it. (B+, or Well done, or Improved, is meaningless.)

These are first steps in building up a relationship and are vital. The desire to please each other offers a strong motivational force. There must be empathy, trust and acceptance.

The role of the teacher

> 'There is no such thing as competence without love.' (John Dewey)

The role of the teacher is important. It would be wrong to read for 'good relationships', 'putting up with anything'. The teacher who tries to fulfil every pupil's whim, to sublimate his own desire completely, is setting up an unreal situation and preventing the development of the pupil. The relationship needs to be of the kind where neither the teacher nor the student has pre-eminence. It should be one where the roles are interchangeable, and each recognises the special position and value of the other. The teacher needs to act as a guide to the pupil, to help to direct his learning. This cannot be done successfully unless the teacher knows the pupils well and learns with them. In practice, this kind of role is much more difficult, if not impossible, if one teacher sees a pupil for specialist subjects and another teacher sees him for pastoral purposes. The two roles cannot be separated. Therefore, if a teacher is to establish a successful relationship he must spend a considerable amount of time with the same group of pupils. This can be done, as can be seen by looking at what happens in many infant and primary schools. Secondary schools, too, need to rethink their priorities.

If a relationship gets off to a reasonable start it can often be helped by getting out of the school environment. A swimming trip, a picnic, helping with a new garden, babysitting, a shared cinema visit, community work. All these activities reinforce the positive element of trust. They not only have the value of adding something to the relationship between pupil and teacher, but show to a peer group that the student can be trusted and successful and his company enjoyed; that teacher and pupil are learning together. It starts to make a chink in the circle of perpetual failure.

The role of the peer group

The role of the peer group also plays an important part in motivation. Usually a group has formed because of something they have in common. In the case of slow learners the thing they have in common is 'failure'; academic failure, emotional failure, physical failure, quite often judged by others a failure to reach the same material standard. They cover up by being introverted, withdrawn; no one speaks much to them. Conversely they can be noisy and difficult; everyone is afraid of them; they are on the defensive and everyone is condescending towards them. They will tell you, 'We're the dummies. We're the thickies.' They reinforce in each other their own belief in their uselessness but a success or trust situation can counteract these feelings. They unconsciously think that if one of their number is trusted, is successful, then maybe they could be too.

The role of the parent

The parent of the slow learner can be placed into many categories: the over-protective, the over-permissive, the wilfully neglectful, or, in the case of handicapped pupils, bewildered, hurt and overworked. Some parents find it impossible to understand why their child is 'slow'. Public attitudes are quickly conveyed to the parents of slow learners or 'bottom stream pupils'. Tolerance and acceptance of people's difficulties is still seriously lacking even with today's more liberal attitudes. Parents are greatly affected by public attitudes and subconsciously reflect these feelings and project them towards their own child. The Plowden Report produces evidence to show that as much as 24 per cent variation in a child's performance can be accredited to the amount of help or lack of help that parents contribute. In a summary of an experiment the Plowden Report shows that when attempts were made to influence parental behaviour, improvement was most marked among the least able children. It follows from this then, that every effort should be made to involve parents in any way possible.

It should be remembered and accepted that many parents of slow learners are themselves the victims of unhappy school experiences. If not actually anti-teacher, then they are 'afraid of teacher'. It is highly likely that they bear a reluctance to come to school, especially on formal Parents' Evenings, where they might be afraid of being an object of shame, or they might be just nervous. To counteract this, it is necessary for the teacher to go to the home, or the club or the pub. An anxious mother is far more likely to feel secure in her own home, thereby responding more openly to genuine discussion than she would if perched on the edge of a hard chair in the school library. Father will relax far more in his local over a pint of beer and therefore will be far more likely to commit himself to some kind of constructive help towards his child. Once the initial barriers have been broken down then it becomes easier to draw the parents into the school occasionally. When pupils are about to be transferred to a new school the opportunity arises to put into practice some kind of plan to set up good teacher/parent relationships. Some of the following could provide a basis:

a) Getting to know the school – a preliminary visit and opportunity for the parent to meet the form teacher or tutor who will spend the greatest amount of time with a particular pupil.

b) Open school – that is the kind of atmosphere whereby parents are always welcomed and feel able to drop in.

c) Home visits for parents who are reluctant to come near the school.

d) A newsletter or some other means whereby parents can be kept in touch with what is happening in the school. It is important that a newsletter for this purpose should be informal, friendly and easy to understand.

e) Meaningful reports avoiding at all costs the Fair, Tried hard, B+, technique.

f) Give simple advice to parents wanting to help their children, e.g.

'Try to hear your child read for about ten minutes each day.' 'Praise him frequently for what he does accomplish'. 'Give him somewhere special to keep his work'.

If we are to get the best from the pupil then we must aim to break down the reserve and build up informal and friendly relationships not only with him, but with his parents.

The classroom environment

The environment plays an important part in bringing about a change of attitude in slow learners towards school. For most, the traditional classroom – rows of desks, hard chairs, blackboard and chalk, and an imposing teacher's desk – holds few pleasant memories and sets the scene for rigidity and inflexibility. Ideally, a complete change of scenery is desirable and if the opportunity allows, using what always proves to be the not inconsiderable talents of the students themselves to bring about this change, it is wholly beneficial. The room could be decorated; old furniture bought and renovated and a small coffee unit built in one corner, a work area in another, a leisure-cum-reading area, a practical area (see diagram).

This, if done imaginatively, can be accomplished for very little cost and provides the basis for giving a sense of identity. It is surprising what local firms will donate if approached personally and it is comparatively easy to persuade people to part with old upholstered suites and chairs. Secondhand carpets can be obtained for about £10 and are well worth the money for the extra feeling of comfort and pleasantness they can bring to a room. If the ideal cannot be achieved because of the inflexible structure of the school, then at least the existing furniture moved around will help break away from the traditional rows. Everything possible should be done to individualise the room and provide within it clearly defined areas.

It is important to have within a room as much display space as possible in order to show the students' own work and to hold frequently changed displays of things which interest them. Initially, it may be necessary for the teacher to mount these displays but it has certainly been my experience that in time the pupils themselves ask to take this job over and they get a lot of satisfaction out of so doing.

Devising some system whereby pupils can make coffee and sit and drink it in reasonably pleasant surroundings is well worthwhile. It not only relaxes the atmosphere but provides a stimulus for talk. I believe that it is inexcusable to turn adolescent slow learners out into a playground during breaks and lunch times. These are the times when they feel most insecure and tend to get taunted or

Diagram

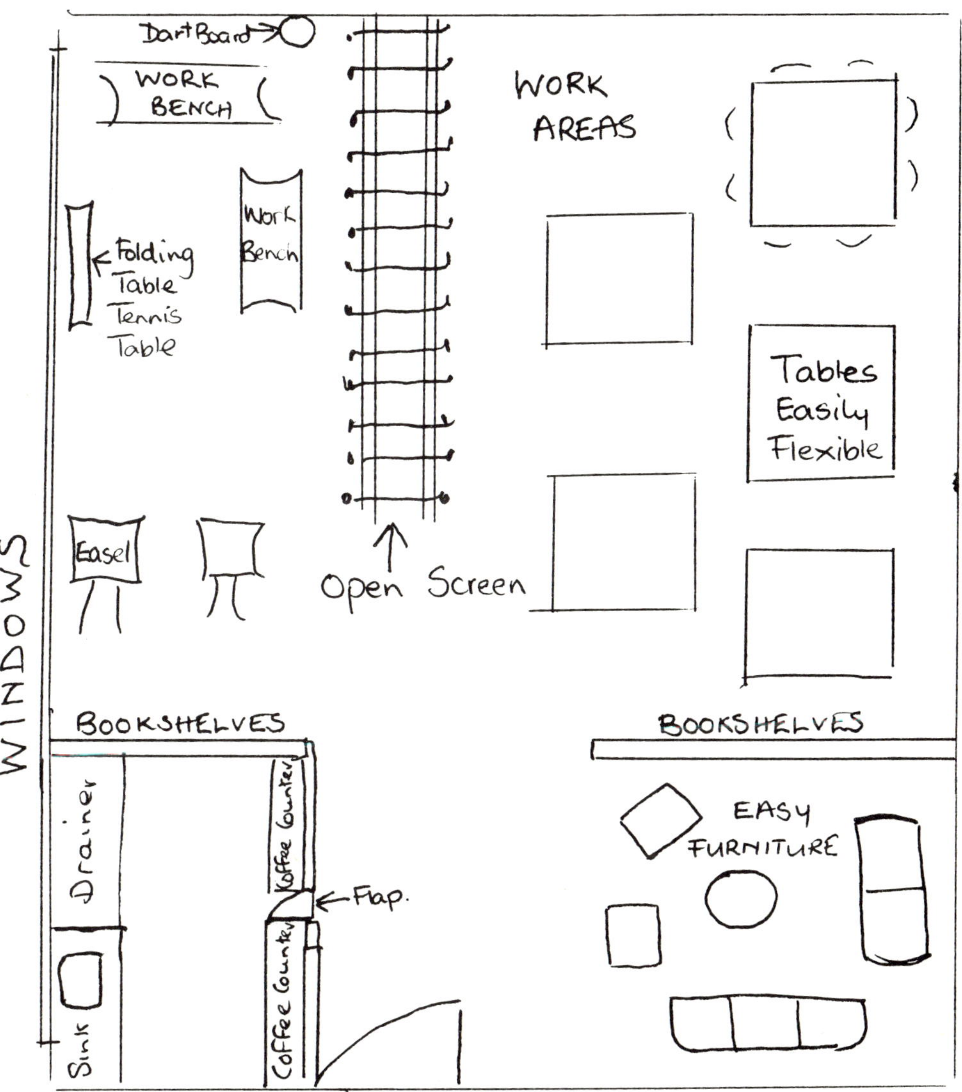

Possible layout of classroom This helps to bring about a change of attitude and a sense of belonging. Using the goodwill of local firms and the 'manpower' of willing students and parents a traditional room in an old school was transformed into this for less than £35. There was never any problem over vandalism.

tempted, so trouble is created. Putting humanitarian reasons aside, it is inexpedient, because in nine cases out of ten, it stores up trouble for the future. A pleasant room, a relaxed atmosphere and the opportunity to talk, have the opposite effect. It creates an atmosphere that brings out the best in pupils and lends itself towards creativity.

Changing attitudes

> 'Children develop most satisfactorily if they are loved for what they are and not what anyone thinks they ought to be.' (Anthony Storr)

Once the setting up of relationships that are mutually tolerant and understanding has been established and an environment that is welcoming and with which the pupils can identify has been provided, then the foundation for a change in attitudes is laid. Without these changes the chance of breaking the circle of failure is extremely limited. Some teachers may seriously resent being asked to change their methods, or provide different kinds of furniture, or abandon a set syllabus, but the question to ask here is, "Has what has been happening previously been successful?" Have the children been helped to learn to think, to make decisions, to solve problems, to be responsible or to respond in a socially competent manner? If they have not then surely we are obliged to re-think our attitudes. Something that teachers need to re-examine very carefully is the validity of class teaching. In many secondary schools class teaching still persists and although I would argue against the validity of this, whatever the academic ability of those concerned, in the case of slow learners, I believe it to be indefensible. How can twenty-five or so young people, who have been grouped together because, in the opinions of their teachers, they are failing to learn at the expected rate, be taught as one? They cannot. They must be seen and treated as individuals. Together with a teacher who knows them really well, acting as their director and guide, they must work out a programme which seems relevant and interesting and leads them towards a satisfying of the needs which have been discussed earlier. Primary school teachers are able to offer a wide number of disciplines to their pupils. They offer understanding, knowledge and a variety of interests. If this is possibly in primary schools then surely it is possible in secondary schools. Indeed the advantage is with the secondary school teacher. Not only do they have their own resources to call upon but they have the specialist knowledge of their colleagues on which to draw and the facilities of specialist departments. If the learning is to be individualised then resources play an important part and these are dealt with in detail later. Undoubtedly, individualised or self-directed learning calls for a high degree of commitment from the teacher and much patience, tolerance and understanding, but the mutual satisfaction that is gained by both the teacher and the pupil more than justifies the effort.

Expectations of parents, teachers and pupils

Teachers, parents and pupils have expectations of school, which, in many cases, and most particularly in the case of slow learners, just cannot be met. Many schools still have the attitude that studying is absorbing as much information as possible, then regurgitating it at an appropriate time in an examination. The more information regurgitated, the more successful the pupil and the greater the number of examinations passed. Not only the pupil, but the school itself, is judged by the number of examinations it achieves, be it the 11+, 'O' level or 'A' level. It is small wonder then that slow learners have little inclination for study of that nature. After all, in the sort of life they envisage for themselves, examinations are unnecessary and even if they did desire them, they realise that they would be unobtainable. Therefore, there is no purpose in studying. Another reason why slow learners are reluctant to conform to the prescribed syllabus of exam-cramming is because of the competitive element. They have failed too often to risk entering a competition which they know, from its very nature, they are bound to lose. It is important, therefore, in trying to break down attitudes like these, that schools, teachers and parents question their objectives. This is much easier said than done. Many parents expect the school to 'get' examinations for their children. Many teachers feel insecure without the structure of a tightly organised syllabus and pupils feel that they are wasting their time working if they are not going to 'get' an exam at the end. Parents are prepared to change their expectations to a greater or lesser degree depending on the adjustment that their child makes to school. If the child is happier, more involved, beginning to contribute more; if the teacher discusses mutual objectives so that they understand better what is happening, then parents will begin to see education as the fullest possible development of their child as a person and will accept and cooperate in this objective. Although among teachers, there is an in-built resistance to change, more and more teachers are being forced to re-think their ideas because of the failure of traditional methods to contain what is sometimes an explosive situation, or they are being influenced by younger teachers, trained to consider the needs of the individual pupil as a priority. This present time, therefore, is providing the opportunity for major re-assessment of expectations and attitudes without which a re-thinking of 'curriculum' cannot take place. Pupils, to a large extent, reflect the attitudes taken by teachers and parents, but for them, the need to gain feelings of freedom, self-assertion and satisfaction, which come from a sense of achievement initiated in self-directed learning, is paramount.

The individual child

Showing respect for the pupil has a reciprocal effect, which in turn has a beneficial effect on the educational process. The genuine interest of the student will be of considerable importance in the efficiency of the teaching process. Interest is not a mere motivational device to lubricate the learning situation. It is the product of a person's education. 'Interests develop whilst one is being educated, as well as being a point of departure for the educational enterprise.' (R. F. Dearden)

It would be a mistake to think that having a respect for the individual pupil or belief in his right to direct his own learning means abdicating all responsibility as a teacher. (See section entitled 'Role of the teacher'.) It does mean, however, the willingness to abandon the teacher's traditional authoritarianism. This is not as simple as it sounds. It means a complete re-thinking of the language in which we talk, question, praise, ask, and receive from, our pupils. It means recognising the individual child as being of equal importance to oneself. It means accepting what they do and say as being of value and not imposing ourselves or our ideas on them. The extract below is from Kenneth J. Weber's book, *Yes They Can*, and to me movingly illustrates this point:

> Meeting Lazlo's father promised to be routine at first. The family had emigrated from Hungary only five years before. Lazlo's accent was still quite noticeable. His father's was thick and he seemed reluctant to speak at all.
>
> Lazlo was in my tenth grade remedial reading class. We had a room called a reading lab (as though reading could be taught like urinalysis), an impressive array of machines (which neither I nor the students understood, but we played with them anyway) and an abundant supply of drill books.
>
> Lazlo's father was attentive as I explained all the wonderful things we were doing for his son. In fact I thought he was quite appreciative – until his first comment.
>
> 'Can you sex chicks?'
>
> My flabbergasted silence led him to repeat the question.
>
> 'Can you sex chicks?'
>
> Only when I ventured a tentative, and uninformed, 'No', did he follow through.
>
> 'Well you know, I can. And Lazlo can too. And do you

know something? We're not going to make you learn.'

With that, Lazlo's father turned to leave. But when he reached the door he paused for one final comment. Pointing a thick, stubby finger at me he said, without animosity, 'That's the trouble with all you teachers; you buggers try to make everybody else just like yourselves.'

Diagnosis and testing

Although the following chapter deals specifically with diagnosis it should be emphasised that testing for testing's sake can be nothing but destructive. In fact, until a teacher knows a pupil well, can discuss the problem with him and mutually want to embark on a programme to solve it, testing can be counterproductive both towards the learning situation and the relationship. This applies to the adolescent slow learner in a streamed situation or situation whereby diagnosis may appear to isolate. There is a very good case, however, at the primary stage to make a concerted effort to discover all children with learning difficulties. If all children at the age of seven or eight were screened, and a proper programme of remedial help worked out and put into practice, if the resources and specialist staffing that are put into secondary schools were injected into the primary situation then a very real effect would be had in the cycle of failure. Some authorities do screen whole age-groups, but too often schools then use this knowledge to stream at seven and not to isolate the problem, and local authorities fail to provide the facilities or resources to tackle it. If immediate and fully-trained help were given to all retarded readers before or when they moved from infant to junior level then the difficulties in secondary schools would be dramatically reduced. If a group should be screened, however, then it is important that teachers should not let their expectations of the child's ability be ruled by their results. Nor is testing of any use at all unless it leads to action. Diagnosis should lead to treatment and a teaching programme devised to remedy the difficulty.

Responsibility of the school

The responsibility of the school to develop a young person to his or her full potential is paramount. This cannot be done without the co-operation of the student and it is certain that there will be no co-operation from students in the later stages of adolescence without a re-thinking of attitudes and methods. A teacher when faced with adolescent slow learners has first to overcome years of conditioning. Young people, conditioned to dislike the school, conditioned to dislike the A streams; conditioned to the role of second-class citizens; conditioned to accepting that they have little to contribute to society. The teacher's first task, therefore, is to try and bring about a change in attitude, a willingness to look at things afresh, to 'have a go' and not give up. In the chapters that follow, there are many materials, suggestions, methods of diagnosing, resources that have been tested and enjoyed by students of various ages. But it should be stressed again that no amount of corrective, remedial, therepeutic programmes will have any effect without a meaningful relationship and a recognition of the pupil's individual needs.

BOOKS FOR REFERENCE (see bibliography for details)

Partnership for Change Ronald G. Cave
A Cure for Delinquents Robert W. Shields
How Children Fail John Holt
The Integrity of the Personality Anthony Storr
Yes, They Can Kenneth Weber
The Age Between Derek Miller
Children In Distress Alec Clegg and Barbara Megson

CHAPTER 2

DIAGNOSIS

Whose concern?

It may seem unusual to include a chapter entitled diagnosis in a book concerned with the slow learner. The diagnosis of any child's difficulties, particularly the problems of the child who cannot read, the remedial or ESN child, should normally be left to the specialist remedial teacher. Ideally, there should be a group of trained specialists within each school who could relieve the class teacher of the responsibility for a detailed programme of work for such children. However, quite a few schools at present have no trained remedial staff. Many primary schools do not have the staffing ratios necessary to appoint a specialised teacher for slow learners. Some secondary schools may also have no remedial staff, perhaps because they fail to recognise the slow learner as a child requiring special attention and resources.

So, from a variety of causes, many primary class teachers or secondary 'subject' teachers will find themselves faced with the problems posed by the slow learner. In order to help him they will need to understand more fully the nature of his difficulties and why they have arisen. The teacher will begin to look in more detail at tasks the child finds difficult, to analyse the particular elements with which the child is struggling, and to search out the root causes of his problem. He has then begun, however tentatively, on the specialised process of diagnosis.

This chapter is an attempt to help the class teacher to understand the child's problem, and to find ways of discovering the cause of that problem – a method of proceeding through the maze of cause and effect.

Why diagnose?

It may be useful first to look at the diagnosis. If any child cannot read, then the answer may seem simple – teach him to read by systematic coaching if necessary. This assumes that the child only lacks instruction. When given this, he will learn. Some children who have had lengthy periods of absence in infant and junior school may indeed only have missed the opportunity to learn. They would naturally be expected to benefit from such instruction. But others may have some more basic difficulty so they cannot learn to read by simple instruction. The need to look at the child's problems in more detail is obvious.

What is diagnosis?

> *DIAGNOSIS N.* The art or act of inferring from symptoms or manifestations the nature of an illness or the cause of a situation – The Oxford Pocket Dictionary.

Diagnosis is an individual process. Each child must be considered in turn. An outline of the problems he is facing is needed, further examination of those difficulties and some careful anaylsis of why those difficulties have arisen must be undertaken. An individual programme of work to correct those causes, as well as the symptoms, of his reading failure can then be prepared. Just as it would be nonsensical to think of a doctor attempting to diagnose the medical problems of all the patients in his waiting room as a group, so too it is absurd to imagine a teacher understanding the reading problems of all the children in any one class or group without looking at each child individually.

Apart from being an individual process, diagnosis is also continuous, and is interlinked with the teaching of the child. It is not useful, therefore, to think of looking at a child's difficulties for the first hour in which the teacher meets him. And to see the next year's work as stemming from that one hour's diagnostic session. The important point is to use the information gained in finding out initially about the child's difficulties in his later teaching. And during that teaching, to look for more clues to the child's problems, which may in turn modify his teaching method. Thus diagnosis and teaching are mutually dependent.

By reference to the diagram below, it is possible to see the crucial importance of the teacher in this process. The person best suited to undertake diagnostic work and the ensuing remedial programme is normally the person with whom the child has established the closest personal relationship, the person who is in daily contact with the child. This would enable the child to benefit fully from the constant reassessments and modifications of both the diagnosis and teaching process.

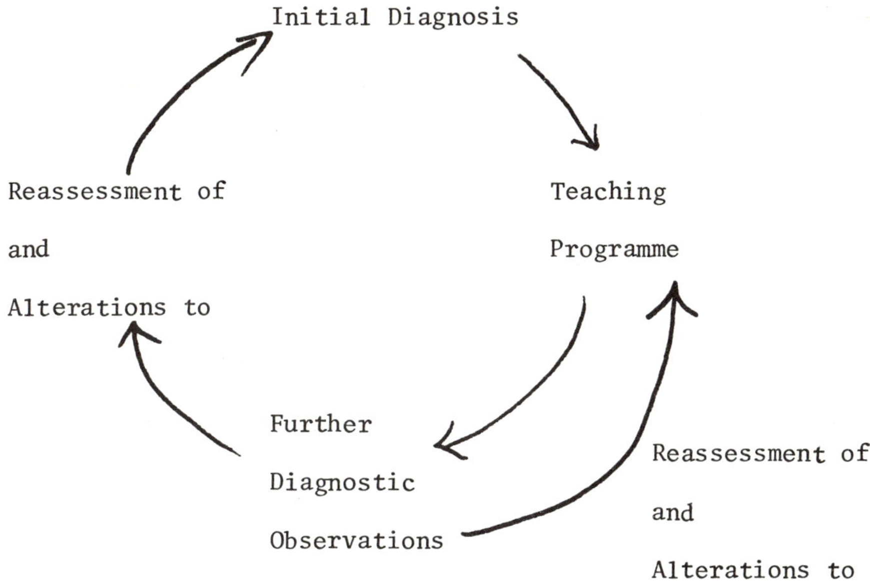

Naturally, when further testing or obervation of the most severe problems is necessary, some specialist staff from the Local Education Authority Advisory Services may need to be brought into the school to add to the teacher's observations – or the child may need to be referred to some outside clinic for further help. The assistance available can be studied in more detail in the chapter concerned with Outside Help.

Diagnosis does not necessarily involve using any standardised tests of reading or any other skill. It is a way of looking at the child's problems rather than any specific set of tests to be carried out. This association of the process of diagnosis with tests stems at present from the role of the educational psychologist within the LEA, and its effect is often to make teachers reluctant to engage in simple diagnostic work since they do not feel competent with the vast range of tests on the market at present. Conversely, it may make a teacher too dependent on testing as the sole method of discovering a child's problems.

An excellent teacher of slow learners may in fact use few or none of the available tests, because he is a skilled observer and knows the child well. He can see the problems within the normal school routine, or can 'stage' situations easily to explore difficulties further. However, most teachers will tend to use standardised tests at some stage, if only as a shorthand procedure. It is important to look closely at the limitations of the tests, to evaluate their usefulness and success in any particular instance. The results of the tests should not be viewed in isolation, but should be interpreted in the light of previous experience of the child. One bold test figure is rarely revealing or useful in itself, but must be compared with previous judgments of, and information about, the child.

Particularly useful indications may be any unusual characteristics in the pattern of scoring on one test, which may give clues to weakness or strengths. The results of a test should raise further questions, rather than be expected to provide definitive answers. Looked at in this light, many tests available today are extremely useful tools for the teacher intent on exploring a child's problems.

What diagnosis includes

---

1. *A Personal Relationship* with the child
   - gaining his confidence
   - talking over his past problems
   - discussing his interests, family, etc.

---

2. *Observation* of the child
   - in everyday classroom activity
   - in situations structured by the teacher

---

3. *Testing*
   - ad hoc tests created by the teacher
   - standardised tests

When to diagnose?

Any teacher would normally embark upon looking at the child diagnostically whenever he first comes into contact with the child who is experiencing difficulty in some form. Depending upon the role of the teacher within the school community, a child with problems may be referred to him by parents, by outside agencies, by the child's previous school or by other teachers or children within his own school.

The whole process of giving help to a child with problems and looking at his difficulties should be begun as early as possible. The young child will not lag so far behind his peers if he is given additional help in the early stages of junior school. Finding out about a child's problems becomes more difficult the older he is, since most children develop additional behavioural problems by being forced to live with, or hide a reading problem over a few years. In some situations, particularly involving an older child, it is not helpful to give a child the impression that you are assessing his performance or problems when you first meet him. He may be well aware that his performance is very low, and an exploration of it may only reinforce his feelings of failure. Just as it is unwise to recommend for this type of child an intensive period of diagnosis, so too it may be foolish to embark on a rigid reading scheme as a 'treatment' for his reading problem. The individual judgment and initiative of the teacher is of paramount importance in both these areas. He will need to be flexible in deciding when to involve the child in diagnosis as well as how to go about the process.

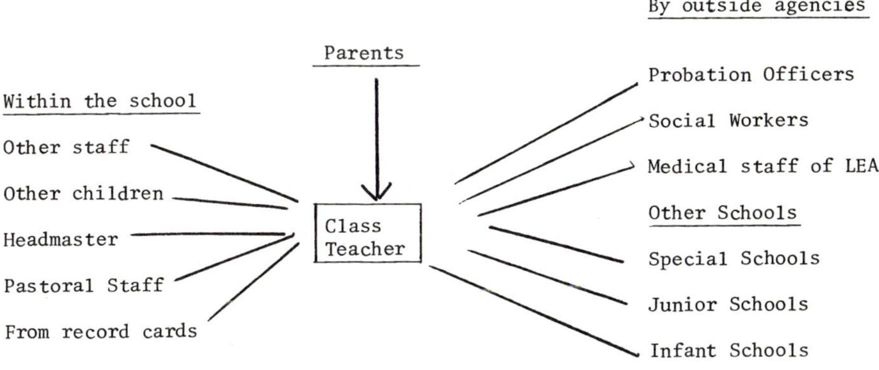

Whom to use to help with diagnosis

The class teacher faced with the need to discover the primary causes of a child's difficulties should be prepared to draw on the training and experience of others, both within and outside the school. All the outside agencies of the educational social service network can be brought in to help. The school social worker may give information on the child's home background; the school nurse and doctor could provide medical details which could affect a child's performance, and can administer eyesight tests; the local audiologist can be called in for hearing tests; the educational psychologist in the Child Guidance Clinic may be of assistance in assessing the child's general level of ability; other more specialised agencies such as speech therapists and peripatetic teachers of autistic children and the deaf can be called in when needed. All these agencies are intended as services to teachers, and should be used for their advice and practical assistance. In a similar way the child's previous headteacher or class teacher should be able to provide more useful background information on the child. And finally, his parents will often be keen to give much valuable personal information when they feel that this will contribute towards helping their child.

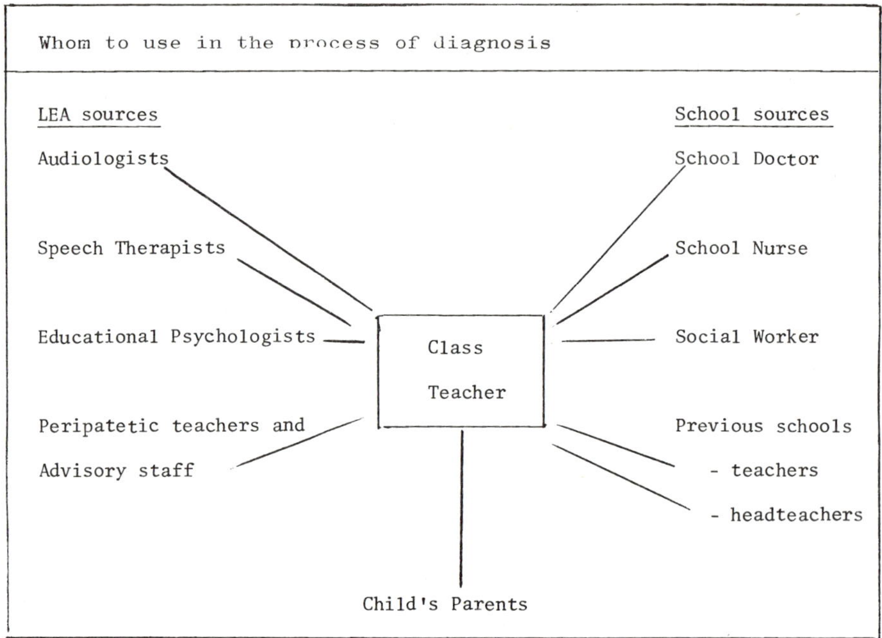

Initial diagnostic screening

In this chapter discussion on diagnosis will centre around the ability of a child to read. Comments on exploring a child's skill in reading will doubtless be relevant to exploring his ability in other areas such as writing and mathematics. Similarly, any basic cause of a child's reading difficulty is likely to affect his achievement or failure in other areas too. For example, the child who is finding even the initial stages of reading difficult, and who is discovered to have problems in the field of perception, will naturally be experiencing some problems in mathematics and related tasks. Any treatment programme designed to help this underlying difficulty should yield dividends in work on number, shape, etc.

The initial step in exploring a child's reading ability is the administration of some form of standardised reading test to find out at which level the child is reading. Most general reading tests provide a 'reading age' as a test result. This reading age score is indicative of the average performance of children at that age, as measured by the test. For example, a child of nine years who is found to have a reading age of seven years on a standardised test, is in need of remedial help in some form, since he is lagging behind his peers by approximately two years. There are two main types of reading screening tests, those which need to be administered to the individual child, and those which a teacher can give to a group or class of children together. Individual tests may look at one of three aspects of reading – word recognition (can a child read a list of words), sentence reading and comprehension (does the child understand what he is reading). Group tests usually involve comprehension, by the child completing a sentence, or choosing one word from several.

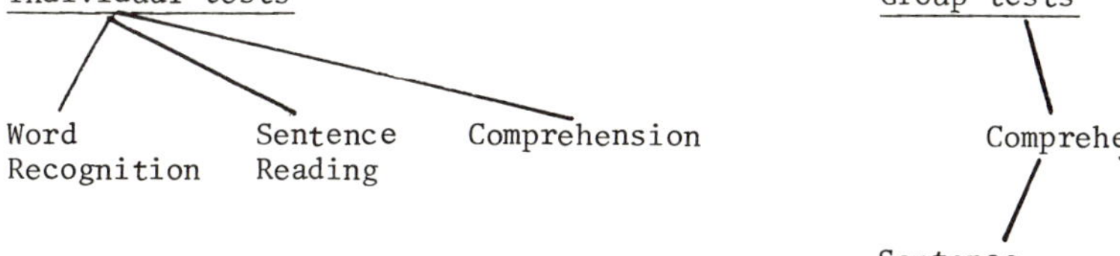

In addition to these reading tests described in more detail below, there are both group and individual tests for phonic ability to which reference will be made later.

PUBLISHED READING TESTS

Individual tests

1. *Burt – Word Reading Test* (rearranged) 1921/58.
   An untimed test. 110 graded words to read. It gives some clues to the phonic ability of the child. 4–15 years. U.L.P.
2. *Carver – Word Recognition Test.* 1970.
   4–8.6 years. Untimed. The test is administered orally by the teacher – child underlines the correct word. May also be given as a group test. 50 items which increase in difficulty. Can be used to look at types of error made. U.L.P.

3. *Daniels and Diack* – The standard test of reading skill. 1958.
   Untimed. 5–9 years. Sentence reading exercise, but sentences in the form of a question for interest only. Gives some indication of the phonic combinations with which a child has difficulty. No reliability or validity given. Should be used with the other diagnostic tests in their *Standard Reading Tests*. Chatto & Windus.
4. *Holborn Reading Scale*. 1948.
   Untimed. One form only. 5–11 years. This test gives two scores – word recognition and comprehension. Harrap.
5. *Neale – Analysis of Reading Ability*. 1958/1967.
   Gives three scores on accuracy, comprehension and rate of reading, and additional tests. Forms A, B, and C. 6–12 years. No reliability data given. Macmillan.
6. *Schonell – Graded Word Reading Test*. 1945.
   100 graded words. Untimed. 5–15 years. Widely used in schools but limited due to the age of the test. Instructions given in *Psychology and the Teaching of Reading*. Oliver & Boyd.
   Additional Schonell tests: R2 – Simple Prose 6–9.
   R3 – Silent Reading 7–11.
   R4 – Silent Reading 9–13.
   R5 – Test of analysis and synthesis.
   R6 – Test of directional attack on words.
   R7 – Visual word recognition.
7. *National Foundation for Educational Research Tests* (obtainable from Ginn & Co. Ltd.).
   Reading Test A. Primary reading test 1. Untimed sentence completion. 38 items graded. No norms available. Of use with first-year juniors.
   Reading Test BD. Primary reading test 2. 1969. Junior second and third years. Norms 8.6–10.3 only. Timed sentence completion.
   Reading test AD. Sentence reading test 1 by Watts. 1956. 7.6–11.1. Silent reading comprehension. Timed 15 minutes. Sentence completion where child chooses one word from a choice of five.
   Reading Comprehension Test DE. Reading comprehension test 1. 1967. Fourth year junior and first secondary. Continuous prose. Untimed. Can be used diagnostically, giving separate scores for global understanding, ability to draw conclusions from what is read, understanding of individual words and phrases, ability to read for detail. Norms 10.0–11.11. Very small print.
   Reading Tests EH 1–3. Secondary reading tests 1–3. 1966.
   Secondary years 1–4. Test 1 vocabulary – untimed sentence completion. Test 2 comprehension – untimed comprehension questions. Test 3 speed – continuous prose, timed 7 minutes or $4\frac{1}{2}$ minutes. Very small print.

Group tests

1. *Daniels and Diack* – Graded test of reading experience. 1959.
   Untimed. Sentence completion. 6–14 years. No information is given on validity or reliability. See *Standard Reading Tests*, Chatto & Windus. Useful as a general reading screening test to identify the slow learner on entry to secondary school. (Cut-off point of 9 years.)
2. *G.A.P. – Reading Comprehension Test*. 1965.
   Timed 15 minutes. Silent reading, with child supplying the missing word. Two parallel forms. 7.8–12.6 years. Could discriminate against child using poor grammar in his writing. Heinemann.
3. *Harrison Stroud Reading Readiness*. 1956.
   6 years. American standardisation. Six tests of pre-reading skills. 5 group tests and 1 individual test. N.F.E.R.
4. *Kingston* test of silent reading. 1958.
   Timed 20 minutes. Tests context understanding, recall, vocabulary and word recognition. 7–11 years. Harrap.
5. *Southgate* group reading tests.
   Test 1 – word selection. R.A. 5.9 years to 7.9 years. Any chronological age. Untimed. Word selection with picture aids. 3 forms. Test 2 – R.A. 7–9.7 years. Any chronological age. Multiple choice, sentence completion. Untimed. 2 forms. U.L.P.
6. *Spooner – Group Reading Assessment*. 1964.
   6.2–11.6. 3 timed subtests, 30 minutes in all. Phonically based. Word recognition, sentence completion and choosing words with similar sounds. U.L.P.
7. *Wide Span – A. Brimmer*. 1972.
   7–15 years. 2 forms. Test of reading comprehension. Nelson.
8. *Young* – Group Reading Test. 1969.
   6.6–13.0. Timed 15 minutes. Word recognition and comprehension. 2 forms. Useful as a group test for children with low reading ages.

Phonic tests

1. *Domain Phonic Test Kit* – J. McLeod & Atkinson. Oliver & Boyd. £2.50. Test and phonic worksheets to remedy phonic difficulties. These sheets may be bought separately.
2. *Get Reading Right* – Jackson. Gibson.
   140 phonic skills sheets, 20 record cards and handbook. £2.19.
   Set of phonic tests 1–11 on the phonic combinations. Accompanying handbook suggests remedial exercises. Books to complete the scheme.

3. *Swansea Test of Phonic Skills*. Congdon, Holder & Sims. Blackwell for the Schools Council. Nonsense syllables used. Expendable workbook for each child. Choice of one word from five, word read orally by teacher.

All the above phonic tests are extremely useful in diagnosis. So too, are

4. *Daniels and Diack 'Standard Tests of Reading'*. 1958. Chatto & Windus.
   - Test 1 General reading – individual.
   - Test 2 Copying shapes.
   - Test 3 Copying sentence.
   - Test 4 Visual discrimination and orientation.
   - Test 5 Letter recognition.
   - Test 6 Aural discrimination.
   - Test 7 Diagnostic word recognition.
   - Test 8 Oral word recognition.
   - Test 9 Picture-word recognition.
   - Test 10 Silent prose reading and comprehension.
   - Test 11 Graded spelling test.
   - Test 12 Test of reading experience – group.

Advantages of individual tests

1. Cost – generally only one test is required.
2. Useful in diagnosis because of personal teacher observation.
3. There is a more versatile number of tests available. They can be used to assess
   – phonic knowledge
   – accuracy of reading
   – rate of reading
   – word attack methods
   – comprehension.
4. They train a teacher to be more observant when hearing a child read.

Advantages of group tests

1. They save teacher time on both administration and scoring.
2. The teacher can more easily keep a record of the child's test for future comparison.
3. These tests are usually very useful in testing comprehension.
4. These tests are more likely to be used regularly because of the ease of their administration.

There are certain important considerations which must be borne in mind when the teacher wishes to chose a reading screening test, in addition to the choice between group or individual test.

Does the test measure only one aspect of reading skill – for example, word recognition or comprehension? Is this the aspect the teacher finds most useful as a screening device? Does the test have norms available for the age of children who will be tested? Is it a recently standardised test? – the norms for some reading tests which have not been re-evaluated in recent years are likely to be misleading. Is the test reliable, i.e. does it yield consistent results on different occasions? Is it valid, i.e. does it measure what it is intended to measure? This rather technical information is contained in the teacher's manual to the test. This should always be read thoroughly by the teacher before embarking on test. It should contain precise details of administration and so on.

All these aspects of a test should be enquired into by a teacher, in addition to the more obvious factors of cost, ease of administration, etc. When the results of the test have been gained, using any one of the tests already described, it is important to bear in mind that these will be useful only as a general guide or screening device to find those children functioning two or more years in reading below their chronological age (unless, of course, one of the specialised phonic tests is used). The results of this initial test and observation will not indicate any specific areas of weakness the child has, nor will it give any indication of remedial action needed. This will be discussed further later, when the next stage of diagnostic action is outlined.

In the same way, if the test used measured only one aspect of reading skill, then the other aspects will need to be explored further by other means. For example, if the test used was one of word recognition only, then comprehension, phonic ability and speed will need to be looked into for each child.

Change in a child's score on these tests is also somewhat misleading. Since norms on reading tests vary from one test to another, even when these are supposed to be measuring the same skill, a child who scored R.A. 7.5 years on the Schonell word recognition test, would not necessarily score 7.5 years on the Burt word recognition test. This makes comparison of scores on different tests extremely difficult. In addition, a child tested on one reading test, for example, the Schonell, scoring 7.5 years, and then retested exactly a year later on the Burt (scoring 8.5 years), may not have gained exactly 1 year in reading age over the period. And naturally, if he were retested 1 year later with a different type of reading test, say the GAP comprehension test, there is more likely to be even more variation in scores since the tests were in fact measuring different skills in reading.

It is important not to be too despondent if a child does not improve his reading ability by one year within the year the teacher is giving remedial help based on his diagnosis of the child's difficulties.

A child who gains nine months over a year's work may be making tremendous strides, since his previous progress may only have been three months per annum. Children's progress often seems to fluctuate while they are receiving help. They often progress rapidly in the first few months, and then seem to be at a standstill for the following six, this in turn followed by another spurt. These points will be explored further when the assessment of a child's progress is looked at.

One final reminder is perhaps necessary that some reading tests are easier for children who have had either a sight vocabulary or a phonic reading scheme; a child tested on the Schonell, as opposed to the Burt, is likely to score lower if he has previously been working on a phonic programme. If he was tested on the Burt, he might score higher, but this test would not reveal his weak sight vocabulary skill. Both these old word recognition tests are still misused at present in schools, sometimes as the sole indicator of progress the child has made over several years. It is far more useful to retest a child on more recently standardised tests, which measure different aspects of the total reading skill.

Having identified the child who is functioning two or more years behind his chronological age in reading work, the teacher is in a position to divide his children up into two groups – those who have made a beginning on their reading, although they are still slow at it, and those who have made no real progress with reading at all. The cut-off reading ages will be about six years to 9.5 years for the slow readers, and below six for those who will be termed non-readers.

The slow reader

Having found that a child has begun to read, the teacher will need to follow up the results of the initial screening test by finding out whether the child has problems in sight reading or phonic word attack skills in particular. For sight reading, a test of basic sight words, from the Dolch or Ladybird list, could be used. Or the child could be observed reading aloud from his current reading book. How does he attack words he cannot immediately recognise? Does he attempt to sound the word out, or to guess at its meaning by using the context of the word to give him clues? Does he say a word beginning with the same letter as the missing word, or one which looks the same in word shape? The strategies he uses in coping with his difficulty will give clues to the teacher as to how the child finds it easiest to read. If he constantly tries to sound out very obvious sight words such as mother or toy, then he has only a very small number of words which he can recognise immediately on sight. His strength in phonic analysis can be used to help his reading, as is outlined in the following chapter on reading methods.

To see how a child can cope with phonic analysis, a phonic test, such as the ones discussed above, may be used. Or the teacher may prefer a list of words of phonic elements (e.g. ship, shop, shoot, etc.), which the child can read aloud. The phonic combinations with which the child is experiencing difficulty will then become apparent. One useful series of books to use in this way is the six short books in the 'Sounds of Words' series published by U.L.P. Children will find difficulty in general within one broad band of phonic elements, for example, with initial letters, or letter combinations, and this will enable the teacher to see where to begin work on word and letter sounds. More details of this may be found in the following chapter.

The teacher now has some idea of the child's reading age and his ability to analyse phonics. Any discrepancy between these two is important for him to note for his remedial programme. He would also need to look at the child's language development to see whether this is weak. A language enrichment or development programme could then be run alongside the reading work. Similarly the child's grammar and vocabulary may be weak. This would be revealed in the classroom or in discussion or drama lessons. The child's spelling ability, or lack of it, is usually interesting for the teacher. In general, spelling tends to lag considerably behind the child's reading age, particularly in slow learners, and strict training is better left until the child has a reading age in the region of 9 years. It is a useful indicator, though, where there is a child who can read well but finds spelling difficult. A child's ability here is easily observed by looking at his 'free' writing: see whether he spells all words phonetically (e.g., nee, rite), or whether he cannot spell very simple sightwords (e.g. when, where).

Handwriting too, needs some attention. If a child's writing is untidy, uncoordinated, although he can read, this will give a clue to his control over finer body movements, and does not necessarily mean that the child is simply untidy in presentation. Whether in fact a child with poor handwriting will benefit from handwriting exercises is a difficult decision for the teacher to make. The child's ability to form and to differentiate between shapes, as shown by the Daniels and Diack test 2–4 for example, will need to be looked into. But cause and effect is difficult to distinguish in this area. A child with poor handwriting may have a generally careless personality, which in turn would affect his reading work. Or the handwriting may be an indicator of general coordination difficulties, which in their turn could have been caused by brain damage or medical problems. The teacher will normally have to seek outside specialised help here.

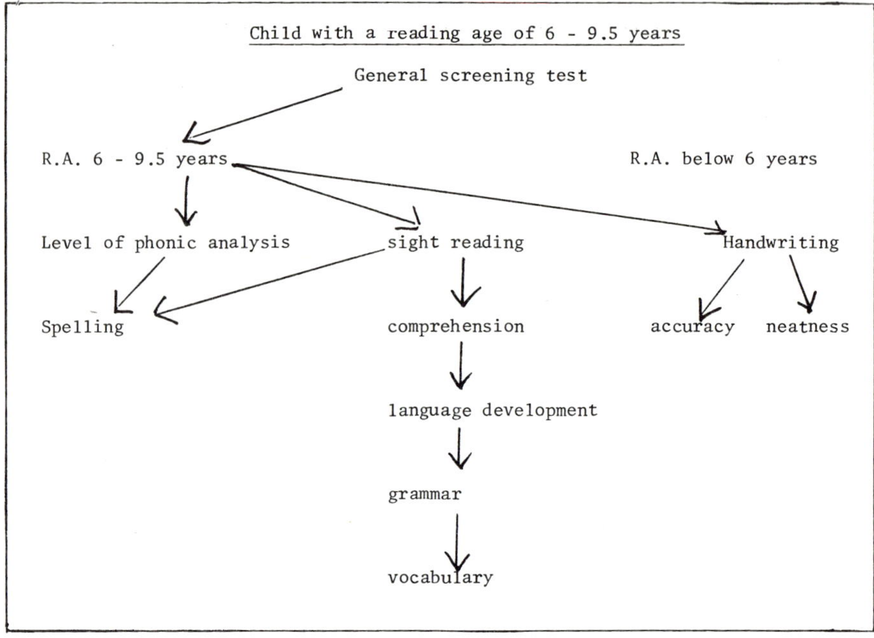

The non-reader

The child who cannot read will probably not react favourably to being given the initial screening test, on which he probably found it impossible to score. Such a child should be picked up from the previous teacher's comments, and school record cards. The teacher who comes into contact with the slow learner often finds the non-reader baffling. If the child cannot read at all, how to begin on reading at such a late stage or find his capabilities? He will need to turn to skills generally considered to be essential to reading ability, and known as pre-reading skills.

Looking at the area of visual abilities first, can the child copy simple shapes, such as those given by Tansley in his book *Reading and Remedial Reading*?

Or more complicated patterns, as in Daniels and Diack's Test 2? Does he have difficulties with specific movements such as circles or diagonal lines? The ability to copy grows as the child matures. It would be perfectly normal for a child below the age of seven years to be unable to draw a diamond. But it would be unusual if he were thirteen. The teacher's ability to interpret the results here is vital.

Can the child copy a visually-presented rhythm? For example

Or, more difficult,

Can he remember a set of objects he has looked at for a few seconds after they have been removed, as in Kim's game? How many of the items can he remember as their number is increased? Can he tell the difference between right and left? And distinguish differences in orientation for both letters and words, as well as simple objects? Daniels and Diack's book is useful here, as are many of the games present in Philip and Tacey and Galt catalogues. The difficulty of all these items can be graded, to gain more information.

How good is the child's coordination generally? In general bodily activities, in P.E. lessons? And at the paper and pencil level? Can he follow a maze at varying levels of complexity? These can be found in most children's comics. How good is he at cutting out figures and shapes? At tying knots and shoelaces? At tracing simple figures? Can he recognise small and capital letters? Does he know the alphabet? How well-developed is his language ability? These would be the sorts of things in the visual language fields which would need to be explored.

If a child was so poor at these tasks that the teacher felt the need to investigate further, then the Frostig Test of Visual Perception is the most useful one. This would need to be administered by a trained tester from the LEA. This test looks at five areas which are likely to affect a child's visual perception and reading. These areas are: visual–motor (can a child follow a maze, etc.), constancy of shape (can he recognise different shapes, even when they are turned round), spatial relationships (in front of, behind, etc.), figure-ground (can he pick out a shape from others overlapping), and position in space (inversions of left-right, up-down, etc.). These tests may be devised from simple games by the teacher so that he may get some indication of the type of difficulties with which the child is faced before calling in help from outside. Frostig also provides numerous paper and pencil training exercises for all areas outlined above, together with very useful suggestions for supplementary work in P.E., craft, etc.

Turning to the area of auditory abilities necessary for reading to proceed (leaving aside for a moment a simple hearing test which would come within the scope of a medical examination discussed later), the teacher would need to know whether the child can discriminate between various sounds, beginning with everyday environmental sounds. The Wepman test of auditory discrimination is particularly useful here, as it covers most of the letter sounds in the beginning, middle and end of words. (For example, can the child hear the difference between bus and buff when these are presented to him orally?) Look at the following chart for further information on this and other miscellaneous tests which are of use in the whole process of looking at a child's abilities within a diagnostic framework.

Miscellaneous tests of use in diagnostic work

Spelling Tests

Daniels & Diack

Schonell Spelling Test

Kelvin Spelling Test. Gibson

Reading Readiness
Harrison – Stroud

Profile – N.F.E.R.

Vocabulary Tests

English Picture Vocabulary. N.F.E.R.
Test 1 5–8.11 years
Test 2 7–11.11 years

Mill Hill Vocabulary

$4\frac{1}{2}$–Adult. H. Lewis

Crichton Vocabulary
$4\frac{1}{2}$–11 years
H. Lewis

Auditory Discrimination
Wepman Test – Chicago Research Associates

Personality Tests

Children's Behaviour Questionnaire – M. Rutter.

Bristol Social Adjustment Guide. U.L.P.

Manchester Scales of Social Adaptation. N.F.E.R.

Progress Assessment Charts. Gunzburg. N.F.E.R.

Visual Perception

Marianne Frostig Test. 3–8 years. N.F.E.R.

If there are any particular sounds which a child finds difficulty in recognising or distinguishing, then the teacher will need to find some short training exercises, such as those outlined in the following chapter. Without the ability to discriminate sounds, the child will not be able to proceed with much success to the stage of phonic analysis. Can the child blend letters to form words? Can he recognise ch ai r, presented orally as chair? Does he know the sound of different letters – in the beginning, middle and ending of the word? (For example, the sound of 'a' in apple, and bat.) This is the beginning of phonic teaching. How does he remember sounds? Can he remember a common tune after a few seconds, a few minutes or a week? Has he any idea of rhythm? i.e. can he tap out a rhythm, simple or more difficult? Can he tap out the rhythm of words and sentences?

The teacher should now know whether a child who could not read was functioning well on both visual and auditory tasks. If he showed a deficiency in one type of work, assuming that there was a marked discrepancy, then it would be wise to call in outside help to examine it further, whilst at the same time, beginning to build up an individual programme to help the child overcome his weakness. The child's dominant sphere – auditory or visual – could be used meanwhile to help him to proceed with his reading work. The indisputable fact remains, however, that reading progress will only move rapidly when the slow learner can use both phonic and sight methods of reading. To do so, training exercises in visual or auditory fields may be a necessary addition to his reading course.

The above suggestions for looking further into reading skills and pre-reading skills can, of course, equally well apply to the child who has made a start on reading. Indeed, should a child fail to make progress with reading tuition, it would be wise to look into these pre-reading skills, to make sure that the difficulty does not lie there.

Thus there is a basic set of steps through which the teacher can work in attempting to look at the difficulties of a slow learner who has not made any beginning on reading.

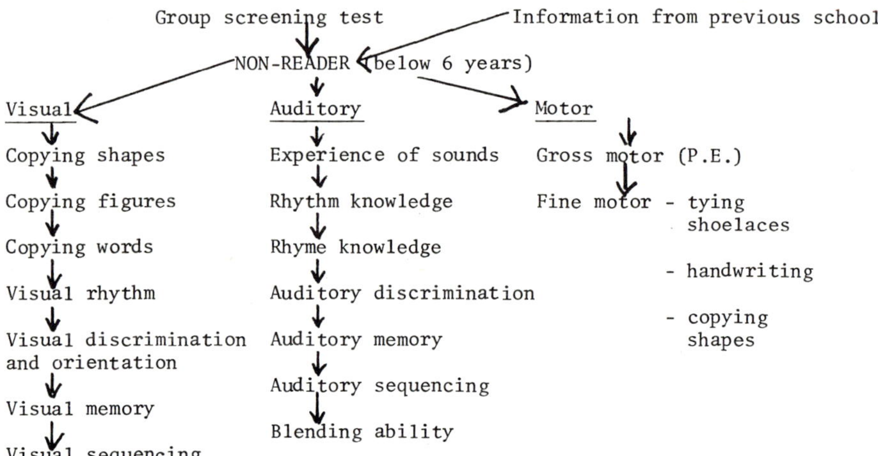

Things to check

More general factors which need to be borne in mind when looking at the slow learning child who has reading problems of any kind are outlined in the diagram below. The medical history of the child will show past health, and particular problems in the medical sphere, or specific infant or birth problems. Such information should be contained on the child's record card, or may be gained after a routine school medical. A recent eyesight and hearing test is essential for children coping with reading difficulties – these can be obtained from the school nurse or local audiologist if no recent test information is available. Turning to the social history of the child is usually also revealing. If the child has had frequent long periods of absence from school, then he may not be a slow learner. He may simply not have been taught the basic reading skills. Information about the child's family circumstances is usually invaluable when it comes to the treatment or training of reading difficulties. Parental sympathy and understanding here will also be useful.

Assessment of I.Q.

Having gone through all the stages in the diagnostic procedure, the teacher may still find that he has not been able to grasp why any child is having reading difficulties. No explanation has come to hand. He may then feel that some assessment of the child's general intelligence is necessary. This may seem apparent simply through everyday contact with him, but often an extremely lively child will

OTHER THINGS TO CHECK

MEDICAL HISTORY

1. Recent eyesight test

---

2. Hearing test

General — for particular blends which may affect his phonic ability

---

3. General Health
Types of illnesses - associated factors. Absence from school this causes

---

SOCIAL HISTORY

Gained from - previous schools
previous teachers
record cards
child himself
parents/friends, etc.

1. Early childhood difficulties - Birth difficulties
- 0 - 5 years

---

2. Parents' relationship to child

---

3. Information on behaviour

---

4. Information on attitude/personality

---

5. Information on reaction to previous failure

---

6. Absence records

---

appear deceptively more intelligent than he in fact is. On further probing, misunderstanding of the words and concepts he uses may be very limited. It is extremely important not to overestimate the importance of an I.Q. indication – the word 'indication' is a useful one. A qualified tester is unlikely to provide anything more, because of the misuse of I.Q. results in recent years. Nor is it necessary for the teacher to have more than a general indication. A figure attached to a child is foolish, even though the teacher may use this figure for the child's assistance.

Intelligence tests available to teachers

Test	*Publisher*	*Age-Range*	*Comments*
Manchester General Ability Test (Senior)	U.L.P.	13–14½	More suitable for top ability range
Manchester General Ability Test (Senior 2)	U.L.P.	14–15	Similar to previous Test
Moray House Picture Test 1	U.L.P.	7	No validity evidence. Not clear as to what test measures
Non-readers Intelligence Test	U.L.P.	6½–9	Verbal abilities test. No reading required
Non-verbal test for B.D.	N.F.E.R.	8–11	
Non-verbal test for D.H.	N.F.E.R.	10–15	No information given on validity
Non-verbal test of intelligence (Sleight)	Harrap	6–11	No information on validity or reliability
Picture Test A	N.F.E.R.	6½–8½	No validation figures
Ravens Progressive Matrices A–T	H. K. Lewis	6–13½	Non-verbal tests mainly assessing perceptual ability and difficulties
Ravens Coloured Progressive Matrices A, Ab, B	H. K. Lewis	5–11½	
Crichton Vocabulary Scale	H. K. Lewis	5–11	For use with coloured progressive matrices
Mill Hill Vocabulary Scale	H. K. Lewis	4–14	For use with standard progressive matrices
Carlton Intelligence Test No. 1	U.L.P.	10–12	Requires literacy

Carlton Picture Intelligence Test	U.L.P.	6–8	Non-verbal. Now out of print
Cattell Group and Individual Intelligence Tests, 1, 2, 3	Harrap	Scale 1, 8–11 Scale 2, 11–15 Scale 3, 15–adult	
Cornwell's orally presented Group Intelligence Tests	Methuen	8–11	Does not require reading or writing skills. Cheap but needs 100 mins. to administer
Deeside Picture Test	Harrap	$6\frac{1}{2}$–$8\frac{1}{2}$	Measures listening comprehension
English Picture Vocabulary Tests 1, 2	Educational Evaluation Enterprises	Test 1, 5–8 yrs Test 2, 7–12 yrs	Test 1, individual Test 2, group verbal test
English Picture Vocabulary Test 3	Educational Evaluation Enterprises	11–adult 11–14 validated	Group test requires no reading skill. Tests mainly listening comprehension
Figure Reasoning Test	Crosby Lockwood	10–16	Does not require reading. Non-verbal
Simplex Junior Intelligence Scale	Harrap	7–14	Difficulties of reliability and validity. Difficult scoring
Simplex Junior 'A' Intelligence Test	Harrap	7–14	Standardisation inadequate. No data or validity or reliability
Simplex G.W.V. Intelligence Tests	Harrap	10–13	Validity and reliability unknown
Simplex Group Intelligence Scale	Harrap	Mental Ages 8–23	Validity and reliability unknown
Valentine's Reasoning Tests for Higher Levels of Intelligence	Oliver & Boyd		An experimental test mainly use for screening higher education entrants
Verbal Test BC	N.F.E.R.	8–11	Masters of Reading needed R.A. $7\frac{1}{2}$–8
Verbal Test CD	N.F.E.R.	9–11	No information on validity

Verbal Test D	N.F.E.R.	9½–12	Requires a high degree of literacy
Verbal Test EF	N.F.E.R.	11–13½	As above
Verbal Test GH	N.F.E.R.	13½–15	As above

N.B. Some tests will only be sold to qualified psychologists or others trained in the use of that particular test. Details given in publishers' catalogues. For addresses, see Appendix V.

An intelligence indication is useful only if it leads on to further action which will help the child. It has no intrinsic use in itself. If, for example, it shows a non-reader to have an average or high I.Q., then it will prove diagnostically useful for the teacher. Any discrepancy between the child's level of ability and school performance should be carefully noted and used for the child's benefit. If an I.Q. result showed a non-reader to be in the educationally sub-normal category, then this would be far less surprising. Too much pressure on this child to achieve results would be only harmful. This is not to assume, however, that the low ability or ESN child cannot learn to read. Many manage functional levels of reading. It merely indicates a general low level of ability which may mean that progress will be slow. This child may be better served by concentrating on his whole education, rather than placing too much stress on reading in particular.

An I.Q. test administered individually to the child by the trained psychologist may show discrepancies within the test itself. A child may score high on non-verbal items, and low on verbal items requiring a more sophisticated use of language. The importance of such findings, and their implications for remedial action, need careful exploration, and should be explained to the teacher by the tester. In general, an I.Q. test is a useful further check on a teacher's own observations. It is when it is used as a screening device or an instrument for predicting the child's future performance, that this measure falls into abuse.

For any further discussion on intelligence testing look at the following references, and examine the manuals accompanying the tests published by the firms listed above.

Useful books on intelligence

The Assessment of Intelligence (West Sussex County Psychological Service, County Hall, Chichester, Sussex, 15p).
Psychological Testing – A. Anastasie (Macmillan, 1968).
Human Intelligence – H. J. Butcher (Methuen, 1968).

Recording information and progress

The question arises of how best to collate the information from tests and observation of the child. Since the standard record card is not likely to prove suitable, a suggested outline record is given below. The extent to which investigation of particular areas is carried out will depend on the child's problems and the judgment of the teacher.

The teacher will thus have built up, over the weeks, months or years spent working and observing the child, a comprehensive view and record of the child's problems and the reasons for these, and perhaps an indication of the general level of ability on which he is working. On the basis of this information, and completely interlinked with it, he will have developed an individual programme of work for the child. This programme should give success to the child, by helping him to use his strengths to practise and overcome areas of weakness.

RECORD CARD

NAME ______________________________ DATE OF BIRTH ______________

ADDRESS ____

____

____

SOCIAL BACKGROUND

INFORMATION FROM PREVIOUS SCHOOL/RECORD CARDS

____

____

____

____

____

POSITION IN FAMILY ______________

DETAILS OF FAMILY BACKGROUND ______________________

____

INCIDENCE OF CHILD'S DIFFICULTIES IN FAMILY? RELATION TO CHILD

____

____

SCHOOLS ATTENDED

NAME	DATES OF ATTENDANCE
______________	______________
______________	______________
______________	______________

COMMENTS ON CHILD'S PERSONALITY AND BEHAVIOUR: ______________

____

PARTICULAR INTERESTS IN OR OUT OF SCHOOL: ______________

____

ABSENCE RECORD - DATES: ______________________

______________ ______________

______________ ______________

A.

MEDICAL HISTORY

EARLY HISTORY - COMMENTS ON WALKING, TALKING, SOCIAL ETC.

____

____

ANY PARTICULAR DIFFICULTIES: ______________________

____

EVIDENCE OF CROSS LATERALITY - DOMINANT HAND: __________
YES/NO DOMINANT EYE : __________
DOMINANT FOOT: __________

TESTS DATES TESTED	HEARING	ANY COMMENTS ON IMPEDIMENTS
	______	______________________
	______	______________________
	______	______________________
	EYESIGHT	ANY COMMENTS ON IMPEDIMENTS
	______	______________________
	______	______________________
	______	______________________

LANGUAGE DEVELOPMENT/EXPERIENCE

DETAILS OF TESTS OR TEACHER'S COMMENTS

____

____

____

____

____

____

____

____

____

____

INFORMATION FROM OTHER OUTSIDE AGENCIES
e.g. Social Workers, Psychiatrists etc..

I.Q. TEST (if given)

DATE OF TEST TEST GIVEN

VERBAL TESTS	SCALED SCORE	PERFORMANCE TESTS	SCALED SCORE
Information		Picture Completion	
Comprehension		Picture Arrangement	
Arithmetic		Block Design	
Similarities		Object Assembly	
Vocabulary		Coding	
		Mazes	
TOTAL		TOTAL	

VERBAL IQ)
)
PERFORMANCE IQ)
)
FULL IQ)

PREVIOUS TEST RESULTS

TEST	IQ	DATE

COMMENTS

RAVENS PROGRESSIVE MATRICES

IQ	DATE OF TEST	PERCENTILE RANK	CLASSIFICATION

B.

PERCEPTUAL DEVELOPMENT

VISUAL DISCRIMINATION

DATE	TEST USED	REMARKS
Object Shape ______	________	________________
Letter Shape ______	________	________________
Word Shape ______	________	________________

AURAL DISCRIMINATION

Everyday Sounds	______	________	________________
Letter sounds	______	________	________________
Word Sounds	______	________	________________

MOTOR COORDINATION - COMMENTS ON

1. General body coordination
2. Specific handwriting coordination

READING ASSESSMENT

* See attached sheet on PHONIC RECORD

1. Initial group test on entry

DATE	TEST GIVEN	RESULT	COMMENTS

2. Further individual testing

DATE	TEST USED	RESULT	COMMENTS

Other considerations

There may be other responsibilities falling upon the shoulders of the teacher in contact with the slow learner, which will naturally vary depending on the organisation of the school in which he works, and his role within it. It may be the teacher's responsibility to pass on the information he has gained on the child to other staff members. For example, a child who has retarded perceptual development will be interesting to the maths teacher since that child will obviously show his weakness in maths lessons.

Similarly, motor weaknesses ought to be pointed out to the P.E. and Games staff, and any general problems, say in hearing or eyesight, to almost all the teachers with whom the child comes into contact. Explaining the implications of this type of information to other people, so that they in turn may use this knowledge in helping the child, is an important obligation for the teacher of the slow learner.

The responsibility for assessing the child's progress over time may also fall to the class teacher. Mention has already been made, in the earlier part of this chapter, of the dangers of over-reliance on reading screening tests in judging a child's progress. The sensitive teacher will use the results of tests repeated to confirm his own continuous assessments of the child, and to modify his teaching accordingly. He will bear in mind the fluctuating rates of improvement each child shows, as well as the difference in rate of improvement he might expect for an individual.

Alongside his own reading or other 'treatment' for the child, an experienced teacher will be keen to use others to help him achieve his desired end. He may call on many people who originally helped in an initial diagnostic assessment, to provide advice and additional assistance. These are listed in the diagram on p. 53.

In conclusion, all the above measures depend for their effectiveness on the teacher having a close contact with the child. Many of the tests require even a one-to-one correspondence before they can yield useful results. The whole staff of the school need to be convinced of the value of flexible timetabling and generous staffing. Without their cooperation, the organisation cannot be developed to cope with the challenge presented to the school by the slow learner.

WHOM TO USE IN TREATMENT OF CHILD

Naturally depends to a large extent on who helped in stage of early diagnosis. Local conditions etc.

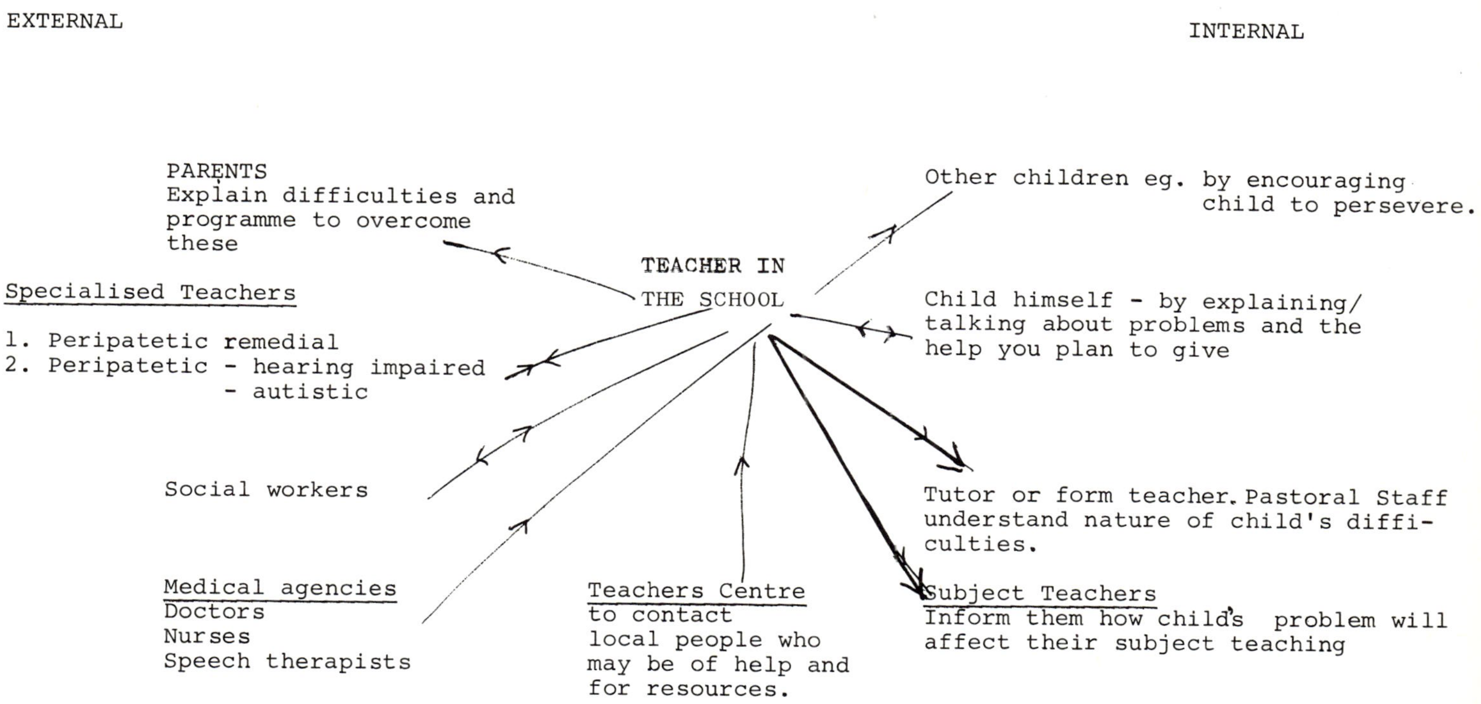

EXTERNAL

PARENTS
Explain difficulties and programme to overcome these

Specialised Teachers

1. Peripatetic remedial
2. Peripatetic - hearing impaired
   - autistic

Social workers

Medical agencies
Doctors
Nurses
Speech therapists

Teachers Centre to contact
local people who may be of help and for resources.

TEACHER IN THE SCHOOL

INTERNAL

Other children eg. by encouraging child to persevere.

Child himself - by explaining/talking about problems and the help you plan to give

Tutor or form teacher. Pastoral Staff understand nature of child's difficulties.

Subject Teachers
Inform them how child's problem will affect their subject teaching

CHAPTER 3

READING

It has been emphasised in the previous chapter, on diagnosis, that any programme for remedial readers must be highly individualised. This will depend on the *specific* difficulties and the general level of operation of each child in the reading group, not to mention the variations of personality and attitudes. (It would seem futile, for example, to rigorously insist that a child who has long been unable to learn a series of flashcards and has built up a negative attitude towards doing so, should be daily forced to attempt this task. This is merely reinforcing failure.) It has also been pointed out that diagnosis must be continuous, preferably not just at the level of regular testing, but rather by sensitive and acute observation by the teacher of the degree of competence and level of attainment of each child.

The first point to be made then is that the reading programme for any child must be based on an assessment of that child's competence and difficulties, and not on a generalisation or norm of the difficulties of a group. A remedial reading programme will only be successful when it fits closely to an accurate diagnosis of the child's specific difficulties and an understanding of his general level of intellectual ability. Moreover there is no doubt of the need to discriminate between specific difficulties and general low-level academic ability. The child with a specific disability may well be expected to proceed at a faster rate than the child of low all-round ability, if diagnosis of his problem has been successful. Again, ongoing assessment will reveal that children 'stick' at different points on the way to reading competence and here also it is clear that no general programme can accommodate this factor.

Reading competence

It is generally assumed that a child is equipped with all the skills of reading when he can score a reading age of 9.5 years on one of the many available standardized reading tests. From this point on it is assumed that there is little systematic work that can be done concerned with the skills and elements of reading. This is not to say, however, that children who have reached this stage have mastered all aspects of reading. The teacher must watch closely to discover those children whose attainment does not progress much beyond this level. These too may be children with specific difficulties:

a) Perhaps the child has not grasped one or two basic phonic sounds.
b) Maybe the child finds difficulty in breaking longer words into their constituent parts.
c) Perhaps the child still has difficulty in fluent reading.
d) Perhaps the child has a poor vocabulary and thus does not understand what he reads.
e) Perhaps the child dislikes reading and just stops doing so.

These few possibilities (there are many others!) are stressed in order that the common situation of pushing a child to the mythical R.A. – 9.5 years and believing all problems are solved is avoided. The problem *may* have been solved, but equally likely some difficulty will remain and a scheme to overcome this must be devised.

Nevertheless, the main concern of this chapter is how children with an R.A. below 9.5 should be dealt with. The problem seems enormous – there are complete non-readers at one end of the scale and children of considerable phonic competence at the other. There are the children with specific difficulties and children with all-round low ability. There are the children who 'stick' at the same point for many months and the children whose years of reading failures have induced an introverted and frustrated air to their problems. As teachers, we must discover not only the correct level of operation for each child and the reasons for this, but also the attitude of the child towards his problem, and develop an appropriate response to this. The sympathetic encouragement given to a timid girl may well not be appropriate to a mature, outgoing boy.

Principles in teaching reading

There is general agreement that several points are common to the needs of many backward readers. Firstly, the course should begin at or below the child's present attainment level. Secondly, children should not be expected to attempt tasks for which they are not prepared. Thirdly the child's self-confidence must be raised by praise and encouragement. Fourthly, children's interests should be used to build an involvement with reading.

It is bearing these points in mind that we must look to see how children who have experienced failure can be taught to read.

Non-readers

The children with the most severe problems will fall into the category in which little or no progress has been made towards reading competence. It is universally accepted that to be able to read the child must first have attained some competence in a number of areas. For example, Tansley (*Basic Reading*) points out that children with poorly developed visual perception – particularly in copying figures and shapes – poor visual discrimination and poor hand-eye coordination are not ready for a 'whole word' approach to reading.

Similarly children unable to copy sound rhythms are nearly always unable to attack 'phonics'. But although children need competence in various areas to cope with reading, preparation for reading does not mean simply waiting for readinesss to develop. This must be an active period associated with the skills needed. These skills are numerous and open to subdivision and overlap, but for convenience it seems reasonable to divide into the following areas (as described in *Teaching Non-Readers* – West Sussex County Psychological Service).

a) Visual/Motor
b) Auditory/Speech
c) Sequencing

These are the areas in which non-readers should be trained, and progress in reading will only be made with increased competence in these skills and their integration with one another.

Practical suggestions for training in visual/motor abilities

(training the child in the discrimination of different shapes and in memorising them; also training in hand/eye coordination)

N.B. In all the suggested activities of this chapter, great care must be taken in grading materials. Too steep grading will lead to lack of success and frustration, but too fine grading will lead to slow progress and boredom.

1. Sets of silhouettes of different shapes can be used for identification.
2. Sets of pictures can be constructed with concealed items in them (hidden pictures).
3. Dot to dot sheets may be compiled for geometrical shapes, pictures, letters, etc. These may be graded by difficulty of shape or by reducing dots.
4. Cut-out geometrical shapes may be used to build up pictures. (Materials for all these activities can be found in children's comics. These can be purchased very cheaply, in bulk at jumble sales.)
5. Simple jigsaws may be constructed for pictures and then later for letters.

6. Show the child pairs of pictures. Some pairs are identical, other pairs only similar. The child has to discriminate.
7. Letters may be used to draw pictures, e.g., S can be drawn as smoke.
8. Odd man out – The child is shown a set of symbols, e.g.

or words, e.g., was was has was, or even pictures and he has to pick out the one which is different from the others.
9. Three card games suggest themselves for packs of shape and/or picture cards: a) Snap; b) Happy Families; c) Pairs (cards are placed face-down and the children try to turn over pairs of identical cards).
10. Copying shapes, figures, letters, without the child looking at his hand.
11. Bingo can be played in a variety of ways provided the players can see the cards as each item is called out. Base cards need to be slightly different for each child. Colours, shape, size, pictures and letters can all be used for this game.
12. Memory flash cards – the teacher shows a flash card with a shape, letter, etc. on it; then it is put away and the child must select an identical card from a pack of his own.
13. The child must complete a picture of objects, people or patterns in which a part has been omitted, e.g.

14. Copying matchstick patterns, either on paper or with matchsticks.
15. Crossing out letters in a random assortment of letters, e.g. 'Cross out all the Ss in red and all the Xs in blue'
XBYSTRSUVSYHPX
CTSSHXAEXRTSPO
This particular activity can be varied considerably and easily graded by using unlike letters (say a and g), like letters (say t and l) and letters that are commonly reversed (b and d).

16. Sheets (probably on a spirit duplicator) can be prepared for identifying

a) similar geometric shapes

b) similar letters

b d d b d

c) similar words

has was hat has hit

d) similar objects

Practical suggestions for training in auditory speech abilities
(training the child to discriminate between different sounds, to memorise them and to say them).

1. The child listens to stories and repeats them as closely as possible afterwards. (Tapes may be very useful here.)
2. The child completes sentences verbally in conjunction with a picture: e.g. John is a———boy.
3. A set of pictures is on the table. The teacher describes one and the child must pick it out from those displayed.
4. The child groups a pack of cards spread face up on the table according to instructions given by the teacher.
e.g. 'Sort out all the red things.'
'Sort out all the things with four legs.'
5. Development of the concept of opposites:
'What is the opposite of – – – – –'
6. The child is asked to give the names of all the things he knows in a given category, e.g. fruit, colours, furniture.
7. The child is asked to match pictures to common taped sounds.
8. A set of objects is placed on the table. The teacher sounds out the first letter of one of them and the child has to identify the object.

9. The teacher reads out pairs of words. Some pairs are identical, some are similar. The child must indicate whether the pairs are similar or identical,

e.g. when then (similar)
thing thin (similar)
heat heat (same)

10. Rhyming. The teacher gives a word and the child must supply a rhyming word to go with it.

11. Happy Families can be played with sets of rhyming words coupled with pictures,

e.g.

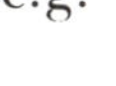

12. The teacher gives the child a riddle with a sound clue: e.g. 'You watch it at home and it begins with t (tuh!)'.

13. Repetition: a) The child has to repeat a sentence or a string of words, or a series of digits; b) The teacher says a series of words then repeats it leaving one word out. The child must identify the missing word,

e.g. this then that those the
(repeat) this then that the

14. The child is asked to add further words beginning with the same sound to a list started by the teacher,

e.g. moon milk mustard.

15. The child is asked to pick the odd man out of a list spoken by the teacher,

e.g. man milk goat mustard.

16. Both 14 and 15 can be repeated using word-endings rather than word-beginnings,

e.g. sight light fight
and sight light side fight

17. I Spy – 'I spy something that begins with the same sound as (bicycle) begins with.' (A limited choice of objects may be necessary for this task.)

18. The child is asked to identify two sounds presented simultaneously.

19. The child listens to, and carries out, a series of instructions.

Practical suggestions for training in sequencing abilities
(training the child to remember the relative positions of visual and auditory symbols).

1. The child must pick out a mirror image from a sequence, e.g.
a) letters

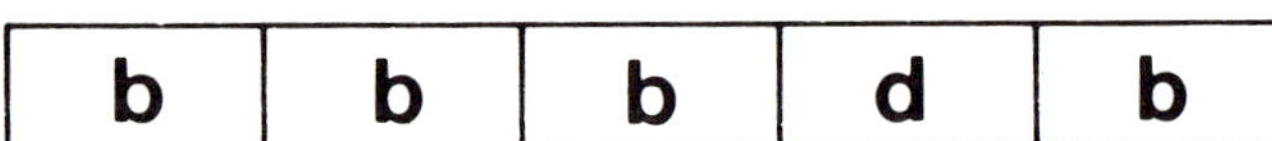

b) geometrical shapes

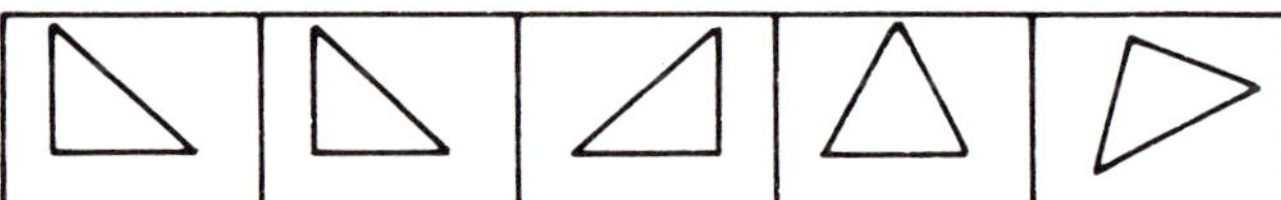

c) pictures

2. The child repeats vocally, or on paper, a series of dots and dashes (some pre-training on morse signals may be necessary here).
3. The teacher taps out a rhythm and the child repeats it.
4. Repetition of words, sentences, digits (as 13 auditory/speech).
5. The child must put in order a series of sequence cards depicting an activity,
e.g. a series of four pictures showing a boy going up some stairs.
6. The child must continue patterns, e.g.

a) geometric

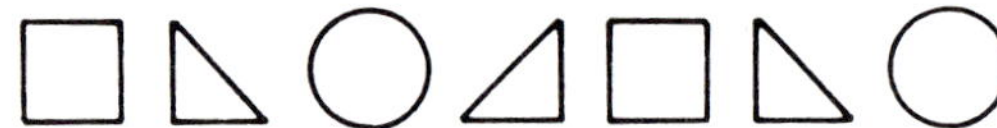

b) non-geometric

7. The child must verbalise a morse sequence of dots and dashes,
e.g. ·—— ··— ·——· ———·· —·—·
8. The child must reassemble something he has been shown on a series of cards. This may be either a temporal sequence or a pattern, e.g. The child is shown four pictures of a plant growing. The pictures are scattered and the child must reorganise them, *or*
the child is shown a pattern of shapes which is scattered and the child must reassemble the pattern.
9. The child must make up picture/sequence jigsaws

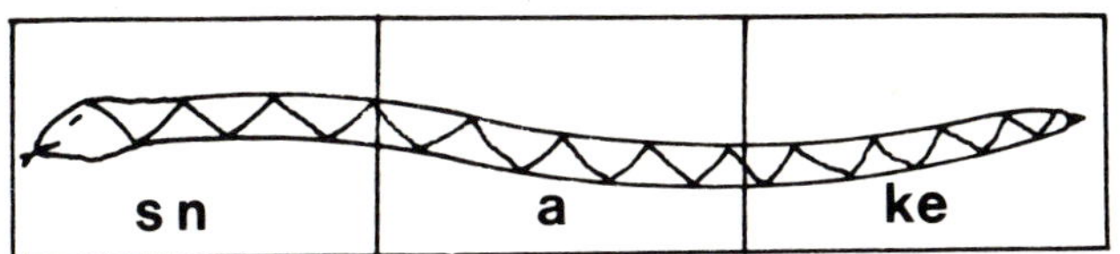

This exercise might be started with pictures and words and eventually with words alone.

10. Activities to develop left/right orientation:
    a) trading from left to right
    b) joining dots
    c) using writing patterns
    d) following the sequence of pictures in comics. Cut up the comics and get the children to place them in the right order.
    e) a variety of duplicated exercises e.g.

mouse to cheese

car to garage

path to house

joining dots for fences

joining dots for railways

Pre-reading materials

There are some publishers who provide a variety of materials for children at the pre-reading training level. However, many teachers may prefer to prepare their own materials along the lines already suggested. Certainly this will prove much more economical. Below are tabulated names of useful publishers of material for children pursuing a reading readiness course and some of the types of material they publish.

Arnold	e.g. Misfits Picture Books New Picture Books Snappy Lotto Picture Dominoes Snappy Snap Early to Read

E.S.A.	e.g. Picture/Word Matching Poleidoblocs Plastic Letters Mosaics Picture Lotto Twinning Frames Dominoes Snap Visual Discrimination Books 1 – 3 Fit-a-Space
Invicta	A variety of construction aids
Galt	e.g. Mosaic Tiles Geometric Shape Spotting Jigsaws Pin Board Remember Remember Colour Dominoes Picture Dominoes Geometric Dominoes Find a Pair Spot the Set
Learning Development Aids	Concept Cards Discrimination Cards Recall Cards Sequential Thinking Patterning
Ginn	Getting Ready for Reading
Philip and Tacey	e.g. Mosaics Tiles Letters Pencil Control Tracing Cards Precept Shadow Letter Chalk Work Tracing Sheets Protus Geometrical Shapes Build a Shape Pelmanism Game Alike and Unlike Strip Books Symmetry and Reversal Pairing Cards Shape Analysis Matching Cards

	Hereward Observation Matching Cards Letter Recognition and Sorting Strip Books Kenny Cellograph Word and Picture Matching Books Polly Strip Reading Books Three of a Kind Strip Books
Philograph	A whole host of activities and boxed games on matching sorting dominoes, etc.
Remedial Supply Company	A variety of materials on paper and on tape

N.B. The activities in the previous four sections are only suggestions. They must be expanded and carefully used in a graded scheme. Some time will be necessary in the preparation of materials but considerable success can be achieved without great expense.

Different types of reading method

A programme of reading readiness should not be carried out in isolation. This would suggest that until the child has mastered all aspects of the programme he will be unable to read at all. This is plainly not true. The reading readiness course and beginning to read should overlap – indeed they must do so otherwise the enthusiasm of the child may well be destroyed. At the same time it is certain that in so far as the child does not attain competence in those skills associated with reading, the progress of the child in reading will be equally limited, and this too will lead to a loss of motivation.

How then are slow learners taught to read? Several different approaches have been excellently tabulated by Goodacre (1972) and are reproduced overleaf.

Although the approaches are markedly different it is perhaps plausible to suggest that they may all be contributory in attaining reading competence. 'Look and Say' is extremely important at the early stages of reading in providing a basic reading vocabulary plus a knowledge of important non-pictorial service words (is, are, where, etc.). At the same time it seems inconceivable that the child can progress beyond a reading age of 8 years if he fails to develop

DIFFERENT TYPES OF READING METHODS

	METHOD	EMPHASIS ON	MAY HELP WITH	DRAWBACKS
DECODING	ALPHABETIC	Names of letters ar-ue-en - run see ae tee = cat	Letter recognition, development of left to right sequence. Durrell has suggested all the consonants letter names except h, g, w and y contain their phoneme or sound plus an extraneous vowel, e.g. b-ee, s-ee for b.c.d.g.p.t.v.z or eh -l, eh-m for f, l.m.n.s.x.	Alphabetic sequence (a b c d) may be confusing, eg. b and d near each other in order sound and shape similar. Child may lose interest in material read if concentrating solely on letter recognition. Some children make idiosyncratic associations with letters which are no help with sound: eg. t is like a hammer
	PHONIC	Sounds of letters ruh-uh-neh (r-u-n = run) or ruh-un-(r-un = run) or ruh-ner (ru-n = run)	Useful for deciphering unfamiliar (from sight) word. Child can try out a word to see if it fits. Does not have to wait to be told. Phonics can be taught systematically, eg. synthesis, word building, word families, incidentally analytic beginning sounds of familiar words	Blending or synthesizing sounds can be difficult for some children. Need for fine auditory discrimination. Boys' auditory ability appears to develop later than girls. 'Irregularity' of English may lead to restriction of vocabulary in readers, artificial style. Child can pronounce unfamiliar word, may not to in oral vocabulary
READING FROM MEANING	WHOLE WORD OR LOOK AND SAY	run run rug (not mat) rabbit	Use of meaningful words: e.g. ice cream. Often pictorial representation an additional clue. Word/picture association. Look-and-say used for non-pictorial words, also service words, eg. are, the you taught as sight words	Individual letters may be ignored, particularly word endings, medial vowels. Leads to guessing. No means of deciphering unfamiliar word. Child waits to be 'told'. Dependency on teacher. Diifficult to differentiate between words similar in length, configuration, eg. cat, cot must keep meaning in the foreground
	WHOLE SENTENCE	The girls run round the tree (N.B. Not dance or skip)	Emphasis on whole sentence and phrases. Children's interests can be used. Meaningful. Fosters appreciation of importance of intonation, phrasing and pitch when reading aloud	Individual letters and words may be left out. Guessing. Written language structure may not be familiar, substitutions may be based on dialect differences – eg. reads we was instead of we were does not help build up letter/sound association
MULTIPLE CLUES	LINGUISTIC	The man will run in the race. The man will r. . . . (letter clue) The man will rabbit (syntactically unacceptable). The man will reach (semantically unacceptable) The man will roll (not probable)	Language as communication. Oral language provides child with clues. Type of word which will make a good 'fit'. Word parts, endings, etc. Signal information, e.g. ed added to a word signals past tense. Written language presents letter strings which become familiar build in sound expectations.	Reading materials sometimes based on words using common letter strings can be artificial. Stressing letter patterns of similar form can be confusing, eg. name, same, bane. Playing down the use of pictures (said to give extraneous cues) may make dull blocks. May underrate difference in speech patterns.

some phonic word attack skills. There is such a barrage of new words it is impossible for 'Look and Say' alone to be sufficient. Linguistic clues too will be very useful by this stage but it is suggested that it is only by using both his phonic skills and contextual cues that the child will consistently unscramble words that are new to him.

In summary, then:

1. Do not abandon a reading readiness course too soon.
2. Do not choose one method of teaching reading to the exclusion of all other. Use the elements of each approach where they can be most profitably utilised in an integrated scheme.

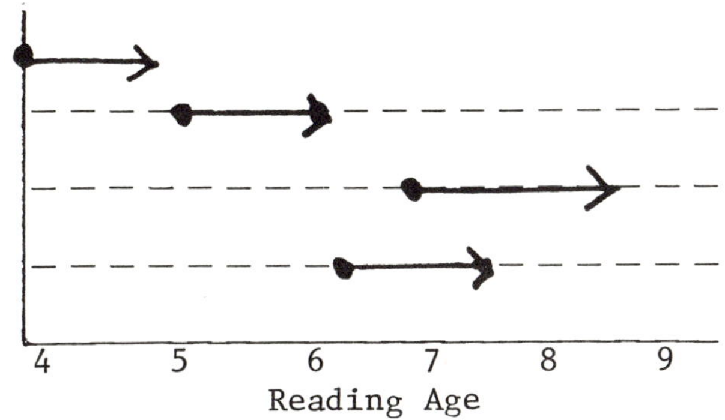

In general as the R.A. goes up the importance of the pre-reading course and 'Look and Say' methods to obtain a sight vocabulary decrease whilst linguistic cues and phonics assume more importance.

Building a sight vocabulary

It is generally accepted that a child will find difficulty in tackling a phonic programme until he has an R.A. in excess of 6.5 years. Until then it is evident that the most successful approaches will be those of 'Look and Say' and 'Whole Sentence'. In this way the child will build up an extensive *sight vocabulary*. Sight words may be described as those words which the child recognises instantly without attempt to break down into constituent parts. It is extremely important at this early stage in a reading scheme to give the child success. It is vital that the teacher buys or prepares a variety of materials to build up an extensive sight vocabulary.

Activities to build up a sight vocabulary (These should be carried out using words belonging to the reading scheme being used).

1) Flashcards: this is a very common method of building a sight vocabulary. The teacher must find a variety of uses for these or the child may well tire of them.

2) Picture and word matching tasks, e.g.

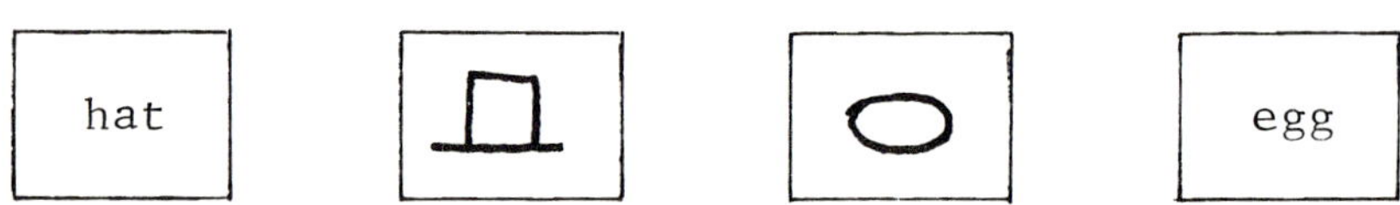

3) Picture/word jigsaws (cut out in card)
These can be easily graded:

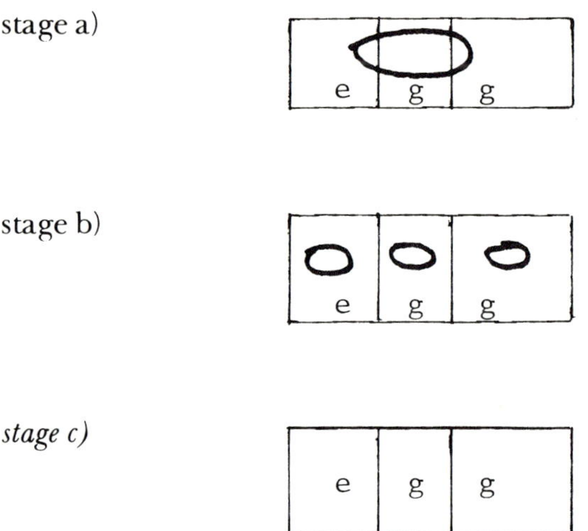

4) Graded Lotto:
The teacher prepares bingo cards based on the restricted sight vocabulary being dealt with at a given time.
5) Dominoes (picture/word type), e.g.

6) Picture/word Snap:
Two packs of cards are prepared – one pack of pictures, the other of words. Both packs are placed face down. The top card is turned over from each pack. When the word matches the picture the child has to read the word. Points can be given.
7) Using the same cards as in 6) the picture pack is dealt out to the children. The teacher turns over the word pack one card at a time. When the word matches a picture in the child's hand he discards that picture. The first child to discard all of his pictures is the winner.

8) A pack of cards is prepared with a word on one side and the corresponding picture on the reverse side. The cards are presented word-side up. Whichever child can read the word wins the card (easily checked by looking at the picture).
9) Any number of 'track' games may be developed by teachers to aid the building of a sight vocabulary. All of these can use packs of flashcards of the words to be learned.

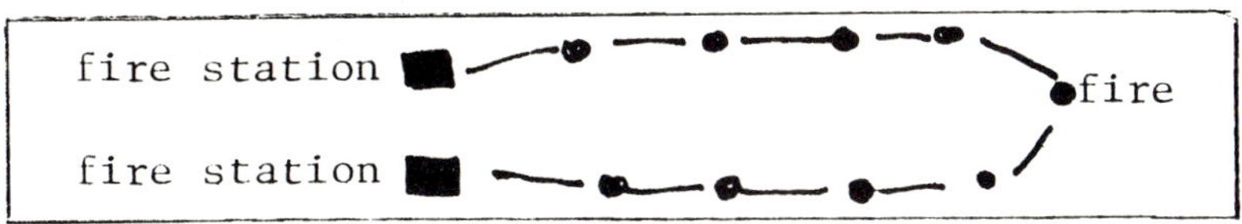

The child moves along the route by reading a flashcard successfully. The object is to put out the fire by 'landing' the fire engine on it.

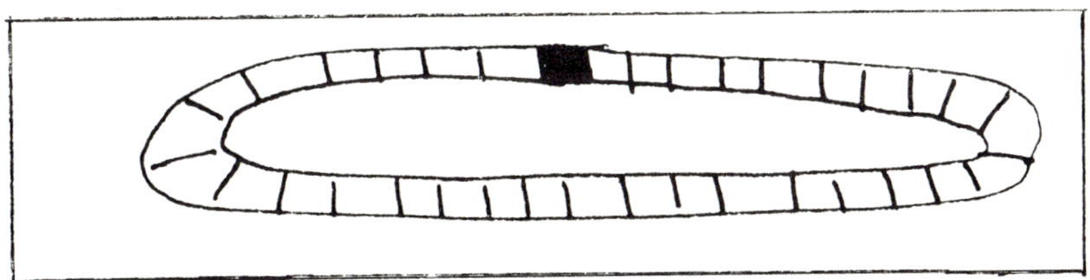

Race Track games may take the form of athletics, speedway, motor racing, etc. Variations on the two themes above are limitless and all can be used equally well with various packs of flashcards. The games may be made much more sophisticated, and hence more attractive to older children, if a dice is introduced to the game, or if different values are attributed to each flashcard.

Before leaving the area of sight vocabulary one or two points must be emphasised. Many of the games and activities involve pictures as well as words. This is satisfactory for nouns but many of the service words (is, has, etc.), common to early reading are difficult to depict. Consequently, the teacher must take care in the games he devises and the words he uses in them.

Secondly, Dolch has produced a list of 220 words, comprising 50% of all the words children ever meet in reading, and the Key Words provide a British equivalent of 300 words which make up 75% of all reading. It is very tempting to believe that extensive 'cramming' on these lists will lead to short cuts in attaining reading competence. Unfortunately, both lists contain for the main part the same service words as mentioned above, and the same pitfalls need to be avoided as many of the words are short, similar in appearance and difficult to depict, e.g., this, that, then, there, these, those, they.

However, careful thought should ensure that many of these words may be *incorporated* into a variety of games. The warning is simply not to introduce too many at one time and over-burden the child – or even worse, to attempt rote learning.

Teaching phonics

It seems likely that the child can cope with reading up to a reading age of 7 years using only a 'Look and Say' approach. Thereafter he will meet such a variety of words that he will need other tools at his disposal to succeed. On the other hand the child will derive little success from a 'phonic' approach until he can do the following (Tansley – *Reading and Remedial Reading*):

a) appreciate and give rhyming words
b) discriminate letter sounds, e.g., 'Which is the odd man out? – man, milk, boy, Mary'.
c) blend words orally from their elements when dictated by the teacher, e.g. cu—a—tu (cat), hu—e—nn (hen).

Once it is accepted that the child is ready for a programme of phonics the teacher must decide the order in which he proposes to teach them. There is considerable agreement over the best order for this, although the various authorities differ in detail. What is important is that the teacher decides on the best order both for himself and the child concerned.

A possible order follows, but this is subject to amendment by both teacher preference and the needs of each child.

PHONIC ABILITY

1. LETTER NAMES:

A B C D E F G H I J K L M N O P Q R S T U V W X Y Z

________________ ________________
________________ ________________
________________ ________________
________________ ________________

2. INITIAL AND END SOUNDS

a b c d e f g h i j k l m n o p q r s t u v w x y z

________________ ________________
________________ ________________
________________ ________________
________________ ________________

3. SHORT VOWELS

a e i o u

4. MAGIC 'e'

a e i o u

5. DOUBLE LETTERS

dd ff ll bb nn gg ss pp rr zz tt

6. ee oo

7. ch sh th wh ph

8. Other two consonant blends - BEGINNINGS

bl br er dr cl fl fr gl gr pl pr sc sk sl sm sn
sp st sw tr tw

ENDS.

ck ct ft ld lm lt mp nd nk nt rt sk st

9. VOWEL DIGRAPHS

ee ea ea (short)

ow o-e oa

ay a-e ai

-y i-e igh

ow ou

oo u-e ew

oy oi

ar er ir or ur

ing ang ong ung

10. 3 LETTER COMBINATIONS:

scr spl spr squ thr str shr

11. ENDINGS

-ble, -dle, -gle, -kle, -ple, -tle, -ed, -er, -es, -est, -ce, -dge, -ge, -ious,-ous, -le, -ly, -ment, -ness, -sion, -tion, -ture, -sure.

BEGINNINGS

be, de, dis, cor, pre, re, ex, sure.

12. SILENTS

k b n w u c g n o t

13. ODDS

qu squ c=s g=j s=sh c=ch ch=c

It has been suggested that competence in phonic word attack skills will give the child added independence in his reading but in any phonic programme some general points should be considered:

1) In the early stages of phonics oral work should be emphasised to confirm that the child is not making associations based on the shape of a word alone.
2) In teaching phonics blending should not be overemphasised but a too analytic approach should not be evolved by the child, leading him to sound out words unnecessarily.
3) Stress must also be made of the use of contextual cues.
4) Phonic elements should be generalised from known sight words. Never introduce a new element by phonic attack.
5) Supplementary free writing, listening and oral work all appear to be important complements to phonic teaching.
6) Supplementary reading should be appropriate to the phonic level the child has reached.
7) Drill and practice must be used in a wide variety of activities.

Activities for phonic training

1) Sets of three dice can be constructed. One dice has word beginnings on, one dice has 'middles' and the third dice word 'endings'. If constructed carefully the dice can be thrown to always produce a 'word' that can be pronounced phonetically *even though* it may not exist in the dictionary. This is a useful exercise for building confidence in phonic attack.
2) The teacher reads out a list of words and the child writes down the first letter, or digraph, or blend.

3) A 'box of sounds' may be useful, i.e. a collection of flashcards for each phonic element in a scheme which can be used in an odd moment. The phonic element being taught may be in a different colour from the rest of the word.
4) Word families may be compiled by letter substitution, e.g. tank, sank, rank.
5) In the early stages of phonic teaching, alliteration may be useful, e.g. The baby bear buys a big balloon.
6) Restricted 'I Spy' may be played using only the phonic combinations which are being taught at the time.
7) Various matching games can be played with picture cards and cards with letters on them, e.g.

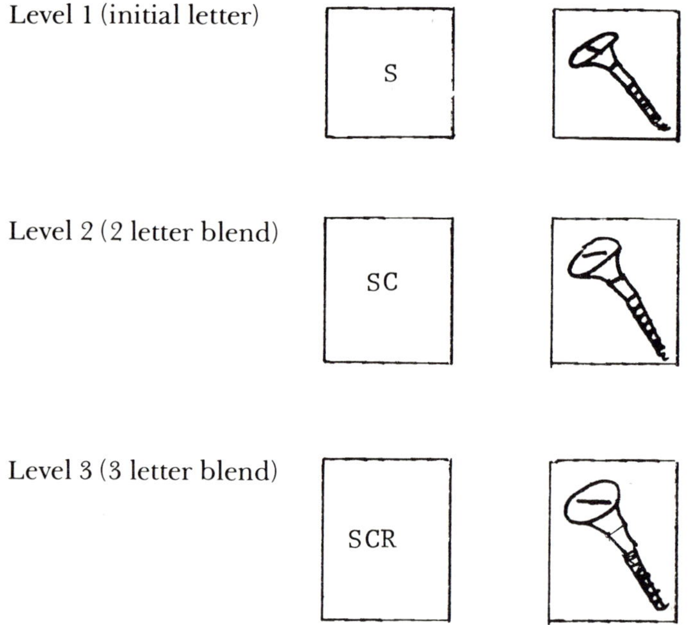

8) The teacher has a set of cards with initial or end sounds on them. When one of these is displayed the child has to point to an object in the room which has this sound in its name.
9) A pack of cards can be made of word beginnings and word endings. Each child is dealt six cards. They may then be used as in 'rummy' until one child has used his six cards to make three full words.

10) Rhyming dictionaries can be made, e.g.

hail	all	ate
pail	call	plate
snail	fall	skate

11) Rotating wheels may be made from cardboard or wood:

A series of these can easily be made to varying degrees of phonic difficulty.

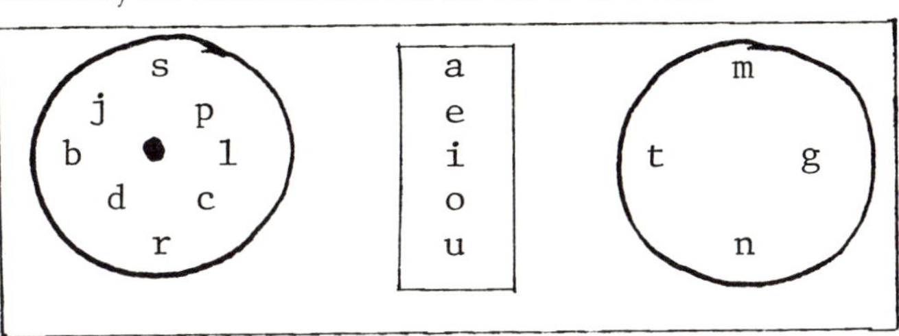

12) Many of the activities suggested in sight vocabulary can be adapted for words of various phonic combinations.
13) The teacher can also produce an abundance of duplicated sheets dealing with individual phonic elements in a variety of ways. A. E. Tansley gives the following extensive list (as used in the Sound Sense (E. J. Arnold) scheme) in *Reading and Remedial Reading* pages 47–48:

1) Putting words into sound families.
2) Finding from given lists words which belong to a given sound family.
3) Spontaneous giving of words belonging to a given family.
4) Finding the stranger in a given list of words.
5) Putting in missing sounds.
6) Joining with a line words beginning or ending with the same sound.
7) Rearranging jumbled words into sentences.
8) Rearranging jumbled sentences into a meaningful passage.
9) Choosing the sight word from several alternatives or given lists.
10) Sentence completion.
11) Story completion.
12) Making up words from given letters.
13) Finding words within words.
14) Adding digraphs to the beginning or ending of given phonograms or pronunciation units.
15) Word sums.
16) Finding words which rhyme or finding the stranger in a list of rhyming words.
17) Exercises on words which belong to various classes, e.g. occupations, food, drink, nationalities, colours, materials, etc.
18) Finding answers to given questions.
19) Making up questions to given answers.

20) Exercises on plurality, comparatives, superlatives and opposites.
21) Finding wrong and right statements.
22) Reading short passages and stories and answering comprehension questions of varying degrees of difficulty.
23) Drawing pictures or making simple models from written instructions.
24) Suffixes and prefixes together with inflected and derived forms of given words.
25) Word squares and simple crosswords.
26) Word puzzles, e.g. 'I have four legs, I am a pet, I go bow-wow, what am I?'
27) Writing a story with key words given.
28) Giving words for given definitions and vice versa.
29) Dictionary work.
30) Changing tenses of given sentences.

Language development

In the section on reading readiness considerable regard was paid to training in the auditory/speech field. It is inconceivable, moreover, that any systematic attack on reading difficulties should not include a parallel language development course. Failure to do so will certainly undermine progress although the course need not be programmed as tightly as, say, a phonics course. The areas which must be concentrated upon are: 1) Description
2) Classifying
3) Logical questioning.

A variety of approaches may be used for language development: discussion, taping, storytelling, drama, puppetry; to say nothing of the variety of classifying games that can be formulated with packs of cards.

Activities

1. Description: a) storytelling (imaginative)
b) story recounting (from tape)
c) object and picture description
d) giving directions.
2. Classifying: a) opposites
b) synonyms
c) dimensions (size, weight, shape, etc.)
d) position (top, bottom, under, over, left, right, etc.)

Classifying lends itself to work with packs of cards.

3. Logical questioning. (Here the aim should be to train the child to deduce by elimination and not to make random guesses):

a) 'Twenty Questions' type games
b) The use of Logiblocs
c) 'Whodunnit' games are also popular with all ranges of children.

Series available for language development

Series	*Publisher*	*Comments*
Zero Books	Macdonald	A series of books designed to stimulate conversation about a variety of situations – in the home, street, etc. Some questions are provided in the script. Amusing and well-illustrated. Particularly useful for younger children.
Concept 7–9	Arnold	Expensive set of language development aids produced in four units. Most useful for slow learners are Listening with Understanding (cassette-based); Communication (variety of games) and Concept Development. Aimed at the primary age-range, this kit can be very useful with younger secondary slow learners. An added advantage is that the units may be purchased individually.
Language Development Programme	S.R.A.	A expensive series of language builders with a teacher's guide.
The Language Project	Macmillan	The Language Project has two elements. 'Language in Action' provides materials for developing aspects of language – listening, speaking, reading and writing. 'Language Guides' is a set of paperbacks on aspects of language and its classroom application for student and teacher. Aimed for children with R.A. 4–9 it may be appropriate for use up until the lower secondary age range.
Talkmore	Arnold	Series of pictures, booklets, flannelgraphs, flashcards for younger children. Reasonably priced.
Pictures and Words	Blackie	An inexpensive language and reading development scheme consisting of display books, pupils' books and teacher's guide.

Peabody Language Development Kits	Available from N.F.E.R.	Three kits available: Level 1 – $4\frac{1}{2}$–$6\frac{1}{2}$ years Level 2 – 6–8 years Level 3 – $7\frac{1}{2}$–$9\frac{1}{2}$ years Very expensive.

Teacher organisation

The general outline of a course in reading for slow learners has been suggested as follows:

a) pre-reading training
b) sight vocabulary
c) phonics
d) language development

At the same time the individuality of the child and the desirability of a course fitting the child and not the child fitting the course, has been stressed. But it is only a framework to be expanded in different places and in various directions for each child. It is precisely because of this that the teacher needs detailed knowledge of each child's temperament, attainment and potential; and this knowledge needs to be under constant revision. This is just one part of the necessary teacher organisation. An intimate knowledge of available materials is vital – a knowledge of which equipment fits which situation, and especially a knowledge of what is available in one's own school. It may be relevant for the less experienced teacher to catalogue available materials under the headings of this chapter in order to become familiar with them. Certainly when dealing with phonics, a notebook of references to workbooks, tapes, duplicated exercises, etc. can be very useful.

Preparing materials

Although a wide variety of materials are available through publishers it is often far more economical and directly relevant, even if time-consuming, for the teacher to prepare much of his own materials.

Teacher-prepared materials will usually appear as disposable paper resources or work cards. They may supplement or replace other materials either as 'follow-up work' for aspects of the child's work, or reinforce features considered to be important by the teachers. But whatever the purpose, the teacher should keep in mind the following:

1) Present material clearly, attractively, and illustrated where possible.
2) Grade the work carefully. Rapid jumps may confuse the pupil.

3) Ensure that each child can meet with some success.

Less obvious than reprographically produced exercises, but equally useful, the teacher can prepare a multitude of games. Some simple suggestions have already been made.

Many older children seem to prefer the sophistication of board games of the 'Monopoly' type and with thought, games of this nature can be advantageously used as either an incidental or definite item of a reading programme. Games may be devised to use:

a) a specific group of words – for a project perhaps;
b) words of a general reading level – from Schonell's lists;
c) specific phonic elements.

Taking an example, it is possible to make a soccer game which can be used in all the above ways.

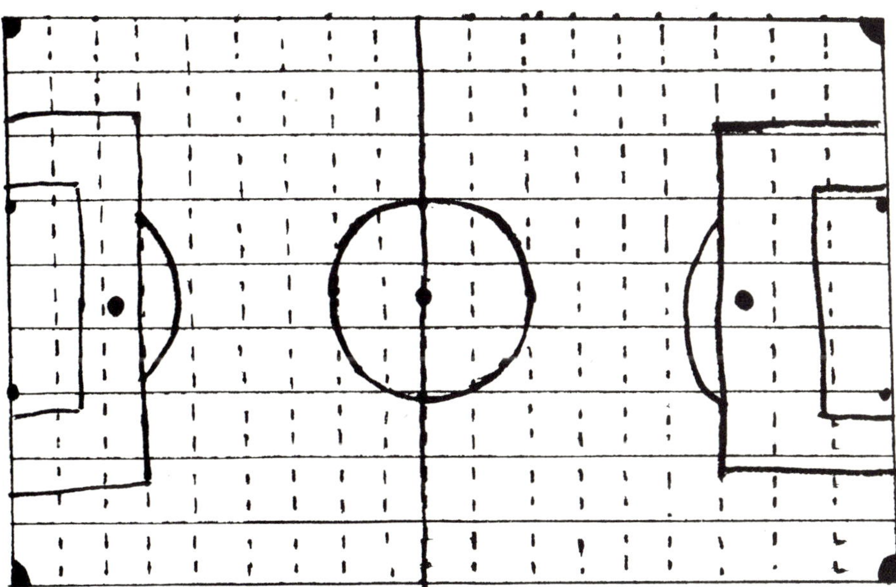

A football pitch is marked out on a squared board 18 squares by 9 squares. The two players attempt to score goals by reading flashcards, e.g.

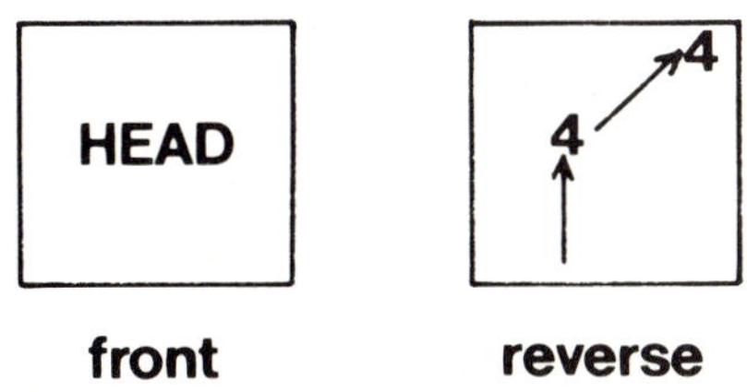

This means that if the player reads or spells the word correctly the ball is moved four squares forward and four squares diagonally to the right. (Different move values should be attributed to each card.)

By producing a number of packs of flashcards the game can be adapted to meet the three above criteria,

i.e. 1) to accustom children to a specific vocabulary – as in a new project;

2) for use at different reading levels – by preparing graded packs using Schonell lists (in this way children at very different levels can successfully play the game together by using packs appropriate to their reading level);

3) as part of a phonic programme by preparing packs of flashcards to deal specifically with individual phonic elements (here again by using different packs, children at widely different points on a phonic scheme can compete with each other).

Used in this way board games have an appeal and a flexibility which can constitute a useful motivational factor in any reading programme. By preparing several games of this nature, reasonable numbers of children can be *gainfully* occupied on a regular basis.

Much can be learned by making one's own materials. This is time-consuming for busy teachers but ancillaries and parents are often able to help in this field once the initial idea has been explained. In my opinion the making of materials should be a practical and important part of every pupil's course. Too often the new teacher is confronted with a need to create new materials without having had any experience of this whatsoever. When this does happen I believe it to be a serious indictment of the course they have followed.

A later chapter on Resources and Materials goes into this aspect more generally.

Useful reading series

A considerable amount of time in any reading scheme will be spent in either hearing the child read or allowing him to read on his own. How then do we select which books a child should read? A number of schemes are available comprising books, workbooks, and a variety of subsidiary material and most children will make some progress with these. However, by the very nature of the problems of many slow learners, numerous children will need to use a wider variety of books at any given level than any of the existing schemes provide in order to consolidate progress. Moreover if the child is to maintain interest and motivation he is going to need to step out of the confines of a single scheme quite regularly. Consequently the teacher will need to be aware of the approximate level of a variety of graded reading series and supplementary readers to ensure that the child meets with reasonable success in his reading, and furthermore the teacher will need to attempt to tie in these books with the phonic programme which is being followed.

Abbreviations

R.A. – Reading Age
I.A. – Interest Age   A equals 8 – 9 years
B equals 10 – 11 years
C equals 12 – 13 years
D equals 14 – 16 years

N.B. An assessment of the R.A. of a book must necessarily be subjective and approximate, and an assessment of the I.A. of a book can only be general and great emphasis must be placed on the emotional and maturational level of the child in deciding which series is appropriate.

Series	*R.A.*	*I.A.*	*Author*	*Publisher*	*Description*
Griffin Pirate Stories	5–9	ABC	McCullogh	Arnold	Serialised stories about pirates. 20 books plus 6 pre-readers. Very popular especially with boys. Part of a scheme along with 6 workbooks. A limitation may be in the specialised nature of the vocabulary.
Look Out Gang	5–8	ABC	Chapman	Gibson	Predominantly phonic based set of six readers. Rather steeply graded.
Royal Road Readers	5–9	ABC	Daniels & Diack	Chatto & Windus	Phonetically based scheme. 12 basic readers plus some 20 supplementaries. Some of the books may be applicable in the secondary school.
Sullivan Programmed Reading	5–9	ABC	Buchanan	McGraw Hill	11 programmed workbooks of American origin. Very finely graded with 11 parallel storybooks. May prove of best use with children with severe reading difficulties.

Series	*R.A.*	*I.A.*	*Author*	*Publisher*	*Description*
Start Afresh	–8	ABC	Butcher	Hulton	6 graded readers.
New Age in Reading	5–10	BC	Clay	Arnold	4 pre-readers concerned with visual and auditory discrimination plus six sets of six readers. Scaled down famous stories.
Far West Readers	6–8	BCD	Rudge	Pergamon	Set of 6 continuous cowboy stories.
Fell Farm Adventures	6–9	BC		Blackie	4 short books for slower secondary pupils about farm life in Cumberland. Limited vocabulary.
Manxman	6–8	CD	Edwards	Dent	6 comic-strip style books. Motor cycle themes, etc. Popular with adolescents. Well illustrated.
Nippers	6–9	ABC	various	Macmillan	Stories designed to relate to real life working-class situations. 5 groups of books graded by colour. Inexpensive, limp-covered, well-illustrated.
Ginger Books	6–9	BC	Briand		9 books, limp-covered. Inexpensive.
Cowboy Sam	6–7	ABC	Chandler	Arnold	Graded supplementary readers on cowboy theme. Popular with junior and younger secondary children.
Out With Tom	6–8	D	Gunzburg	Methuen	Set of 18 readers based on vocabularies of social usefulness.
Oxford Colour Reader	6–8	ABC	Carver & Stowasse	O.U.P.	6 grades with 6 books to each of the first 4 grades. 28 limp-covered books in all. Colourful, making much use of pictorial cues in the early stages, the series incorporates puzzles and other written work. Can be very successful with some pupils.

Series	*R.A.*	*I.A.*	*Author*	*Publisher*	*Description*
Oxford Graded Readers	6 –8	CD	various	O.U.P.	The 9 titles of the 500 'Headwords' and 750 'Headwords' senior level are appropriate for older slow learners.
Rescue Readers	6–10	ABC	Webster	Ginn	18 books (limp) in 3 series with accompanying work-books for the first series (rescue stories). Attractive and well-illustrated, these books are suitable for boys and girls.
Sea Hawks	6–8	BCD	McCullogh	Arnold	2 introductory books, 4 graded readers and 4 library books. Attractive and well-illustrated sea stories. May be used as supplementaries to Griffin Pirates and Dragon Pirates.
Space Age Readers	6 –8	BC	Segal	Blond	2 books plus 2 workbooks.
Step Up And Read	6–9	BCD	Jones	U.L.P.	6 readers (steeply graded) phonic cards and 3 books of Companion Exercises. More suitable for boys than girls. Phonic scheme.
Tales and Adventures	6–9	BC	McCullogh	Hulton	Blue and Yellow series. Folk tales with appeal mainly for girls.
Tempo Books	6–9	BCD	Groves & Stratton	Longman	Phonic based graded readers. Set of 10. Carefully controlled vocabulary.
Tim's Gang	6 –8	BC	Kirby	Nelson	3 books about a group of boys whose hideout is on a demolition site.
Beginner Books (Dr. Seuss)	6–8	AB(C)		Collins	Humorous books designed to show slow learners that reading can be fun.
Wild West Readers	6 –8	ABC	Prothero	Wheaton	A series of 12 graded books.

Series	*R.A.*	*I.A.*	*Author*	*Publisher*	*Description*
Adventures in Space	7–8	ABC	McCullogh	Hart-Davies	4 sets of 3 books dealing with space travel. Comic strip layout. Limp-covered.
Bandit Book	7–9	BCD	various	Benn	Two series: 'One Star Bandit Books' with a limited vocabulary and 'Bandit Books'. Library style books using teenage slang.
Burgess Books	7–9	ABC	Burgess	U.L.P.	Set of 8 supplementary books with workbooks. Amusing and in short chapters.
Challenge Books	7–9	BCD	Smith	Holmes McDougall	27 short adventure stories. Black and white illustrations. Mainly suitable for boys.
Crown Street Kings	7 –8	CD	Oates	Macmillan	9 paperbacks each describing an episode in the life of a family. Humorous cartoon-like illustrations.
Data Books	7–10	BCD	Young	Schofield & Sims	18 basic books and 6 workbooks. Aimed to be used as a follow-up to a basic reading scheme. Controlled vocabulary and sentence structure.
Famous Ships	7–9	BCD	Smith & Newton	Oliver & Boyd	Four titles. Short books, limp-covered.
Dr. Fobbin	7–11	AB	Smith	Macmillan	Supplementary readers. Set of 7 short books.
Far and Near Readers	7–12	ABC	various	Chambers	17 books in 2 series. Paperbacks.
Go Readers	7–8	CD	Calman	Blond	4 books in restricted vocabulary. Racy style with teenage appeal.
Good Company Readers	7–11 plus	BCD	Elliott & Cannon	Johnston & Bacon	8 readers and 8 'development' books.

Series	*R.A.*	*I.A.*	*Author*	*Publisher*	*Description*
Inner Ring	7–9	BCD	Pullen & Rapstoff	Benn	38 stories in 6 series including science, sports and facts. Realistic stories of fair appeal to teenagers. Illustrations black and white but adequate. Hard back and limp covers.
Inswinger	7–8	CD	Gregory	Hulton	6 paperbacks on a football theme. 6 workbooks also.
Interest Books	7–8	BC	Segal & Peacock	Warne	4 books for boys, 3 books for girls.
Jimmy Books	7–9	BC	Morton	Benn	4 books about a 'naughty' boy. Well illustrated.
Lively Reading	7–10	BC	Sealey	Nelson	16 books in 4 stages with 4 workbooks. Well illustrated information readers. Very popular with boys.
Look Out Gang	7–8	ABC	Chaplin	Gibson	6 books. Phonic approach.
Onward Paperbacks	7–9	CD	Crosher	Cassell	Attractive paperback style supplementary readers. Illustrations rather infrequent.
Panorama	7–10	BCD	Charlton	Holmes McDougall	Series of 3 books.
Patchwork	7–10	CD		Cassell	Series of 6 attractive well-illustrated paperback supplementary readers.
Scope Books	7–9	ABC	Burgess Elliott & Cannon	Oliver & Boyd	4 books. Stories, comic strips and games. Appeal to many children.
Signal Books	7–8	ABC	Niven	Methuen	Set of 6 books in two graded series of 3.
Story for Today	7–8	D	Abbs	Heinemann	Set of 6 books on modern teenage subjects.

Series	*R.A.*	*I.A.*	*Author*	*Publisher*	*Description*
Structural Readers	7–10	BCD	Allen	Longman	Almost 50 graded supplementary readers and plays. Paperback, attractively presented.
Teenage Twelve	7–9	CD	Richardson	Gibson	Set of 12 phonically based readers. Based on Dolch word list. Slim books, short chapters. A detrimental factor is the heavy typing of specific phonic elements.
They Were First	7–9	BCD	Smith & Newton	Oliver & Boyd	12 slim, limp-covered books. Popular appeal dealing with personalities such as Gagarin, Bannister, etc.
Trend	7–10	CD	Bird	Ginn	Set of 25 graded paperback supplementary readers. Attractive and popular. Australian origin.
Trigger Books	7–8	CD	various	Ulvers-croft	5 books published, so far, in a paperback series.
True Adventure Series	7½–8½	BC	various	Blackie	47 titles in this series.
Joan Tate Varieties	7–9	AB	Heinemann		6 paperback books for younger children, aimed at presenting topics within everyday experience.
Adventure Road to Reading	8–10	ABC	Petheram & Byers	Hulton	6 books. 4 for boys, 2 for girls.
Adult Readers	8 plus	D	various	Readers Digest	12 books plus teacher's manual. For adolescents and above.
Ann and Jenny Books	8–10	D	Boyers	Ginn	6 books for girls in a magazine style. Popular series.

Series	*R.A.*	*I.A.*	*Author*	*Publisher*	*Description*
Bookbuilder Books	8–8	BC	Crosher	Methuen	Mostly for boys. 4 titles. Jumbled story follows each chapter.
Booster Books	8–10	BCD	Chalk	Heinemann	Adventure stories. Strong phonic element throughout. Should be used in conjunction with Booster Workbooks 1–5.
Can You Solve It?	8–9	ABC	Belmont & Akhurst	Ginn	6 Detective stories which set problems in deduction.
Club 75	8–9	CD	various	Macmillan	12 paperback books catering for the interest of young teenage boys and girls.
Crusader	8–9	BC	various	Blackie	32 adventure stories.
Everyday Life	8–9	BC	Adams	Cassell	Set of 12 information books.
Forward Books	8	BCD	Crosher	Methuen	Short adventure stories.
Fun and Adventure	8	BC	Wright & Wilson	Macmillan	2 books of collected articles.
Fun and Fancy	8–9½	BCD	McIntyre	Macmillan	2 anthologies for slow learners.
Instant Reading	8–9	BCD	Chalk	Heinemann	10 amusing supplementary stories.
Jet Books	8–10	BCD	various	Cape	12 adult-style paperbacks.
Kennett Library	8 –10	CD		Blackie	40 modified classics; limited appeal.
Life with Dan Berry	8	BC	Jones	Blackie	2 titles. Realistic situations.
Magnet Readers	8–9	BCD	Burnham	Pergamon	15 books divided into: Scotland Yard, Science and the Sea.

Series	*R.A.*	*I.A.*	*Author*	*Publisher*	*Description*
Noel Parker Finds Out	8–9	BC	Cliffe	Cassell	3 stories of a young detective.
Pictorial Classics	8–9	BCD	various	O.U.P.	Shortened Classics.
Readers Delight	8–9	BCD	Taylor	U.L.P.	Collections of stories, jokes, puzzles and poems.
Simon and Dorothy Stories	8–9	BC	Emmeus	Blond	4 books mainly to interest girls.
Tales Retold for Easy Reading	8–10	CD		O.U.P.	30 titles in two series. Classics and crime. Based on 1500 and 2000 'Headwords'.
They Work With Danger	8	BCD	Smith & Newton	Longman	Frogmen, astronauts, etc.
What Happens . . . Series	8–9	BCD	Smith & Newton	Hart Davies	Information series.
Windrush Books	8–9	BCD	various	O.U.P.	8 books, each a complete story. Low priced supplementary reading material.
Active Readers	9–10 plus	CD	various	Ginn	12 adventure stories in two series.
Between Ourselves	9–10	D	Bradley	Oliver & Boyd	3 books on personal relationships for secondary girls.
Cresta	9–10	CD	various	Holmes McDougall	8 readers.
Emergency Ward 10	9–10	D	Kenyon	Blond	4 books based on an old T.V. series.
Focus Books	9	CD	various	Holmes McDougall	4 titles.
Joan Tate Books	9 plus	CD	Tate	Heinemann	Paperbacks suitable for girls. Few illustrations.

Series	*R.A.*	*I.A.*	*Author*	*Publisher*	*Description*
On Your Own	9 plus	D	Booth & Akers	Nelson	3 topics for school-leavers; bank, wages, holidays.
Pacemakers	9–10	CD	various	Burke	5 paperbacks with an appeal for girls.
Practical Everyday Reading	10	D	Smith	Holmes McDougall	4 books concentrating on social vocabulary, newspapers, advertising, shop floor, entertainment, etc.
Shorter Classics	9–10 plus	CD	Thomas & Thomas	Ginn	23 titles.
Simplified English Stories	10 plus	D		Longman	Simplified Classics and modern novels. Originally produced for those learning English as a foreign language.
Spotlight on Trouble	9–10	D	Gunzburg	Methuen	8 stories of real-life problems.
Streamline Books	9–10	D		Nelson	Simplified well-known novels. 17 titles.
Titans	9–10	CD	Mosley	Ward Lock	4 adult-style novels.
Topliners	10–12	D	various	Macmillan	Adult-style paperback. Great appeal for teenagers. 30 titles.
Wide Horizon Reading Scheme	9–12	BCD	Ridout & Serrailier	Heinemann	10 books. Good stories. Poorly presented.
A Year with the Slaters	9–10	CD	Watts	Longman	12 books.
Bulls Eye	9–10	CD		Hutchinson	6 paperbacks.

Workbooks and activities

Publisher	*Title*	*Description*
Arnold	Sound Sense	Phonic
	Thinking and Learning	
	Dragon Pirates	Support for Schemes
	Griffin Pirates	Support for Schemes
Blackie	Read Write Remember	Sight vocabulary
Cassell	John Smith Spelling 0 – 5	
E.S.A.	Training in Basic Cognitive Skills	Pre Reading
	Training in Basic Motor Skills	Pre Reading
Cambridge Art Publications	Fun with Phonics	
Gibson	Remedial Refresher Cards	
	Spell The Word	
	Choose The Word	
	Word Games	Phonic
	Sounds Right	Phonic
Ginn	First Interest	Accompany readers
	Rescue	Accompany readers
	English Workbooks 1 – 8	Background support
	Better English	Background support
	Word Perfect	Phonic
	Phonic Workbooks 1 – 6	
Hart Davies	'Soundabout' Card Games	Phonic
Heinemann	Booster	Phonic
Harrap	Spelling Books	
Hulton	Workrate	Accompany Inswinger series
Longman	Read, Write, Draw	Background support
Macdonald	Happy Families (cards)	
Macmillan	Essential Read Spell	
Nelson	English for Primary Schools	Background support
	Moving on with Reading	Background support
Oliver & Boyd	Reading to some Purpose	Background support

Publisher	*Title*	*Description*
Oxford University Press	Adventures in Writing Oxford Junior Workbooks	Accompany readers Sight vocabulary, early phonics
Philograph	Telling Words Word Family Workbooks Find the Right Word	 Based on 'Word Families'
Remedial Supply Company	A large number of workbooks available covering many aspects of reading	
Schofield & Sims	Data Spellaway	Accompany books
S.R.A.	Phonic Word Games	
University of London Press	Sounds and Words Step Up and Read	Phonic Phonic – also part of bigger scheme
Warne	Reading and Doing Using Books With A Purpose	 Training in 'reference'
Wheaton	First English Workbooks	Phonic
Wills & Hepworth	Ladybird Workcards Ladybird Workbooks	

For American material see App. VII.

Reading laboratories

A number of publishers have produced more expensive aids to reading development, usually in the form of Reading Laboratories.

S.R.A. – Science Research Associates have produced many laboratories. Originally of American design they have recently been 'Anglicised'. The laboratories take the form of graded reading cards followed by comprehension checks and word study skills, incorporating phonic and structural word analysis and vocabulary building. Listening skills are also built into the programme, as are materials to increase reading rate. At each level of the laboratories there is a wide variety of workcards, allowing children to remain as long as necessary at each stage.

(Handbook to Lab. Ia, p. 8): 'Repetition is essential in learning any skill whether it is operating a typewriter or learning to read. Skills that present little difficulty require little practice, whereas more difficult ones must be performed again and again before they can be mastered.'

The S.R.A. labs. are firmly based on the Reinforcement Theory of Learning and for this reason are recommended for concentrated daily use over a short period of a few weeks rather than regularly through the school year.

(Handbook to Lab. IIa): 'With proper timing, there is a carryover of one day's learning to reinforce the next. During the earlier stages of a learning process practice is most efficient when it is clearly spaced.'

Certainly experience suggests no use for S.R.A. on a casual basis – unless used as directed by the handbook it is merely a 'keep the kiddies quiet' device. But used properly it can lead to dramatic improvement in reading for *some* children – although others will achieve little success and considerable frustration. It takes, in fact, considerable effort to maintain motivation throughout an entire S.R.A. course.

Ward Lock Reading Workshops (Ward Lock)

The Reading Workshops are similar to the S.R.A. Laboratories in format, being based on a reading passage followed by questions and presented in four-page card folders. Also, a similarity with S.R.A., the Reading Workshops attempt to motivate the child by self-checked cards and the compilation of a percentage graph upon card completion.

Reading Routes (Longman)

Reading Routes is a box of 144 comprehension and project folders taking a pupil from R.A. 7.5 up to 12 plus years. Again it is based upon graded folders in 10 grades of difficulty. Again it is hoped to maintain motivation by pupils self checking and filling in 'percentage success' graphs. Reading Routes differs from S.R.A and Reading Workshop in its claim to be project based (project suggestions are given for each card) and by its admission that 'although pupils enjoy working steadily through the cards in this colour sequence, if too rigid a pattern is followed it may sometimes lead to a loss of interest or a pupil marking time.' Hence it is suggested that children *may* depart from this pattern to follow one of the routeways (Ordinary and Remarkable: Transport and Invention: Nature: Famous People: Animals: Story and Fable) at another level. However, great care must be taken when doing this to ensure that the child does not simply meet with the frustration of attempting something which is far too difficult for him on a topic that interests him.

Scholastic Individualised Reading Sets (Scholastic Publications)

These sets contain 100 paperbacks, a set of teacher's cards, a set of pupils' cards, 2 records and 2 book display cases.

The sets aim 'to develop children's motivation for reading by presenting them with a wide range of attractive, well-illustrated books with a variety of themes'. The books are loosely graded into 4 levels. Their presentation and layout *are* attractive to children. Each book has a comprehension type work card to go with it. A useful set of books, but in no way do the Individualised Reading Sets claim a systematic approach to reading in the way that S.R.A. does.

Stott's Programmed Reading Kit (Holmes McDougall)

This kit contains 29 items plus a teacher's manual. Cards in each item are laminated and (very useful) pre-cut where necessary. Items are graded in difficulty and the kit is arranged in colour sets to make the sequence easier to follow.

Stott's kit is a phonic based set of games and activities which attracts a wide variety of children throughout the primary and early secondary age range. It ranges from the beginnings of reading to an R.A. of about 9 years. It is at the early stages of reading where the kit is most useful, providing a wide variety of enjoyable and carefully graded activities, whereas in the later stages grading seems much looser. One advantage of the Stott material is that it can be purchased either as a complete kit or as individual items.

Other aids and equipment

The Stillitron System (Stillit Books Ltd.)

The Stillitron System is a reasonably priced system consisting of self-contained texts using programmed learning techniques and reinforcement by immediate feedback of green and red lights for correct and incorrect responses. The Reading System contains 6 phonic based 'Word Control' Readers and 4 action stories. A wide variety of other systems are also available. A master grid is produced so that teachers can prepare their own material for Stillitron use.

The Stillitron is immediately attractive to children – no writing, just applying stylus to grid and receiving immediate visual indication of success or failure. It has tremendous novelty value – but children may soon tire of it and its lack of robustness is a severe limitation.

Language Master (Bell & Howell)

The Language Master is a tape machine which plays back pre-recorded segments of card mounted tape lasting only a few seconds. This allows words and illustrations to be set above the tape giving the child an opportunity to link what he sees with what he hears. The two channels of the tape also allow the child to record his own response and then compare it with the teacher's pre-recorded item. The Language Master can be used with a junction box and/or headsets.

A variety of prepackaged material is available through the publishers for use with the Language Master, e.g. Word Study Kit
Find The Word
Ladybird Key Words

Also sets of blank cards suitable for teacher-prepared material are available. An expensive piece of equipment, the Language Master, by virtue of the short duration of the tapes, is a patient teacher that can be used where much repetition is necessary. On the other hand this may limit the variety of approach and older children can soon get bored with it. It is probably of most use in the initial stages of reading.

Synchrofax Audio Page (Arnold)

The Synchrofax is an expensive piece of taping equipment but has considerable versatility. It consists of a tape machine on which is seated a card the size of an A4 page. On one side of the card is a four-minute tape, the other side being blank. Thus a commentary can be prepared to accompany a piece of work presented on the blank face. The Synchrofax lends itself easily to pre-reading training, sight vocabulary acquisition, phonics, spelling, comprehension, creative writing, etc.

Readmaster (Arnold)

Designed to assist speed reading.

Autobates Teaching Machine

Simple non-electric teaching machine with several available programmes.

Cassette Recorders, Headsets, etc.

Less convenient than Synchrofax or Language Master, for items of short duration a cassette recorder can be used to great effect for a variety of work especially in conjunction with work cards, or for simply listening to stories.

Clifton Audio-Visual Schemes – Brown & Bookbinder (E.S.A.)

Two tapes for use with programme cards and student workbooks. Tends to be repetitive and therefore may be difficult in use with older children.

Interest Books

As we move away from a teacher-centred type of education and towards a child-discovery-centred approach, the importance of books grows. Children who cannot have access to information, because of their low reading ability, are likely to become frustrated. Thus the teacher must be aware of what is available in terms of project books, what age-range of children they are suitable for and what reading ability is necessary to cope with them.

Publisher	*R.A.*	*I.A.*	*Series*
Arnold	7	7–11	We Discover . . .
Baker	9–10	11–15	It's Made Like This
Benn	8	8–16	Inner Ring Facts
Black	8	10–15	Industrial Archaeology
	7	6–10	Let's Read and Find Out
	8	8–16	Learning Library
	7–8	7–12	Little Learning Library
	7–8	8–14	Sevens Series
Blandford	10 plus	9–14	Colour Series
Bodley Head	9–10	9–16	Natural Science Picture Books
	8	8–14	The Study Books
Brockhampton Press	9	9–16	Picture Reference Series
Burke	7	6–10	Do You Know About
	8	9–16	Let's Visit
	7–8	7–11	Our World
Cassell	7	7–14	Animals of Many Lands
	7 –8	8–14	Everyday Life Books
	9	10–16	Living Through History
	7	7–11	Other Children In . . .
Chambers	7–8	6–10	Our Book Corner
	8	7–11	Starting Science
Chatto & Windus	8	8–14	Young Learner Books

Publisher	*R.A.*	*I.A.*	*Series*
Collins	8–9	8–14	Wonder Colour Books
Dent	9	11–16	Behind the Scenes
Faber	9	9–14	Your Book of . . .
Gibson	6	6–10	Little Animal Books
Ginn	6	6–12	First Interest Series
	9	9–14	Machines At Work
	9 plus	10–16	Topic Books
	9	9–16	Wider Interest Books
Hamlyn	13–14	9–16	Spotlight Series
Hamish Hamilton	8–9	8–16	Look Books
Hart Davies	8–9	8–14	Animals and Their Homes
	9–10	11–16	Finding Out About Science
	7	7–14	Observe and Learn
	9	8–16	Record Holders in the Animal World
	7	8–14	What Happens . . .
Holmes McDougall	7–9	7–14	Travels in Time
	7	7–10	Magpie Books
Longmans	10 plus	10–16	Explorer Series
Lutterworth Press	6	6–11	Wrigley Books
Macdonald	7	4–11	Beginners World
	7–8	7–14	First Library
	7	8–14	Introduction to Nature
	8–9	8–14	Library of Sport
	9 plus	10–16	Junior Reference Library
	7	5–11	Starters
	10 plus	10–16	Visual Books
	Pre Readers	4–12	Zero Books
Macmillan	8–9	9–14	Active History
	8–9	9–14	Discovery Project Kits
	8	9–14	Exploring the Past
	Pre Readers	4–7	First Words
	8–9	8–14	History Workshop
	7	7–14	Livng and Growing
	7	7–11	Observeand Discover
	7	7–11	Our World
	7	6–8	See How It Grows
	7	6–11	See How It's Made
	7–8	9–16	What Do They Do?

Publisher	*R.A.*	*I.A.*	*Series*
Methuen	7	7–10	Concept Science
	7	6–10	Look Around Books
	7–8	7–11	Matter of Fact Books
	7	8–14	Stand and Stare Books
Mills & Boon	8–9	8–14	Junior Science Books
	7–8	7–11	Junior True Books
	9–10	11–16	Let's Look At . . .
	8–9	8–11	Look, Read and Learn
Nelson	8–9	13–16	Interest Books
Oliver & Boyd	7–8	8–13	Open Gate Library
	9 plus	8–14	Science From the Beginning
	7	8–14	What Happens When
O.U.P.	9 plus	8–14	The Changing World
	9 plus	8–14	People of Britain
	9	8–14	People of the World
	8–9 plus	9–14	Rivers of the World
	7	8–14	Inside and Outside Books
Parrish	7	7–8	Junior Colour Books
Schofield & Sims	8	9–14	Everyday Things
	8	8–12	In History I
	9	11–16	In History II
Philips	7	7–10	Unit Books
Studio Vista	6 –7	6–10	Come Inside Books
	9	9–16	Dutton Paperbacks
	8	9–14	How to . .
Transworld	10 plus	10 plus	How and Why Wonder Book of . . .
U.L.P.	8	8–11	Dolphin Science Books
	8–9	11–16	Topics Through Time
Ward Lock	8	9–14	Information Books
Warne	Pre Readers	4–12	Words and Pictures
Watts	8	9–14	The First Book Series
	7	7–11	First Look At Series
	9	9–14	Let's Find Out About
	7	9–14	Let's Go
Wayland	8	13–16	Choosing A Job

Publisher	*R.A.*	*I.A.*	*Series*
Wheaton	7	7–13	Read About It Series
Wills & Hepworth	7–10	8–15	Ladybird Easy Readers
Worlds Work	8	11–14	Children's University Books
	8	8–14	Zim Science Books

Reference Books

P. Bell, *Basic Teaching for Slow Learners*, Muller.

E. Goodacre, *Hearing Children Read* and *Methods*, Centre for the Teaching of Reading.

J. Hughes, *Reading with Phonics*, Evans.

Leicestershire Schools' Psychological Service: *Books for Slow Readers in Secondary Schools*.

A. E. Tansley, *Reading and Remedial Reading* and *Basic Reading*, Arnold.

West Sussex County Psychological Service: *Phonics*, *Teaching Non Readers* and *Reading Schemes*.

CHAPTER 4

LEARNING DIFFICULTIES IN MATHEMATICS

'Just what do I teach the bottom stream in Mathematics?'
'What's the point?'
'Shouldn't we give up trying to teach this subject?'
'It's a difficult subject – I was no good at it at school – I hated Mathematics.'

The problem: the subject, anxiety or limited ability?

Mathematics seems to have been one of the main sources of anxiety in the educational lives of many. Ask any adult what he thought about Mathematics at school and he will express either a positive liking for the subject or a positive dislike – even fear of it. The majority will say the latter, and the anxiety continues. Parents cannot but feel anxious whilst employers and Further Education establishments demand some mathematical qualification. Teachers who have never enjoyed Mathematics have to teach it; for the majority of secondary schools still band/stream/set for Mathematics, thus grouping together those with the most diverse difficulties, and then will give that class to the least confident – the new member of staff or the least experienced or qualified. Not that experience or qualifications necessarily make the best teacher, but without them, confidence and understanding of the problems may not abound. Where does the teacher go from there? You have a group of students who will undoubtedly say they're 'no good' at Mathematics (because they're in a lower stream); who may say that they hate the subject; they find it boring or useless and they don't want to do it. You may also have been given a syllabus which 'the others' are doing, and told not to expect your pupils to get through it, but to do the useful topics – social arithmetic, preparation for work; anything to keep them occupied. A chore which may well become a nightmare.

That paints the worst, but nonetheless frequently true, picture of the state of Mathematics teaching for those condemned as 'slow learners' with 'poor motivation', 'lack of concentration', 'reluctance to learn'. Is it surprising that anxiety exists for both students and teachers when the expectations of the school are for little success yet society demands it; when every lesson becomes a frustrating battle or a waste of time because the student and/or teacher has given up the search for a solution? Anxieties building on a history of anxieties to propitiate the myth that Mathematics is a difficult subject for all but the gifted few.

Is it a difficult subject?

Every subject can be challenging but few seem to create as much fear or frustration as Mathematics. Is it 'examination Mathematics' which causes the frustration? Certainly, if we consider the skills which each student has already acquired which are essentially mathematical in nature but totally disregarded as such. For instance, when a child learns to speak, he learns to *abstract* from highly complex situations, a group of sounds which label what he sees. He learns that one label can apply to many seemingly different situations ('chair', 'Mother', I).

He *transforms* verbs to give different tenses. He is able to select, make deductions, understand games and their rules. All these seem too obvious, too trivial, to be worthy of consideration in Mathematics, yet here is direct evidence of success in complex mathematical activity and implies a potential to acquire similarly 'complex' procedures.

It is likely too, that most students are competent in telling the time and using money, and have no doubt retained those skills from an early age. Yet they are both highly complex skills and pose challenging teaching problems when a student, possibly through over-protection, hasn't acquired them by early adolescence.

Premature formalisation

All this is not to deny that many learning problems exist in Mathematics but rather to deny that the ability to learn Mathematics is only 'given' to the few. One of the main problems is premature formalisation which has confused. No one expects a child to walk until he is ready to. No one expects an amateur football star to be able to take the pace of a first-division league game in his first week. Yet children are expected to have acquired certain Mathematical skills by a certain age and all difficulties can be traced back to a confusion which has been ignored or misunderstood. The time of teacher, parent and student is thus best employed in seeking out the source of confusion; and it is a rewarding occupation, for each difficulty will reveal a new dimension of the subject of which all might have been unaware before. Helping someone to walk again or to speak – after an accident or illness, poses fascinating if occasionally bewildering problems about activities which we take for granted. Just which muscles do we use? How, why, when? Helping someone to understand some Mathematics can be equally fascinating. If the procedures of the past had been appropriate they would have been retained. Since they have not, a completely new diet is required – a new approach, different topics, Mathematics through other subjects, starting points based on the students' interests. But above all, concern, interest, trust and confidence that all is possible if the appropriate route is sought.

Patterns for teaching

It is important that the class be seen as a class of individuals. Irrespective of the system of the school, the general pattern of teaching or streaming, it is unlikely that class-directed activities will be at all successful except for the one or two for whom the level and subject matter is appropriate. A 'disciplinarian' who strikes fear into his class may 'contain' the boredom and frustration and their inevitable disruptions, but he/she is in no way solving the problems. Indeed he/she is likely to be adding to them. Not to class-teach will inevitably involve the teacher in far more preparation of materials and resources; individual programmes which may require access to other departments, close knowledge of the students and their interests, patience, energy and time. It is not an easy task to overcome fear, positive dislike or apathy and to help the students recognise and overcome their particular problems in Mathematics. But, once a pattern of working has been established, once the students are aware that the teacher is both interested and confident; that some activities can be enjoyed 'without pain', then the responsibility becomes a shared one. Edith Biggs in her book *Freedom to Learn* recommends several procedures for moving from a class-directed approach to one in which the needs of the individual are recognised. These are related more to primary than to secondary education but are equally applicable and recognise the differing circumstances, needs, talents and fears you might meet as a teacher.

Recognising the problem areas

The problem of diagnosis of difficulties common to all or to many disciplines has been discussed in an earlier chapter and procedures recommended. It is essential to be aware of the reading ability of each student and his level of visual discrimination. Some students may be gifted mathematicians but their studies have been impaired by their inability to read the questions or to recognise differences in notation. Some students may be quite adept at numerical work but have been 'turned off' other mathematical work and just aren't interested. Others may have never understood arithmetical procedures but could easily come to terms with some aspects of Mathematics. The available tests do little to diagnose either of the latter problems. Even if we ignore those Arithmetic/Number/Mathematics tests which rely on reading or interpretative skills, most tests entertain such a narrow view of number that at best they reveal little and at worst they reinforce confusion.

A typical test will include *graded* additions revealing many misconceptions of number and its structures. For example, one might see:

Test 1 – a page of examples like $7+8=$ i.e. additions of 1 digit numbers.

Test 2 – a page of examples like $17+23=$ i.e. additions of 2 digit numbers.

and so on to

Test 6 with $\begin{array}{r} 208 \\ +\ 37 \\ \hline \\ \hline \end{array}$ and then $\begin{array}{r} 213 \\ 224 \\ +\ 19 \\ \hline \\ \hline \end{array}$ or $213+224+19=$

A different array from horizontal to vertical is certainly one inconsistency, but the major inconsistency lies in the fact that the tester really believes he is grading the tests. *Should* there be any real difficulty with tests 2 to 6 if the student has retained the necessary understanding to do the first? The more numbers, the more carrying, the harder the example, according to the system. The more numbers, the more confusion, the more boredom for the students. Testing is uneconomic, certainly does not form a logical sequence and may be the root of the problem of why only a few students are 'good' at Mathematics according to the tests. Some students have a particular gift for perceiving simple patterns from complex ones, for making order out of a chaos – an 'order' which agrees with that of the tester. A few number puzzles at the beginning of the session and careful observation could as quickly and more efficiently reveal those students with particular difficulties with number, and, those who don't want to do any work of this nature.

Examples:

Find the missing numbers

i) 2, 4, 6, –, 10, –, –, –, –, –,

ii) 2, 6, 10, 14, –, –, –, –, –, –,

iii) 1, 2, 4, 8, 16, –, –, –, –, –, –,

iv) 100, 200, –, 400, –, –,

Circle the odd one

i) 3, 12, 21, 14, 9, 15

ii) 2×3, $12\div2$, 6×1, $\frac{1}{4}$ of 24, $2+5$

iii) $\frac{1}{2}$, $\frac{1}{4}$, $\frac{2}{3}$, $\frac{1}{5}$, $\frac{4}{7}$, $\frac{8}{5}$

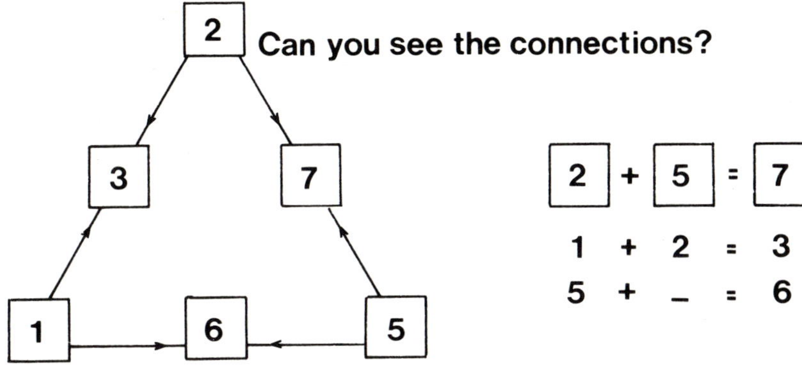

Now fill in the missing numbers for these:

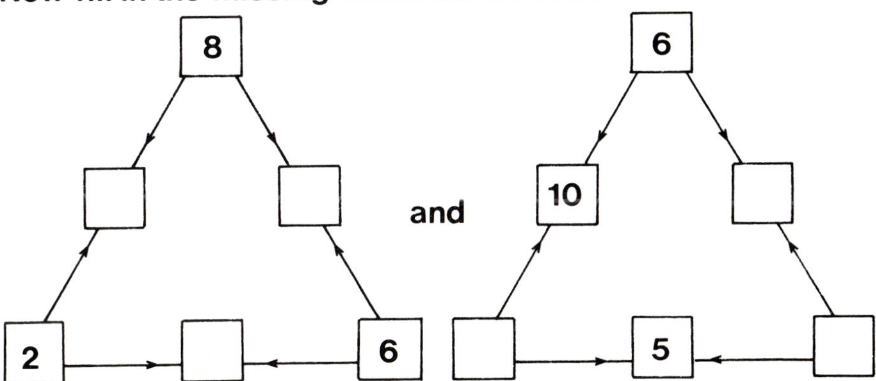

Can you see how these number squares work?

2	5	7
3	6	9
5	11	16

now try these

2	5	
7	4	

etc. and then more complex ones like

3		5
	4	
8		

Cross number puzzles

///	1	///	2	///
3		///	4	5
	///	///	///	
///	6		7	///
///		///		///

Clues across:

3. 1+2+3+4+5
4. 4×8
6. (10×10)÷1

Clues down:

1. 5+5+5+5+5
2. 30–17
3. 40+40–41
5. 4×5
6. (2×3)+15
7. 20÷2

The 'problems' then can be divided into two main groups – students who say 'I can't do Maths but if you're willing to help me, I'll try again' and those who say they've never enjoyed it, they dislike it intensely and they don't want to do any more. The solutions for both will ultimately lie in the relationship between student and teacher – a trusting and caring relationship where the problems are recognised and accepted. It is as important for the student to understand the teacher's difficulties in making each topic interesting and worthwhile for him, as it is for the teacher to understand the student's likes and dislikes, strengths and weaknesses. But the starting point for each problem area may be different.

'I can't do Maths'

What can't the student do? What can he do? Can he add, subtract, multiply, divide? Can he use money? Tell the time? Can he draw? Can he use a compass? Can he measure? . . . No test exists which could usefully diagnose why the student says that he/she can't do Maths, but research into what he has been faced with before and observation of how he tackled the number puzzles give you many clues as to the nature of activities which might help.

For example, does he count on his fingers? If he does then you can build on that activity by evolving a system whereby he uses his fingers more efficiently. Gattegno in his book 'The Common Sense of Teaching Mathematics', advocates not 'counting' the fingers, because this can be a confusing model and the index finger of the left hand may come to mean 9, irredeemably, but of using different arrays of fingers to show all the numbers.

For example, for 4 or

4 shown
6 folded

4 shown
6 folded

It shows the complements of 10 also, and knowing the complements – even if 'knowing' means the student refers to his fingers – will make all addition speedier and less cumbersome. Also there is no reason why the fingers should represent just the units; you can use them to represent tens or thousands or tenths or . . . so 4 tens + 6 tens give 10 tens (or one hundred), 4 tenths + 6 tenths give 10 tenths (or one unit) and so on.

Perhaps the student can cope with addition but is unsure of himself and needs to practise. If this is the case there are many opportunities for practising addition without resorting to the unchallenging and frequently boring pages of sums. Shopping; doing some simple accounts for a school activity or tuck shop; cooking; darts, pinboards, football scores, even new mathematical topics such as coordinates and vectors.

If there is difficulty with addition then there is likely to have been a history of failure with subtraction, multiplication and division also. If subtraction is seen as adding on, then the problem can be tackled as before. Multiplication and division are likely to be more problematic than addition and subtraction, but reticence to explore them may be overcome if you introduce sophisticated aids such as hand or electronic calculating machines and slide rules. You can use them to give the answers and then with the answers there you can search for patterns, i.e. for ways of triggering off the memory without rote learning. For example in (say) the 9 times table the pattern lies in the digits adding up to 9 and the tens digit is one less than the number you're multiplying by. $9 \times 2 = 18$ ($1 + 8 = 9$, 1 is one less than 2) $9 \times 4 = 36$ ($3 + 6 = 9$, and 3 is one less than 4).

Does the pupil understand numbers? Do you?

Like words, numbers can assume many meanings, in as many different contexts. Until the context becomes clear and is fully understood by the student, the numbers will confuse, the importance of their notation will be lost along with many opportunities for extending the student's numeracy. Estimation is not only fun, but a necessary arithmetical tool of far greater importance than an ability to know your tables. Unless there is a definite pattern or array few people could accurately guess the number of objects in a group if the group size is bigger than 7. Guessing the number in a crowd at a football match, the number of minutes you have lived, the number of hairs on your head; then asking about recording and relevance can lead to a wealth of activity. Does it matter if you're 100 out? Certainly it would if you were concerned with money. Numbers as values in money, time, space, weight, reinforce (or introduce for the first time) the necessity of notation, and the meaning of concepts (which may be ever changing, like money values). If the students are interested in cars then a discussion on the relative merits of a Mini (say) costing about one thousand pounds and an XJ6 Jaguar at five thousand pounds could lead to an investigation into fuel, seating capacity, acceleration, pollution, resale values, running costs, weight, wear and tear on the road surface; braking distances, accident statistics. Is an XJ6 worth five times a Mini in all or many or some respects? Similarly discussions on salaries for, say, a miner earning forty to fifty pounds maximum a week and a footballer earning three to five hundred pounds. Then there are astronomical numbers of infinitesimally small objects (atoms, viruses, blood cells) and astronomically large distances and weights wherein both consideration of notion and errors could lead to fatalities – a fatal blood count – missing the moon by a mile!

Geometrical topics

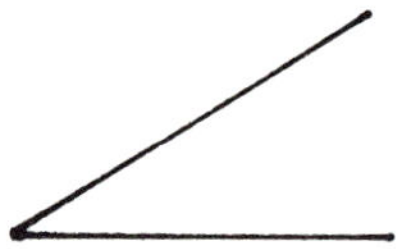

Errors in distances can lead to measurement of shape and space and thence into the wider sphere of geometrical concepts. Angle measure is often one that has confused – so often it has been presented as a diagram like this. Angle becomes a shape rather than a measurement of rotation. Many students will believe that the lines must be the same length, that there can only ever be two lines in a diagram, that 'angle' is the space between the lines. Angle as a measure of rotation is best achieved by having something that turns. Dials, wheels, gears, spirographs, magnetic compasses, provide opportunities for making models, designs, orienteering, surveying, constructing efficient pulleys, understanding maps, mazes, buildings. Geometry is the Mathematics of perception of the space in which we move and cannot be restricted just to two-dimensional drawings on a piece of paper. Unless the students make models, study their surroundings, become involved in the classifications and the need for them, the two-dimensional representations will be meaningless. Perception, distortion, illusion, can include a wealth of Mathematical work besides physiology and psychology. A short time with a camera – taking shots from different angles, pictures from magazines, films, slides, give the two-dimensional forms which can form the basis of inquiry into perspective, viewing from a distance, enlargement (– and both combine to lead into use of trigonometry) and distortion. When the student wishes to record his observations, then the need for protractors, compasses, set squares, rulers, emerges. A good pair of compasses seems essential since poor equipment adds to the frustration. A protractor, which is circular and one-directional is also a useful tool since semi-circular, two-directional protractors are a common source of confusion. (They can easily and cheaply be made from thin paper and a pointer attached by a paper fastener and the scales reproduced on a Banda, say.) Modern geometry has introduced symmetries and transformations as part of the curriculum, and both lend themselves to practical work in both two dimensions and three dimensions. Cuisenaire's 'Prisms and Cubes' give opportunities for buildings and discussions and activities like this:—

Use 4 cubes to make these:

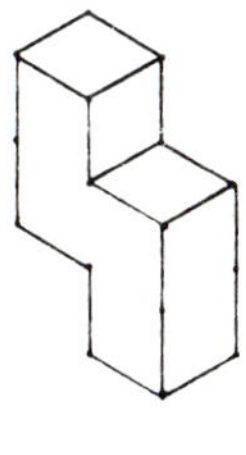

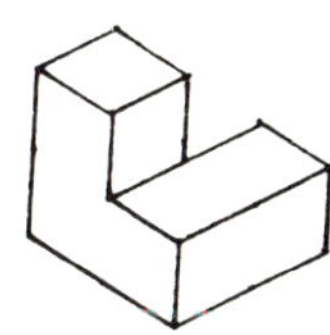

How many different shapes can you make?
Can you draw them?
Isometric dotty paper makes sketching solids easy.

From the 3-D sketching booklets by G. Giles (Fife Maths Project), lead into two-dimensional representation of three-dimensional forms in a logical and exciting way – a welcome introduction to technical drawing. Without formalisation the mathematical awareness, vocabulary and experience thought to be inaccessible to many and certainly to the 'slow learner' can be made readily accessible. Producing patterns by paper-folding (parabolae, ellipses), interference patterns, curve sketching, envelope techniques (for example, sliding a set square down a ruler so that one edge passes through a fixed point giving a parabola), plotting loci, give experiences upon which you can build later.

Algebra

'Too much abstraction!' is the general criticism of algebra and many teachers and parents will say 'What's the use of teaching algebra to students who have found other branches of Mathematics difficult?' Yet algebra is only expressing relationships, minimising the use of words and abbreviating – thus making general rules, something we do every day. It is certainly easier to retain one rule than it is to remember many examples, which may, or may not, recur in the same form. But it is certainly not easier to retain one rule when one hasn't understood it.

The confusions are hardly surprising. For many years at school children are faced with – say – $3 + 4 = 7$, and, 34 means three tens and four units – no other answers are possible. Then suddenly letters are introduced and all the rules change so that $a + b$ can have many answers, ab means a times b; signs are omitted, brackets appear in abundance and algebra is a completely new world, instead of being a generalisation of the old.

But if symbols are used in which variables are acceptable, then perhaps algebra is possible. For instance, H (= home team score) A (= away team score) are used to report football statistics in the paper; temperature (T), time (t), are both obviously changing.

Would this prove difficult? – You are told that the home team scored 4 goals, but not how many the away team scored. Some possible scores are H A (4, 0), H A (4, 2), H A (4, 7). Write down some more possible scores and mark all the scores on a graph.

Instead of writing 'the home team scored four' we write $H = 4$ for short . . . . . it is a short step to labelling a graph $H = 4$ and then moving to $H+A = 3$ and $H+A \geqslant 3$ and so on. The 'real situation' may seem too contrived when $3H+2A = 8$ appears but at least it is a beginning of awareness of equations, inequalities, graphs. You can then move to the notation employed by Banwell & Saunders in the 'Making Mathematics' series of books— □ △ — shapes in which you put numbers. This would be best employed though, with some exploratory work – a search for the rule for a pattern or an experiment. A mathematical balance (Invicta) provides opportunity for initial exploration, so do pulley systems with variable weights, and all situations in which simple relationships exist between two variables.

The algebra of sets is a source of confusion too, again because of the inflexible approach to numbers the students have been taught but also because the student is not aware of the sorting and classifying opportunities of his task. Remind him by using a logic block set and some of the more sophisticated 'logic' games suggested by Dienes and move towards the rotation by use of counters or objects and moveable circles and the solution to this:

Draw a venn diagram to show the sets A B & C if
A = (1, 2, 3, 4, 5, 6)
B = (0, 3, 6, 9)
C = (1, 3, 5, 7, 9)

Could only be this

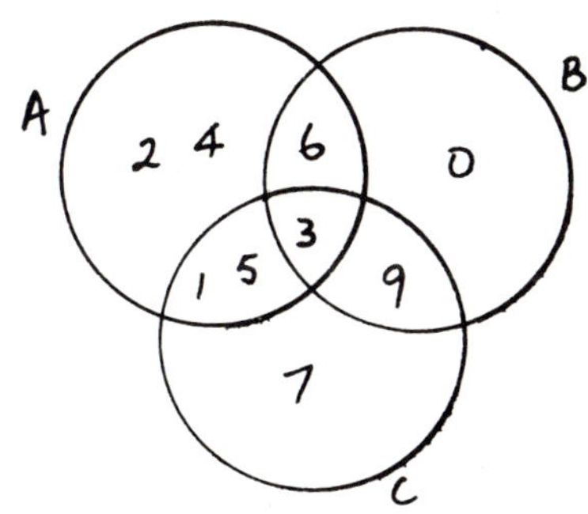

and not this

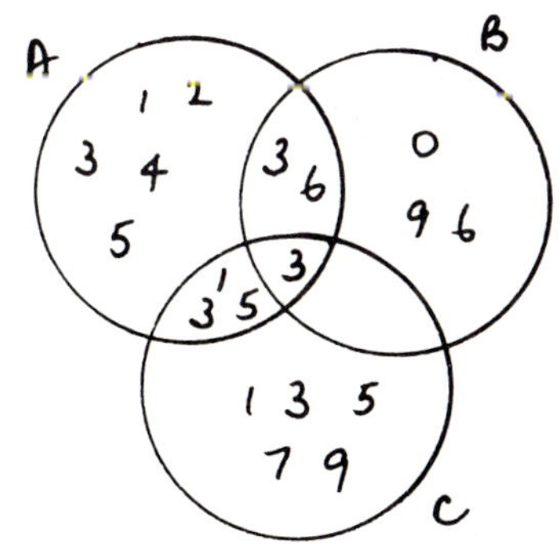

Where the student has correctly worked out AnBnC, BnC, AnB and AnC but has repeated numbers within each set.

Once the notation is established you can move to 'truth tables' and on to circuit boards and complex logic problems. Practical work followed by formalisation leading into practical application being the 'golden rule'. It is impossible, in one chapter, to define all the possibilities that exist for exploring the many basic mathematical topics; it is only possible to suggest some starting points for each main area and to emphasise the need for discussion, practical work, use of apparatus before formalisation. Topic booklets, workcards and apparatus are referred to in Appendix I.

'I won't do Mathematics' – the reluctant learner

There is no need to call an activity 'Mathematics'. Indeed, since one of the commonest failings in the teaching of Mathematics is to restrict it to such a narrow field of activity, the teacher of the reluctant learner can introduce a wide variety of activities which the student will not recognise as Mathematics! It is, however, essential that the activity starts from the students' interests and that every temptation to *contrive* Mathematics from their interests be avoided. Students' interests are obviously wide-ranging from the 'pop scene', fishing, football, fashion, to astronomy, community studies, vehicle engineering. Each one cannot avoid a wealth of mathematical thought and action, though it need not be made explicit. Rather, the teacher should be aware of the potential and introduce new ideas when interest flags or further involvement seems possible. For example, measuring a football pitch to scale is likely to be a very dull and meaningless activity to a football fanatic – unless he wished to make a magnetic or blow-football table. Assessing chances of success for certain popular teams or even working out transfer fees and the percentage the player gets, may *not* be dull or meaningless. Working out hire purchase prices and agreements from catalogues may seem to the teacher to be of use for the future, but unless the student has the opportunity to buy, his motivation is likely to be limited. It might however be of interest to a student whose parents 'run' a catalogue for a company, or the student who wishes to do so in the future. There are a range of activities to choose from. For example, sociological surveys *can* provide opportunities for discussing estimation, sampling, displaying and interpreting data, deductions from other surveys, generalisation to other situations. The numerical work is relatively simple or can be aided by a calculating device, but, since we are considering reluctant learners in Mathematics, the emphasis must be on the sociological rather than the mathematical results. Games of logic or chance need not look mathematical nor do they need extrinsic motivation or rewards or prizes to be exciting. Patterns and designs can be translated into three-dimensional forms. 'Curve stitching' (using nails and wood) requires precision, use of a protractor and ruler, skill in hammering in nails and encourages a flair for design. Shopping – like Monopoly – seems to have a fascination at any age; puzzles and games rarely fail to convince that every student can and will persist with an activity for hours.

Then it might be possible to involve some students in helping others. If it is possible for the students to arrange to work in a creche, playgroup, junior school or school for the mentally handicapped, then his/her involvement will lead to questions about how he/she can help, and will inevitably lead to a study of what they themselves learnt, and how and when. A student who has really struggled to understand Mathematics is often a better teacher than one who has never struggled.

A student may try many activities and then give up. He/she may reject all suggestions. The teacher has to maintain interest throughout and in a trusting situation it is unlikely that all will fail. A little success and enjoyment after years of boredom or frustration will have the effect of releasing a fund of energy and enthusiasm for other activities.

Mathematics – as a tool for life?

This is one of the hardest questions for educationalists and parents. If we ignore for the moment qualifications (examination results), have we not a duty to prepare our students for the complexities of life ahead? Part of the problem inevitably lies in the fact that we cannot even guess what life will be like for each student when he leaves school. Also, even if we assume that rents, mortgages, taxes, wages and electricity meters will still exist in the future, the motivation for carrying out the often tedious and complex arithmetical procedures is unlikely to exist while the student is still at school. They can become just arithmetical exercises and it is unlikely that the procedures will be retained for use when the problems arise. However, a sociological survey of the area – some relatives, pensioners, people in need – *could* provide motivation. Even a weekend or a holiday job provides its wages slip and a cooperative effort between staff most concerned with the student and his future (careers, sociology teacher, tutor,) should ensure that the student leaves school at least aware of all the necessary details from renting accommodation and running a car to obtaining unemployment pay or social security benefits. Where opportunities arise before this, such as a group visit or camp, then problems of budgeting can be tackled along with timetables, plans for activities, quantities of food, fuel and general supplies.

Several surveys* have revealed that the commonest mathematical rules required are those to do with money, time, addition and counting (very little multiplication, subtraction or division), very simple measuring and basic budgeting:–

A. *Survey by Wilson* in 1919 – 4,000 adults over 14 days.

Results

1) 83 per cent of the problems dealt with buying or selling goods.
2) 11 per cent involved the use of money in other ways.
3) 6 per cent dealt with quantitative measurements.
4) Addition and multiplication were the main processes used.
5) There was some use of common fractions, and bills had to be made out or understood.

B. *Moore* – 1957 – studied personal, social and business usage of arithmetic – sample 88 men and women. Two questionnaires. Form A anticipated usage of arithmetical processes. Form B recorded actual daily usage.

Results

Out of a total of 2,837 problems encountered by 88 adults in 7 days, 1,513 problems were concerned with money – of which 1,208 involved only shillings and pence. 281 problems with pounds, shillings and pence, were mainly (a) solved by addition or subtraction and (b) performed mentally. Other problems involving number made most use of addition, followed by subtraction, multiplication and to a lesser extent, division. Only 6 per cent of all problems involved capacity, linear measurement and fractions (some use of logarithms and square roots was reported by 3 technical men). Fractions most used were halves, quarters and eighths.

C. *Thompson* – 1962 – studied usage of arithmetic by ESN boys aged 14 plus.

Results

a) Most problems were oral. Exceptions were a very simple form of budgeting and the completion of time sheets.
b) Number work was restricted to reading and understanding numbers and the use of addition and counting.
c) Simple measuring instruments were used occasionally, mainly in the home, and only addition of length was required.

* Wilson – reported in Kirk, S. & Johnson, G.O., *Educating the Retarded Child* (Houghton Mifflin, Boston, 1951); Moore, N.A., *Survey of the Usage of Arithmetic in the Daily Life of Adults* (Unpublished dissertation, University of Birmingham, 1957); Thompson, G.E., 'What arithmetic shall we teach our educationally sub-normal children' in *Special Education*, Vol. LI, No. 3, 1962.

d) Ability to tell the time was necessary and some needed to interpret timetables.
e) The language of number was frequently required.
f) Some general items such as rent, rates, insurance and hire purchase were met without being thoroughly understood.

Beyond these the teacher should judge for him/herself how to give the student a richer understanding of life – and for each student the curriculum will be different. There is no reason why a student who has struggled with Arithmetic (say) should not become involved and excited by a course of linear programming and other mathematical forms.

There is also no reason why any student who so desires cannot attempt some form of examination though what this entails in the present system of examining in Mathematics should be clearly explained to the student and his parents.

In England and Wales there are a variety of syllabuses for O-level (and in Scotland O-grade), varying in content and approach but having in common an extensive syllabus and only one form of assessment, the examinations. With such extensive syllabuses a student who has encountered difficulties for several years is likely to feel unsure about each new topic and will require more time and in-depth study – neither of which an O-level (or O-grade) syllabus permits. It is a great sacrifice to the learning process if the examination takes over and all learning – of necessity – becomes rote learning for the examination. The student is unlikely to retain or understand the topics and a difficult examination would be likely to destroy rather than enhance confidence. However, if the student must have an O-level qualification for his chosen career, and in consultation with parents and teachers he decides to take a chance, then he must be given the opportunity of doing so. In England and Wales there is, though, an alternative, in that a Grade 1 CSE is equivalent to an O-level pass (there is no equivalent in Scotland). CSE syllabuses are more varied, can be partly continuously assessed, partly examined; schools can submit syllabuses related to the school's course. An example of a typical CSE syllabus is given in Appendix II. The project work inevitably relies on student choice and the examination is on 'basic' Mathematics which can arise from all the situations discussed before.

However, a grade 5 CSE is no substitute for several years of mathematical enjoyment without frustration and there are an ever-increasing number of opportunities for gaining qualifications at a later stage if the student wishes to pursue them. He will certainly not do so if he has failed, been crammed, or dislikes Mathematics.

Preparation of Resources

If the student is to be convinced of your concern then the resources must emulate your intention, as too, must the environment in which he is to work. Workbooklets need to be carefully and attractively designed – and for those with limited reading ability, they should be sparing in the use of words and new vocabulary introduced through diagrams and activities. A booklet, worksheet or workcard cannot replace adequately a sympathetic teacher who 'reinforces', re-explains when necessary. It is too easy to put too much in a booklet either placing too great a burden on the teacher's time for continual explanation or confusing to the extent that the student rejects it.

The booklet on Coordinates reproduced here is the author's fifth attempt, for a group of 11–12 year olds.

Worksheets can be very dull if they are the only resources. Project folders containing photographs, pictures from magazines and articles, will add considerably to the resources. Wall displays (changed frequently, and preferably of students' work) enliven the environment. Games and puzzles should be seen as an integral part of the course; calculators, surveying equipment, slides, film loops and films – indeed all media should be employed, and every opportunity of working with other departments and the students' interests should be seized!

Details of resources will be found in Appendix I.

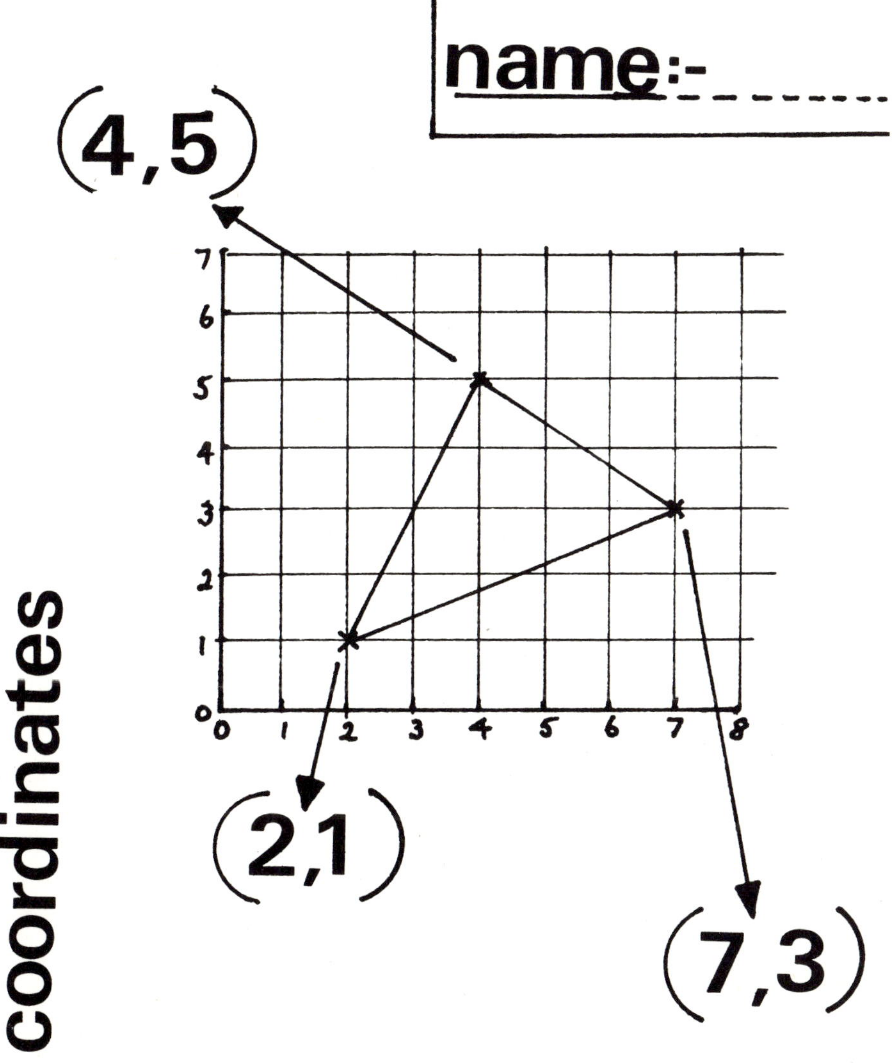

coordinates

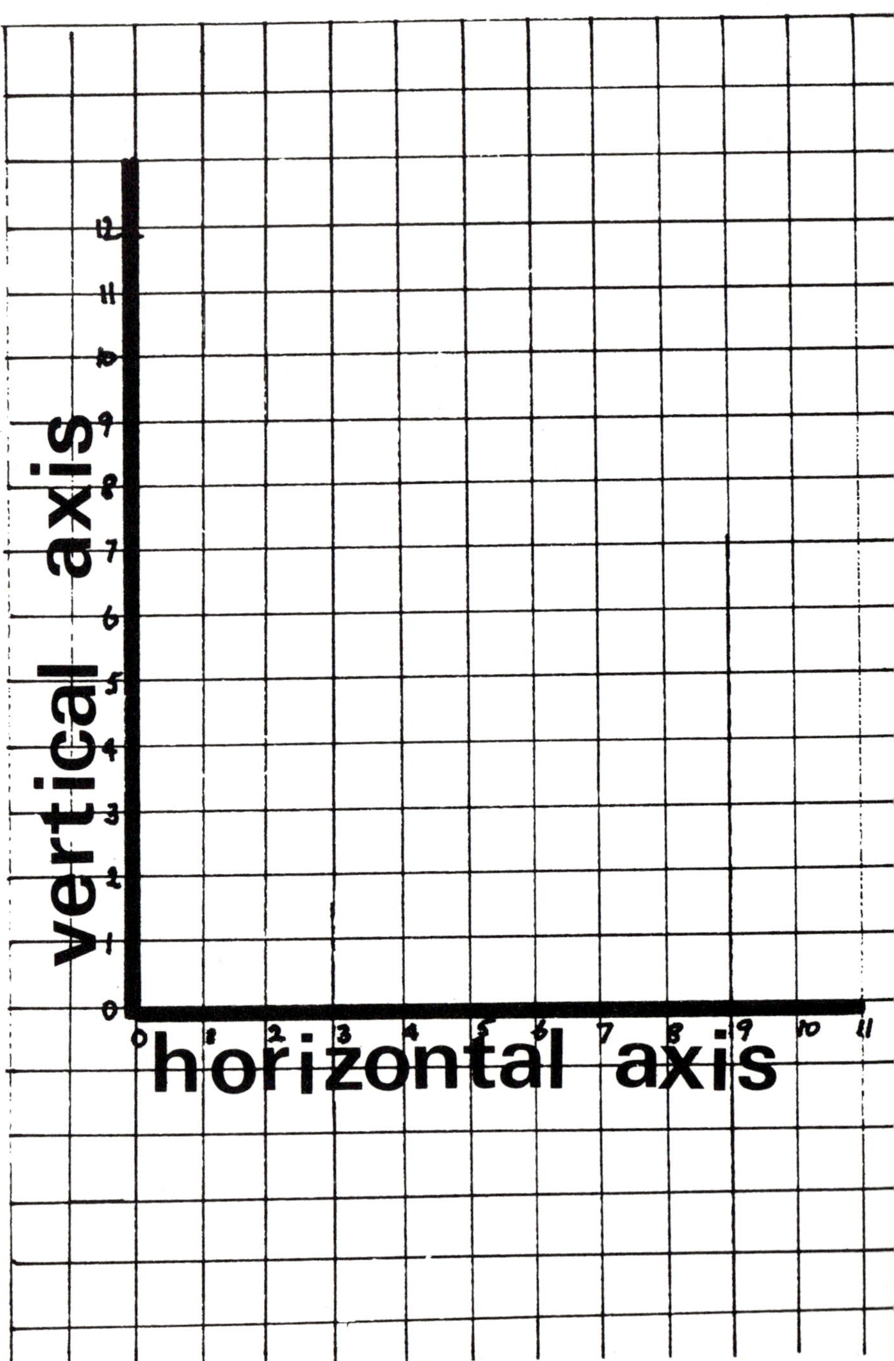
vertical axis
horizontal axis
0
1
2
3
4
5
6
7
8
9
10
11
12

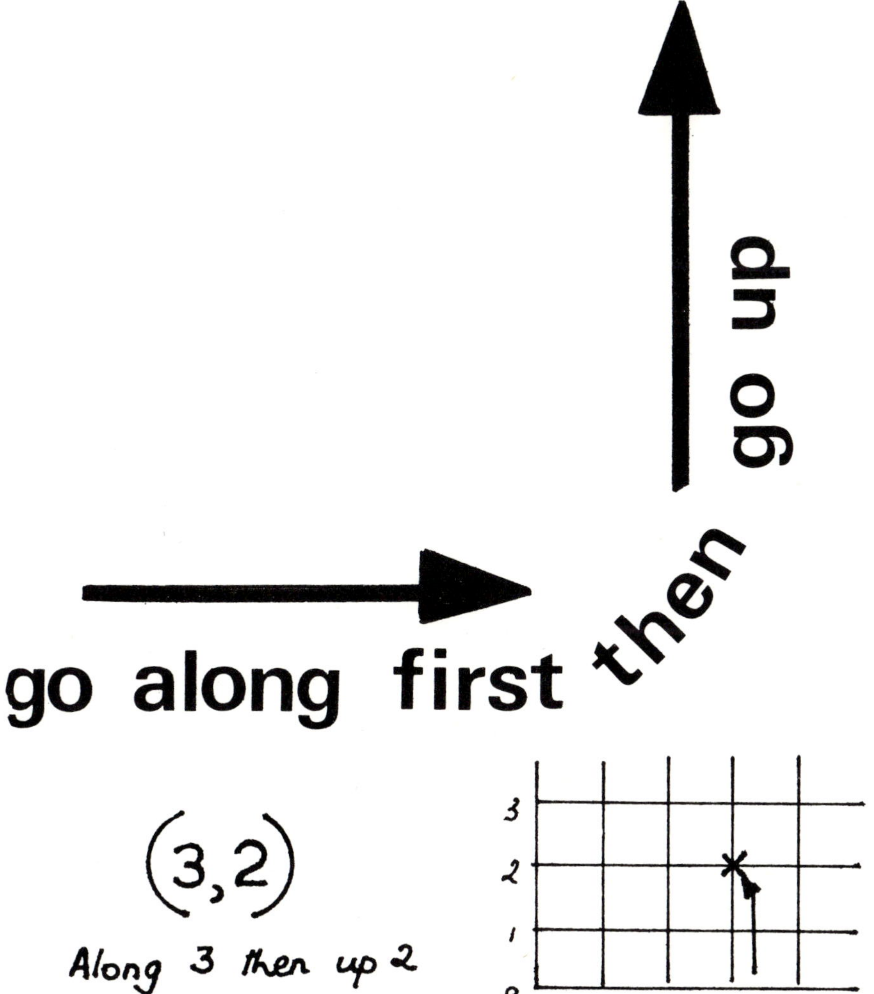
go along first then go up
(3,2)
Along 3 then up 2
0
1
2
3
0 1 2 3 4

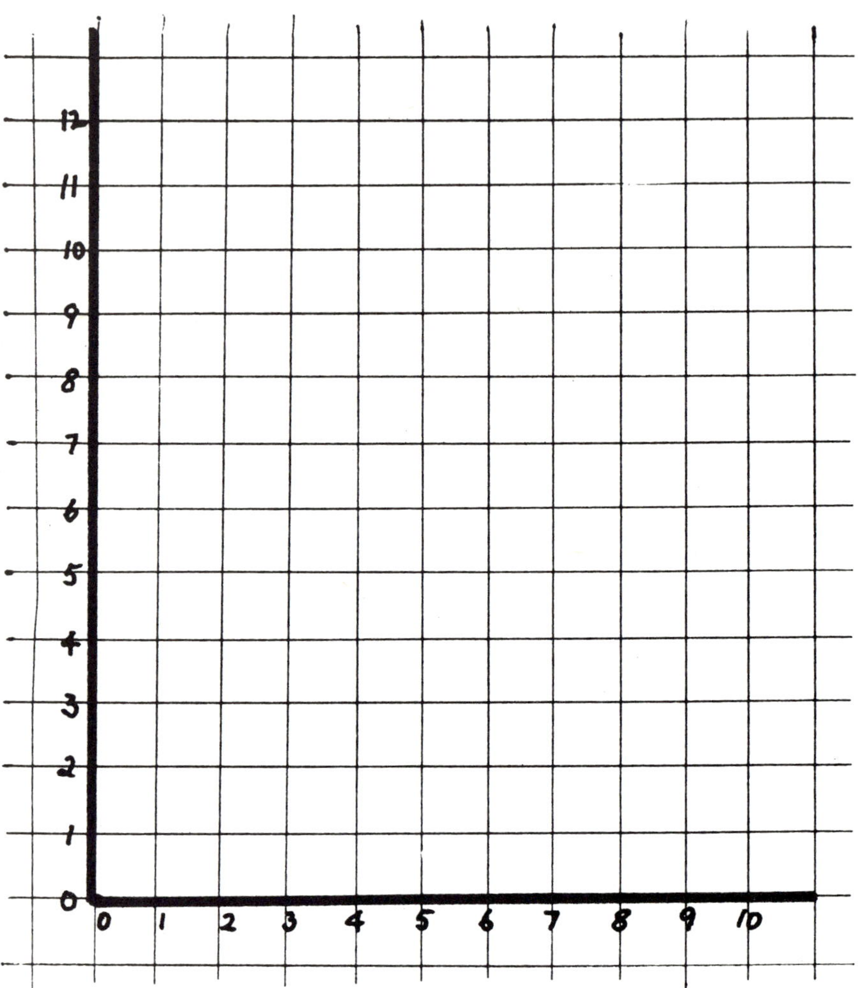

Plot these points. Find the shapes.

1. (2,1) → (2,4) → (4,3) Join them up.

2. (6,3) → (9,3) → (9,6) → (6,6) Join them up.

3. (4,8) → (9,8) → (10,12) → (5,12) Join them up

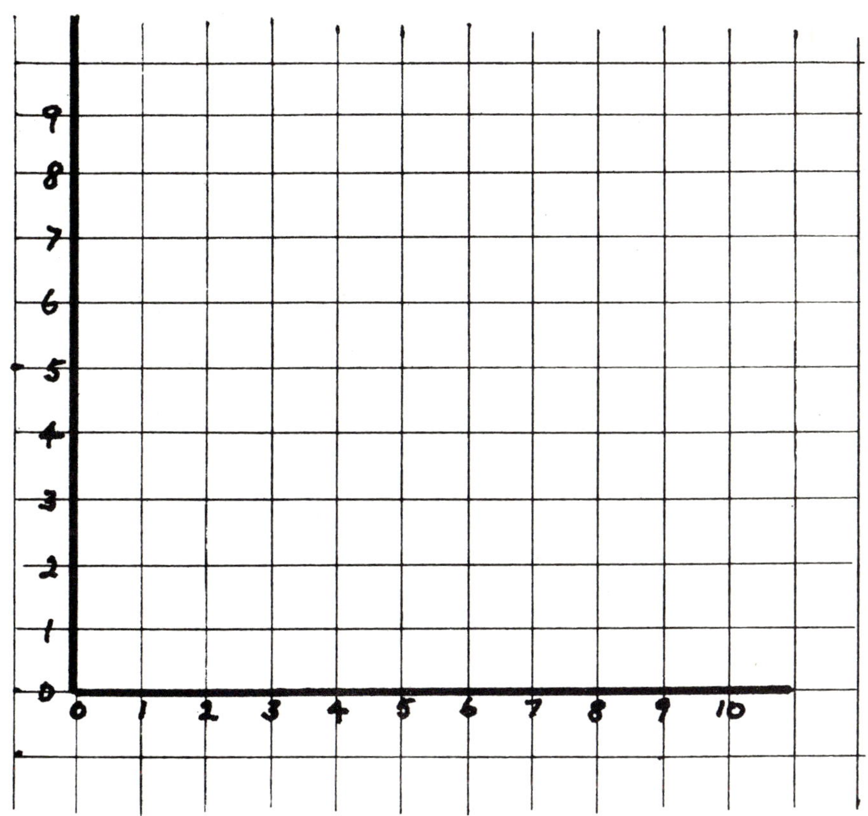

Make a star. Join them up in order.

(5, 0) → (6, 2) → (8, 1) → (7, 3) →

→ (9, 4) → (7, 5) → (8, 7) → (6, 6) →

→ (5, 8) → (4, 6) → (2, 7) → (3, 5) →

→ (1, 4) → (3, 3) → (2, 1) → (4, 2) →

→ back to (5, 0)

sink the battleship !

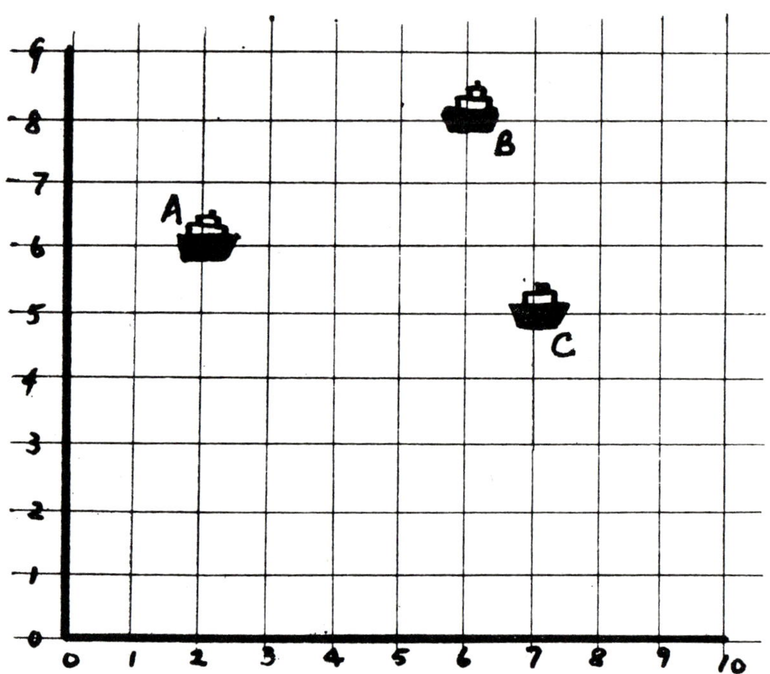

Where are the battleships ?

A is on the point (2, 6)

B is on the point (_, _)

C is on the point (_, _)

Play a game of battleships.

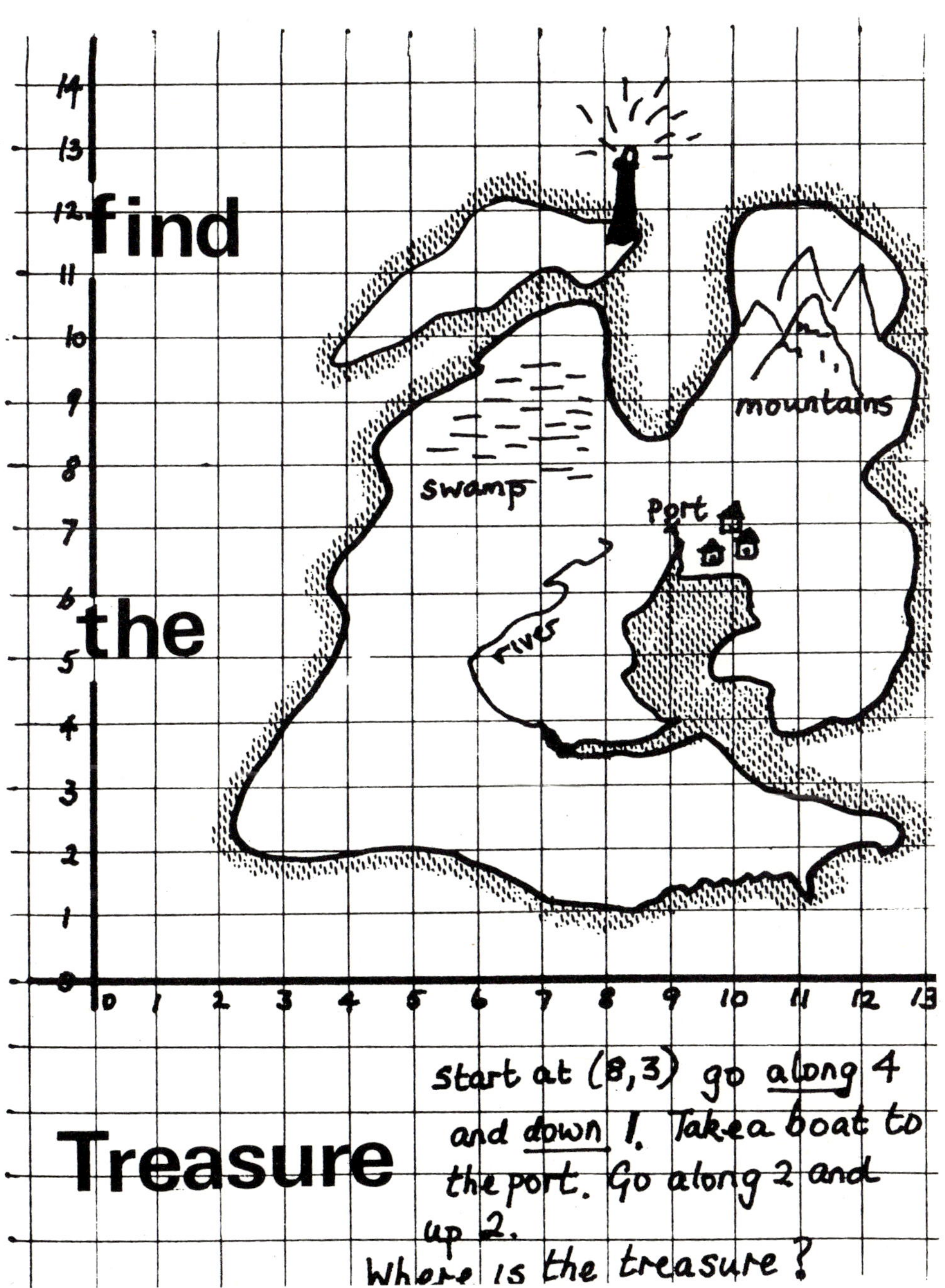
find
the
Treasure
14
13
12
11
10
9
8
7
6
5
4
3
2
1
0
0 1 2 3 4 5 6 7 8 9 10 11 12 13
swamp
mountains
port
river
Start at (8,3) go along 4 and down 1. Take a boat to the port. Go along 2 and up 2.
Where is the treasure?

Horizontal axis.

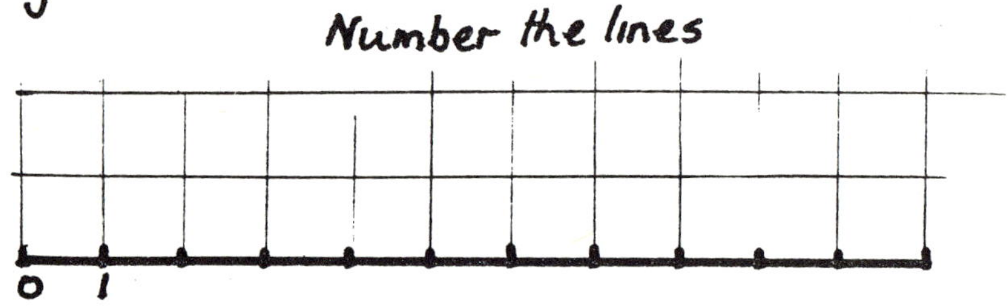

Now number all the marks on this:-

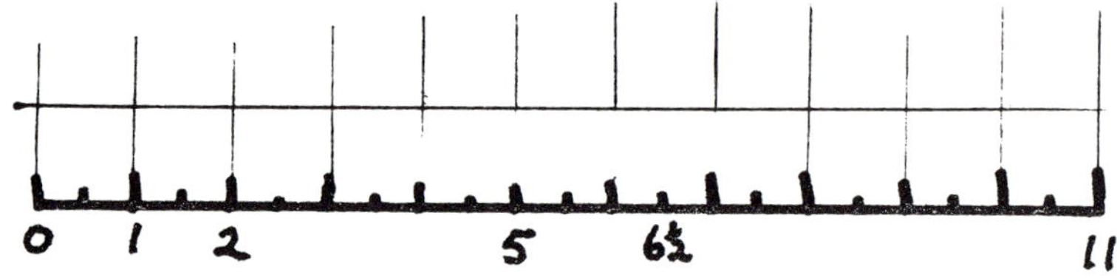

Vertical axis

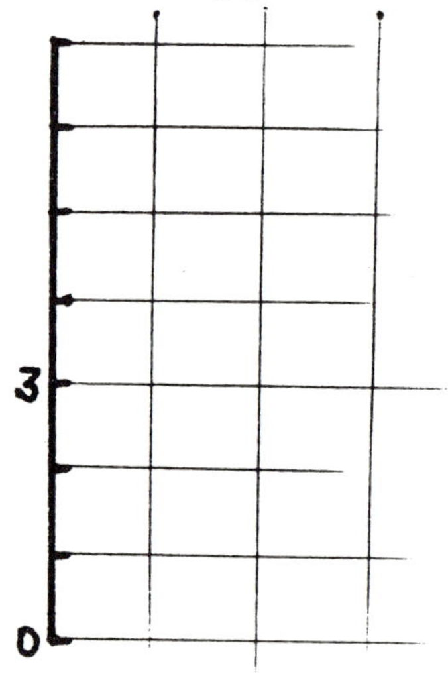

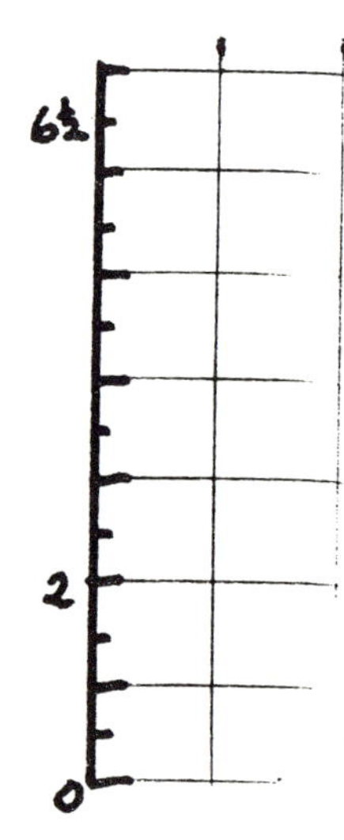

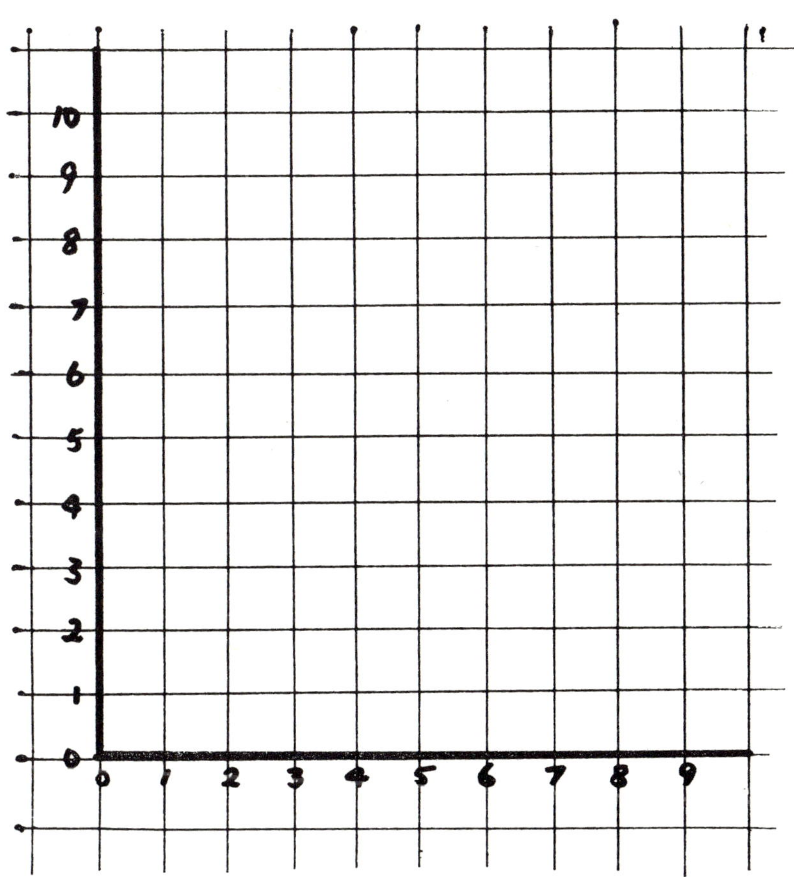

Plot these points:

$(2\frac{1}{2}, 4) \rightarrow (7\frac{1}{2}, 4) \rightarrow (5, 8\frac{1}{2}) \rightarrow (2\frac{1}{2}\ 4)$.

Then these:

$(2\frac{1}{2}, 7) \rightarrow (7\frac{1}{2}, 7) \rightarrow (5, 2\frac{1}{2}) \rightarrow (2\frac{1}{2}, 7)$

What is it?

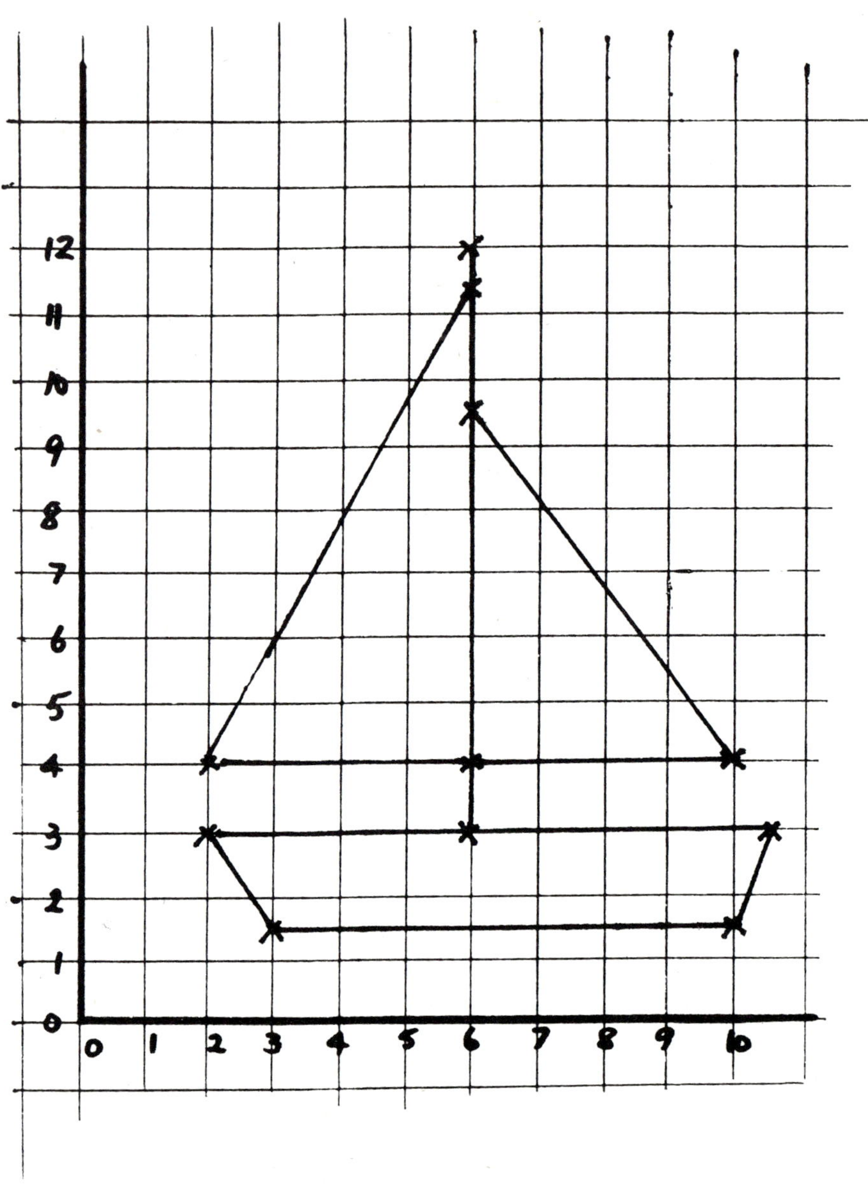
12
11
10
9
8
7
6
5
4
3
2
1
0
0 1 2 3 4 5 6 7 8 9 10

There are 11 crosses on the picture opposite.

Write down the coordmates of each one:

(_ , _)

(_ , _)

(_ , _)

(_ , _)

(_ , _)

(_ , _)

(_ , _)

(_ , _)

(_ , _)

(_ , _)

(_ , _)

CHAPTER 5

SOCIAL STUDIES

The growth in importance of social studies

If we accept a definition of social studies as simply 'the study of a given society', the study to include the past, the present and speculations and hypothesis about the future of the institutions and systems of that society, the importance is obvious. It is particularly important that slow learners who so often are on the periphery of our society should be drawn into a fuller understanding of the way it functions. Pupils very often groan at the mention of History, Geography, Economics. They question, quite rightly, the relevance of knowing the succession of kings after Henry VIII. Why does a factory worker need to know the topography of South Africa, or a shop assistant the international balance of payments? They don't! The teacher's time would be better spent in adjusting the curriculum rather than justifying it. In general, the two criteria which should be used when designing a social studies programme are:

1) To cater to the present interest and needs of the individual pupils and

2) To prepare the pupils to meet the future problems that will face them as adults.

Accepting these as valid criteria, then the following, as outlined by Scott Brown, a remedial teacher of some experience, should prove useful:

1) To provide materials that are people-centred. Abstract situations should be reduced to human dimensions. Materials and methods should be structured so that slow learners deal with human behaviour from which they can then abstract concepts and generalisations.

2) To stress historical and social conflict (presenting opposing positions, juxtaposing contradictory evidence, presenting opinions

unpopular among pupils), thereby necessitating that pupils assume value stances and make defensible choices among alternatives.
3) To help pupils perceive relevance by placing constant stress on linking past and current events and by encouraging the use of past/present analogies.
4) To make classroom dynamics relevant by tapping pupils' feelings and experiences (real-life personal experience, television programmes, current music, fads and language), by stressing public issues of importance to youngsters and by the use of learning modes like role-playing, simulation games, creative projects and skits. Space does not allow for a detailed discussion of each subject that falls under the social studies umbrella, but under the headings below are some programmes which may prove helpful as a springboard in developing your own.

History

1. Start with what the pupils know already and build from there. Remember, we all fear the unknown, so in starting with what is known already you take away one obstacle in the way of learning.
2. Always relate historical material to present-day situations. History is completely irrelevant unless related to present-day situations, and the pupils will not hesitate to tell you that. Slow learners have problems conceptualizing but by correlating the past with contemporary situations they have talked about, read about, and watched on television, they may understand.
3. Cover broad areas showing some sort of change, social upheaval, or peculiar life-style. Leave out specific dates, names, incidents. If the pupils show interest go back later and fill in the details.
4. Involve the pupils in preparing the materials. Have them collect mementos, newspapers, pictures, etc. from their parents, grandparents and neighbours. The more the pupils get involved, the more they learn.
5. Visit places of interest that will highlight what you are discussing. Trips of this nature are extremely meaningful to pupils, and get them very enthusiastic. Chances are the pupils will remember more about the trip than about the whole unit.
6. Emphasise the human side of any situation. Pupils do not relate to government and political ramifications of situations, but they do relate to the human side of the same situations.
7. Divide the class into interest groups and let them study on their own. The teacher will have to help provide the resources for this venture, but once started, the pupils usually produce excellent results.

8. Bring in speakers who you know will be interesting. A dull or too academic speaker will bring out the worst in the pupils and should be avoided at all costs. Someone who can tell anecdotes and non-academic stories will be appreciated and well received; the more off beat the better.
9. Use drama as much as possible. Let the pupils write and act in their own plays about an era or situation. Role-playing, often neglected, has great educational merit and should be used. Assign pupils detailed roles to play using information they have learned and set up the situation. This is a good way for the pupils to 'feel' the situation.
10. Use audiovisual materials to the fullest. When studying an era, try to get a feature film depicting that era. Newsreels and well-made documentaries usually go over quite well also.

Since most pupils know about major wars, a good place to start the study of history is with a major war. Very few pupils are uninterested in war, and most are very enthusiastic. Here is a skeleton outline for a World War II unit:
1. Discussion of World War II. Starting with an open-ended discussion will give the teacher clues to what the pupils already know and what their interests are. Let the pupils give direction to the discussion even if it ultimately gets into relating war stories.
2. Break the class into groups by interest to plan individual or group projects. From the discussion on the first day the pupils should have found other pupils with similar interests. Let them plan and carry out a project reflecting this.
3. Discussion of the new weapons developed during World War II. How were they different from World War I? What does this say about society? Most students will be turned on with this discussion and will use this as a project.
4. Study pictures, newsreel and accounts of London during the blitz. This follows up the previous discussion on weapons and shows how destructive they were.
5. Visit the Imperial War Museum in London. Follow this with a tour of London highlighting the places destroyed during the War and how they have been rebuilt.
6. Discussion of life during the War. Try to imagine what it was like to live during the blackouts and bombings, as well as everyday life.
7. Bring in a speaker to talk about life during the War. Since the pupils have previously offered suggestions on how it might have been, they will be interested to find out if they were correct.
8. Create a World War II display. Ask the pupils to bring in as

much World War II material as possible. Many of the items will be valuable and will have to be watched with care but the pupils will really get into this project. Once everything has been collected make a display for the whole school.

9. Find out what people ate during the War that was different from today and let the pupils make it and eat it.

10. Show a feature film about World War II. Pictures such as 'Tora, Tora, Tora', and 'Battle of Britain' are the best.

11. Visit Coventry Cathedral and the new city. Try to find pictures of the city before and after the war and compare them to what the city is today. Talk to town officials to find out how the war affected the people in the city.

12. Fight the War. Divide the class into the Alliance and the Axis countries. Fasten the country's name and flag to the pupils and let them play a game of football. (Hope the Allies win.) After the game the pupils will better remember which countries were involved on what side.

13. Discussion of the group projects.

14. Assign pupils the role of diplomats at the peace conference. Give them detailed information of what each country wants out of the conference. Let them bargain and come to terms.

15. Review and wrap up the unit.

Economics

Economic difficulties are at the heart of many marital problems. Yet few schools offer a course in the day-to-day economics one will need as an adult. It is time to correct this fault. A good economics course for slow learners should have a double thrust, one aimed at informing the pupil of the present state of the economy and the reasons behind it and the other aimed at providing information for future survival in the economy. Newspapers and magazines are good sources of information since much is written on a day-to-day basis on these subjects. The teacher must remember, however, that economics is a difficult area and he must be prepared to offer a maximum amount of help and encouragement to the pupil. The following are areas one could consider teaching to slow learners in an effort to prepare them for after leaving school:

1. *The Rights, Privileges, and Obligations of an Adult*

Most people do not know their rights, privileges and obligations until it is too late and they are in trouble. To remedy this a solicitor can be asked to speak to the class on the laws of contracts, credit, debts, and any other area of concern to the class.

2. *Social Programmes*

Most of the pupils do not know what is available to help people who are unemployed, or too ill to work. Nor do they know the laws governing these programmes. Using the local M.P. as a resource person, go into the laws and the history of the laws of any relevant social programme. The application forms used for these programmes should be duplicated to be filled out by the pupils. This section should be geared to familiarising the pupils with agencies that are there to help in time of need.

3. *Renting or Buying a Flat or House*

An estate agent could be of help here. He can go over the contracts, prices, and procedures necessary in finding somewhere to live. The things to look for in renting and buying, such as plumbing and wiring should also be dealt with. Most agents will be more than happy to talk to the pupils since they comprise potential clients.

4. *Insurance*

Here is an area most of us get into without knowing much about it. The three areas to get into are: Why? When? and How Much? Insurance agents may be used as resource people. If possible arrange a debate of representatives from rival companies on why their insurance is best.

5. *Trade Unions*

We all hear about trade unions but do we know much about them? Probably not. Therefore, a section of the course should be devoted to the history of unions and what they are doing today. The discussions should focus on the benefits of unions versus the problems caused by unions. Arrange for a union leader to debate with an anti-unionist.

6. *Banking*

The main part of this section should be on the services provided by banks. The local bank manager or officer of the bank can be asked to explain checking accounts and how to open and use one, credit buying, and applying for loans and mortgages. A behind-the-scenes visit to a bank during working hours would be interesting.

7. *Taxes*

Here is an area of great concern to us all. Yet most of us only know how much we pay and not what the taxes are used for. A government official should be asked to explain the different types of taxes and the way the local rates are set. He should also explain how tax money is spent locally. For a project, each pupil can fill out the income tax forms and send them in. By doing this now he will learn early and not panic when the real time comes.

8. *Jobs*

This will probably be the most important part of the course. Where are the jobs, and how to get them, are points that should be stressed. A teacher or actual employment manager from a local firm should conduct mock interviews. Each pupil could also fill out a mock job application. It is surprising the number of pupils who do not know how to spell the name of their town or school. Finally, the class should visit as many potential employers as possible. In this way they will see the type of jobs that will be available.

Geography

Geography is an area that offers a broad range of possibilities for getting out of the classroom and doing things, from map making and reading to week-long field trips in the mountains. The study of continents and nations will be meaningless but the study of local towns and estates will be close to the pupils' lives and hold at least some interest for them. The scope and range of the course should be narrow enough so that anything studied in depth could be visited. What sense is it for pupils to learn about places and things they will never come in contact with and yet remain ignorant of their everyday surroundings? With this in mind, a suggested goal of the course might be: to help the pupil understand his environment. This includes man-made as well as natural surroundings. The course should answer the following general questions: What is the origin of the town in which the pupils reside? Why and how did it develop? What elements fostered or inhibited its growth? What changes are taking place in the environment because of the growth of the town? The following are some ideas that may be used in an urban geography course for slow learners.

1. *What is urban geography and why study it?*

The teacher is bound to be asked that question and should be prepared to explain beforehand.

2. *Map reading*

Anyone who plans to travel to the next town should know how to read and plot a course on a map. For fun and experience the students should be asked to plot the fastest routes to given locations. They should also be asked to plan a tour in which they must see certain geographical formations such as hills, rivers and cliffs. If at all possible the class should take the tour.

3. *The geographic features that dominate the area*

Take a coach tour of the surrounding area, to see the geographic areas of the town and country. Be sure to see all of the local city. Be sure the pupils understand what is being seen and why it is being seen. A promise of return visits for in-depth study of certain areas will encourage the pupils to work at the course. If a coach tour is not possible then a bicycle or walking tour can be attempted.

4. *The town*

A study of the history of the town using old maps, records and pictures can be fun for all. Each town usually has one person who knows the history of the town and can supply endless stories of great interest. He should be asked to act as a resource person and be used to the fullest. Projects such as making charts and graphs chronicling the development of the town should be encouraged. At the same time a map of the present town can be constructed. This map should include the business, industrial, agricultural and residential areas. The Planning Officer could be asked to speak to the class on how the area developed and the future changes in the zone. Try to find a residential area that will be torn down in the near future and follow its demolition.

5. *Make a land survey map*

Using the school grounds or neighbouring area, make a map showing the hills, slopes and contours of the grounds.

6. *Study a slum*

Trace the rise and fall of a slum area in the local city. Explore the history of the area and the reasons why it turned into a slum. End with a photographic essay of the conditions of the houses and environment.

7. *Study a new estate*

Find a new estate just built or in process of being built, and study the reasons behind its being built in that area. Try to discover what effects, if any, it will have on the town and environment.

8. *Study local industry*

Talk to a representative of a large firm operating in the area and find out the reasons for its being where it is. Hopefully this will lead into a discussion of the availability of power, natural resources, tax rates, population and a host of other considerations.

9. *The estate*

Study the history of the estate or house each student lives in. Each student should be responsible for his own home and using town records find out as much as possible about it.

10. *Plan a town*

Using all the information learned during this unit, the class should plan a model town.

At the end of this unit the pupils should know about the past, present and potential of the area in which he lives. This ought to help him understand the changes that have occurred and will occur and help reduce the culture lag that goes with change. This study should also help him decide if he has any job future in the area in which he lives.

Possible individual projects:
1. Photographic study of a city showing the different aspects of city living.
2. Photographic study of the variety of the surrounding landscape.
3. Collecting and cataloguing the plants found in the local geographic area.
4. Study the culture of any racial, ethnic or religious group that is different from the majority of people living in the area.
5. Study the culture and geography of a region or country other than your own.

Sociology

Sociology comes closest to being the perfect discipline for the slow learner, for in studying sociology one can bring in diverse and relevant material that does not fit easily into other disciplines. In what other strict discipline can one discuss and learn about modern prisons and courts, or present-day violence, crime and juvenile delinquency? Family living and even sex education, if extended to look at broad social problems such as venereal disease, abortion, and pre-marital sex, come under sociology. These areas hold the interest of pupils longer than any area I know. They also are areas which slow learners need to know about. The goal of the course, then, should be to inform the pupils about the problematic side of their society and where to get help to deal with it.

The following are general ideas for a unit on violence for the slow learner:

1. *Why study violence?*

The slow learner, in many instances, is faced with violence every day: at home, from his alcoholic father; in school as he or his friends vandalise the lavatory; after school, as he terrorises or is terrorised; on television nightly, or on the cinema screen. Studying violence, the consequences of violence, and the alternatives to violence, may give the student a new understanding of what he sees around him. Hopefully, the course will also open his eyes to alternatives to violence.

2. *Discussion of violence*

The discussion should start out by probing the pupils' views on violence to property, animals, people, and nations. The pupils will have taken part in an incredible amount of violence and will want to talk about it. Try to get at the reasons behind the violence as well as how the students felt before and after the act. This type of discussion will be enlightening to both the teacher and the pupils.

3. *Role-playing violent situations*

With the help of the drama instructor set up role-playing situations in which all pupils will play the victim at least once. If done properly, this can be very effective in getting the pupils to feel the effects of violence. This can do much to turn pupils away from the use of violence.

4. *Read local newsclippings about local violence*

The amount of violence in one area is very enlightening. After talking about what has been read, try to draw conclusions about the area, regarding population density, and socio-economic levels.

5. *Walking tour of the school and town*

The purpose of the tour is to look for vandalism. Where does it occur? How much is there? Is it concentrated in certain areas? Now draw conclusions from what you have just seen.

6. *Northern Ireland and the I.R.A.*

The history of Northern Ireland should be studied first. Attempt to draw conclusions about the people involved in the I.R.A. and in Northern Ireland in general. Can the pupils offer solutions and explanations for the situation?

7. *Violence on television and in films*

Discuss how seeing violence affects them personally. Do they ever want to imitate the acts they see? Do they feel indifferent, or are they repulsed by it? A relevant film can be shown to the pupils, followed by a discussion of censorship.

Photographed, developed and printed by a 14-year-old pupil in connection with a project on race and immigration.

8. *Study of the Teenage Gang*

Many teenage gangs exist today whose only goal is to be violent. These groups are written about and depicted in films continuously. Using these as a resource material study the social phenomenon and let the pupil decide the reasons and value of the gang.

9. *Talk with a psychologist*

Discuss the reasons for violence. Possibly the pupils will come out of this with a better understanding of themselves or their parents. Possible places to go for help to cope with their situation may also be discussed at this time. Society's options for dealing with violence should be discussed as well as what the future may bring in dealing with violence.

10. *Talk with a solicitor or probation officer*

This discussion should deal with the laws concerning violence. The legal resources available to victims of violence should also be discussed.

11. *Visit to Court*

Visiting a court in session is fascinating and the students will want to spend several days there. If the magistrate is not too busy he may be willing to talk to the pupils and explain what is happening.

12. *Visit a prison*

Before visiting the prison a discussion should take place on the conditions of prisons. Then travel to the prison to see for yourselves. You will probably have to cut through a sea of red tape, but the experience will be worth it. If the students can talk to a prisoner it will make quite an impression. If this is not possible, an ex-prisoners' organisation may be able to help.

13. *Suicide*

Again using role-playing, set up situations to discover how people must feel to take their lives. Discuss the effect suicide has on the family and friends of the victim.

These ideas may sound stereotyped and 'course'-based but they are not intended as such. They should be seen more as avenues of exploration that the pupil can embark on, using his own interest as a starting point.

CHAPTER 6

HEALTH AND SEX EDUCATION

Quite often in schools, the very words 'sex education' are emotive. There are the teachers who fall into the anti category, those that feel it is the prerogative or job of the parents and nothing to do with them. This is understandable; many teachers were brought up to never ask questions about sex, never to discuss it and certainly never to teach it. Among my colleagues a large proportion never discussed reproduction, menstruation, masturbation, with either parent or anyone else in their family. Their knowledge was gleaned solely from magazines, books and peers, and many will admit that even today they still have misconceptions. There is, too, the other extreme; those who feel we live in a permissive society, therefore it is the done thing to encourage young people to have as much experience of sex as they are able to get. In my view both these extremes are wrong. Sex, as with all other subjects, or perhaps more than all other subjects, begins with relationships. Only when the atmosphere is relaxed, the relationships mutually caring, do the right questions begin to emerge. As teachers we are not, therefore, to make judgments, to condemn, or encourage, but to provide information, present alternatives and outline the results certain decisions may have. Students need to thoroughly understand the pill, how it works, what it involves, its social consequences and where to obtain it, should they wish to take further advice. This, however, is not sufficient in itself. They need to be able to talk, and think, and feel compassion; to understand themselves and one another and to see 'sex' as something that is an extension of this, not as an end in itself. Even allowing for the best will in the world, heartache cannot be avoided and I believe that when a young girl finds herself pregnant she needs to be accepted and loved; she needs the teacher she knows well to help her over that most difficult hurdle of 'telling Mum'; often an initially angry, upset and bewildered Mum, a Mum who needs counselling – 'How am I going to tell her Dad?' – 'What can we do?' – 'Where have I gone wrong?' – 'I had to get married, now she'll have to!' The mother, like the daughter, needs support, information and advice. She needs to know the available options – continuing the pregnancy, abortion, a home tutor, financial assistance, the law. A teacher of 'slow learners' needs to know the answers to all these questions and to be able to offer support when needed. Very often that will be the sole support the student or family gets. Slow learners are certainly not 'slower' at sex, however amusing a picture that conjures up. They are certainly slower to realise the consequences. They are often more anxious to please and therefore so much more vulnerable.

A beginning – A two-year course

Appendix III outlines a two-year course dealing with many aspects of Health and Sex Education. I do not believe that a course such as this can be successful in itself, but very often it can provide a starting point to the questions and worries that most adolescents have and which many find difficult to articulate. The course is divided into two parts.

Part 1

The first year is the basic course – Health and Sex Education – and uses professional people such as Health Education Officers, nurses, midwives, health visitors, social workers, etc. During this first year a comprehensive range of subjects is covered and a diary is kept by the pupils of the subjects covered.

Part 2 – Project, Social Involvement and Practical Work

The second year of the course is of a completely different nature from the first year. Being optimistic, one hopes that something during the first year will have particularly caught the interest of the pupil and that he will wish to pursue this particular interest in depth. This forms the basis for the 'project'. (If the pupil wishes, this work may form part of the work submitted for C.S.E. – see Appendix III, section on distribution of marks.)

The following extracts are from two projects, chosen by the pupils themselves and from which I believe they gained far more than a C.S.E.

'A Diary of Edith – – – – – by Jenny – – – – –

Why I chose this subject

I chose the study of old people because I am very concerned about the problems of the elderly. I realise that one day I will be old and I hope I don't have to face the problems a lot of old people do today. I wish a lot more people would realise this fact too. I feel that our society is unfair to old people. A lot of old people have done a lot for their country, they should not be forgotten, but should have some sort of reward. More people should be made to realise the facts of the problems of the old. I aim to show the facts and problems and possible alternatives.

Edith – – – – was a typical old person with problems, probably more towards her family then herself because of her senility. I visited Edith almost daily and I became very close to her. I only wish more could have been done for her.'

Below, reproduced in their original form, are entries from a diary that was kept from September 18th 1973 when the project was begun, until February 21st 1974, the date of Edith's funeral:

24th September 1973, 4.45 p.m. 'I don't know if I could go round these ones on my own, they do at school a bit.' That's the begining of today's fasinating conversation. 'Are you speaking to me? I heard people say they couldn't do it, it's rediculous' she's saying. 'I'm sorry', she said that because I looked at her. 'Yes, I know, there's somebody outside the door now.' I've just told her there's not and she's chattering her teeth now but I don't think she's cold. 'I can hear, I can't bear it, when I get the money.'

P.'s just slapped her for scratching and she said 'You're a little girl arn't you' so P. told her she was a bloke.

I've just given her a chocolate and she said 'For me? Oh, you're a kind girl' and she started crying. It made me feel really nice for some reason. I've just given her another one and she said 'I'll keep this one, it's very kind of you, you're so kind, I'll save it for my house, you are kind, thank you. It's so difficult, you don't know what to give, still, I suppose it comes to you, I suppose someone helps you, I hope so. There's somebody coming again lady.' C.'s just told her to go to the loo so she said 'the who?' She went upstairs but came straight back down again so C.'s took her back up again.

10th February 1974. She looks terrible, very dozy. The doctors

have decided that they're not going to give Edith the operation because she's not strong enough and they're hopeing her hip will go back into place on its own.
I'll say hello and ask her if she's alright. 'Yes thank you dear, Oh, you're a good girl, such a lovely girl, you're the best I know you're such a lovely girl.'

It's awful, she looks like she's in pain. She's taking deep breaths, I hope she's okay. I can't stay long because I have to go and see an aunt in another ward.
17th February 1974. Today Edith passed away, as far as I know in her sleep. I was very upset when I heard and I coundn't stop crying and thinking about her, even though it probably was for the best.
21st February 1974. Today was Ediths funeral. Ediths two sons, C., P., and I went in the Funeral car and although it was quiet and sad it was a beautiful funeral with lots of gorgeous flowers. I couldn't believe she was in the coffin.

Conclusion

I have been making this study over a considerable length of time and I feel that I have learnt a lot from it, especially about the facts of old age and the problems of old people with dimentia, such as Edith ----.

I had always had close contact with Edith ---- but I had only seen her problem in isolation. Through this study I think I have found out about the problems of old people in general, how our society treats them and how they feel, although more emphisis has been put on old people with dimentia. As you can see from my last chapter I have made suggestions from how I think things could be changed and improved for the old with this problem.

Overall I have enjoyed the reserch and writing of this study although it is quite a sad aspect of our society.'

Lack of space prevents me from printing more. I only wish that all the diary could be printed, for I feel that the understanding, compassion and writing that this pupil gained from her contact with a senile woman, a person whom society in general shrinks from, has a lesson in it for us all.

Another aspect of the course is 'Social Involvement'. Every pupil chooses some kind of community work with which to become involved. The possibilities here are enormous as so many organisations are only too willing to cooperate. Reprinted below is a fifteen-year-old's description of her experiences:

People That Matter by Jenny – – – – –

I remember well my first visit to Glenfrith Hospital. It was a dull afternoon in September, cold but crisp. Caroline, a teacher, took us to the hospital. We were laughing and joking all the journey, perhaps because we wished to hide how nervous we were deep inside. The main building is a big house. A long drive way down to the house is surrounded by trees. It looked like something out of a film set. You wouldn't know the occupants were hundreds of mentally ill people.

Eventually arriving, we walked round the grounds with Caroline, meeting and chatting to various patients that were walking or keeping themselves busy. We visited the children's ward. A little boy sat outside on the slabs and watched us attentively, not responding to our smiles. I remember the terrible smell in the children's ward. They were in rooms and rushed to the glass door as we approached, pressed their faces against it. Some just sat there in the corners and didn't even notice us.

We walked back past the main house towards the industrial ward where I was to spend my alternate Wednesday afternoons from today. From the outside, it resembled a small factory with muffled glass windows and the double main door. Entering, I was confronted by the same smell as the children's ward, only not so strong. I felt sure to spend an afternoon in this stench would make me sick. I wasn't quite sure what to expect. I'd met mentally retarded people before, but never worked with them and spent long stretches of time with them.

We were introduced to Mr. Allen who, with two nurses and a Mr. Johnson, ran the occupational therapy. He told us about the occupational ward and its functions. He showed us adjoining rooms where specialist workers made wicker baskets and toys. My first impression of the ward was that it was so drab, very clinical. They had made a bit of an attempt to liven it up with posters and now they've acquired a radio with speakers, but the walls were still that drab grey-green colour. They seemed to be relatively happy and were very anxious to meet us. We made notes and walked round attempting to talk; most of them were very pleased to talk to us. I noticed their need for touch and affection. One girl, Diane, started to pour out her problems. Now I realise it is her way of acquiring sympathy and attention. To every new visitor she puts on the crying act. They were all partaking in some small activity, e.g., packing cocktail sticks and making boxes.

At about 3.15, they all had tea and one of the women washed

up. I found them beautiful people and so affectionate. I soon learnt all their names pretty well and their particulars, what they did last night, who their boy friends/girl friends were. Once you gained their confidence it was all go. You couldn't shut them up, it was great.

Weeks passed and each time they had something new to say to me. I wrote letters home for them, joked with them. I suppose it was wrong, but I started to write to a girl who was on the ward. She is 21 and her name is Jennifer. I think in a way, Jennifer was my favourite, even though I knew I shouldn't have one. I got to know them all by name as the weeks passed and really looked forward to my visits.

Christmas was in the air and there was an unusual happiness around, even though Jennifer was upset because her father was ill in hospital and she thought she wouldn't be allowed to go home. One afternoon, she gave me a Christmas card she had written in and although I could not make head or tail, she knew exactly what she'd written to me. I still proudly possess the card and the envelope.

They loved to tell me about their homes, but never really spoke about their lives in the hospital. Occasionally, I would find out with a lot of persuasion, how long they had been at Glenfrith Hospital and where they had been before them came here.

I noticed that they got upset easily if more attention was paid to another patient, so I had to work out a timetable sort of, to get round to everyone, spending equal time with each.

Well, I'm still visiting Glenfrith and good news! they are decorating the industrial therapy unit, they've had radio speakers in, Jenny's dad is better and everything seems roses.

'Shangton

My second social involvement involves the new mentally handicapped village organised by C.A.R.E. in East Langton. I can't explain the difference between Shangton and Glenfrith, it is incredible. I found also that in Shangton, I was accepted quickly and found a lot of new friends. Jeremy was an easily found acquaintance and couldn't do enough to help me settle into my new environment. A girl called Claire who worked in the sewing room took us around the village and showed us everything, she described everything down to the last detail to us. I way so surprised and pleased the way the people were allowed to walk around and get on with things on their own. The cottages were fabulous and it gave one a sense of belonging.

There were six male – six female to a cottage and two houseparents, just like a large family, which I'm sure helped the patient's condition, it gave a sense of security and love. Nothing was clinical. Each person had their own bedroom with washbasins and can stick posters up. Donny Osmond was a favourite, most have their own record players and 'Crazy Horses' blasts out from all directions. A £1 a week pocket money is handed out every week and Saturday afternoon always offers a treat, either shopping in nearby Market Harborough or just a ride in the village's donated mini-bus. Each villager has his/her own job to do, whether it's helping in the kitchens, in the greenhouses, workshops or sewing rooms, and regular help with Mr. Jack Townsend, the man who donated his land for the C.A.R.E. village project on his farm. The relationship held between the houseparents and villagers is unbelievable. Some of the villagers get to become Junior staff, which gives them a sense of responsibility. Jeremy is in charge. He has been in the C.A.R.E. villages, first at Blackerton in Devon, now in Shangton. I have only worked in the village for three previous weeks up to now, but already feel a part of this exciting and brilliant new idea. We clearly need more of these villages to improve our relationships with mentally ill and handicapped.'

The third aspect is a practical project. The student may make anything that he chooses, that he feels will be of use to the community. Debby organised a Christmas party for the children of the nursery she had been working in:

Christmas Fun by Debby – – – – –

On Thursday, December 14th 1973, we organised and prepared a Christmas party for some of the children who attend the creche. The children were aged from three to five years old. The party was from three o'clock untill four o'clock. We organised pass the parcel for a game, we had two parcels and they enjoyed it tremendously.

We took quite a few photographs of the children playing pass the parcel, photographs of the food set out and photographs of the children. All the children were happy and excited. At the end of the party, we gave all of the children a little Christmas stocking. Inside the Christmas stocking there was a packet of sweets, little hand made Golly-wogs, a balloon and a lolly pop.

Menu

Beef Paste sandwiches
Cheese spread sandwiches
Sausage Twists
Sausages on sticks
Cheese savors
Cheese and onion crisps
Jelly and Blancmange
Small iced cakes
Chocolate fingers
Train cake
Ribena to drink

The Time Plan

Time	*Things to Do*
11.00 – 11.15 a.m.	Make the Swiss Roll and the Sausage twists
11.15 – 11.45	Make the little cakes and wash up. Bring out the Sausage twists and the Swiss Roll
11.45 – 12.15	Make the drink and put it in the fridge to cool. Fry the sausages and put them on sticks.
1.15 – 1.30	Decorate the cakes and the Swiss Roll
1.30 – 1.45	Wash up and dry up
1.45 – 2.15	Put the chocolate fingers, savors, crisps out and set the table
2.15 – 2.30	Do the sandwiches and finishing touches
2.30 – 2.45	Meet the children

Appendix III gives an outline and examples of the different parts of the course, which is recognised by the East Midland Regional Examinations Board.

Summary

As stated earlier, this course is not intended to be the means of teaching Health and Sex Education step by step. It is intended as a basis for discussion and further enquiry. It offers, in the second year, complete freedom of choice and flexibility to pursue any line of enquiry. Students of all abilities have taken part from the academically bright to the severely E.S.N. and I hope all have gained a greater insight into some aspect of life.

Sharon's conclusion at the end of her project on V.D. sums up the value better than I can:

'I think if I hadn't done this project I wouldn't know hardly anything about V.D. at all. I would still be going around not sitting on toilet seats and touching door knobs etc. and probably having sex and thinking I hadn't a chance of having V.D. But the whole aspect of V.D. is not taken seriously enough. If it was talked about more it would broaden peoples minds to the whole topic.

When I visited the clinic as part of my project I found it wasn't as bad as I thought. I expected some nasty old doctor there to be drilling into my head that I was a naughty girl and if I got it again I would be in for it. But it wasn't at all like that. The nurses and doctors were very friendly and they didn't seem to mind me being there. I wasn't in the 'black book' at all. They were all just like ordinary people like you and I, and they were there to help people and cure them of this horrible disease.

CHAPTER 7

DRAMA AND PHOTOGRAPHY AS MEANS OF COMMUNICATION

A. DRAMA

Many schools these days have appointed a specialist Drama teacher but the time the teacher has does not always match the time pupils require or want. Drama plays an important part in the learning process of all pupils, but with slow learners it is perhaps of even greater importance. It is another form of expression; another form of communication. Teachers who are not specially trained are often apprehensive about attempting drama. They remember their own schooldays of elaborate plays and excerpts from Shakespeare and feel unable to cope. Drama today is very different from this, and the following may provide some ideas when the pupils say:

'Can we do Drama?'

Any teacher who has shown a willingness to take a class or a group of pupils for drama is familiar with this question arising again and again, sometimes when the teacher has planned something quite different or when he feels least able to meet the demands of a lively group for drama. Certainly pupils gain considerable satisfaction and pleasure from an activity which can sometimes appear wild and uncontrolled to an onlooker. And often they want to repeat the activity called drama, even doing the same play over and over again without becoming bored. I remember one group of adolescent boys who made a play about a haunted castle full of monsters, which ended Hamlet-like with all of them dead except two. They repeated this play, which would usually last for an hour, week after week, and emerge exhausted and satisfied. Another group of boys in an approved school repeated the same play about escape many times and never seemed to tire. The teacher can sometimes do little more than stand back and marvel.

But it is frustrating if the teacher really can do no more than look on. Any good teacher wants to understand what it is that motivates pupils for such intense, concentrated work, and he wants to be able to become more involved in helping to make drama work when it breaks down or fails to get started, and to direct the group to face new challenges, to make progress in drama.

Each teacher will eventually come to his own understanding about how drama works for him and for each group of pupils, but he needs to know some of the ways in which drama is often started so that he can build confidence as a leader, an 'enabler' and an initiator.

Community Drama

In order to obtain maximum influence as a teacher on the work that is progressing whilst retaining the option of not interfering at the inappropriate moment, the teacher needs to be able to keep the pupils as one group. If the group is large, more than 20, then a play about a community is a good way of doing this.

A helpful way of starting such a drama is to begin a discussion about an object such as a key, a ring, a hat, a photograph, which is produced by the teacher. The discussion requires to be positively directed by the teacher, until he feels the group is beginning to find its own direction. He can open doors by saying that the object is, perhaps, thousands of years old and challenging the group to describe some of the incidents that have occurred in its life: he can define a specific area that seems to be fruitful by asking the group to be more detailed – How old was the man? Was he able to defend himself or did he need to ask for help? Whom did he ask? Was he proud, and did he find it difficult to ask for help?

Such questioning will often help a group to get to a starting point for a play which may start with the teacher saying, 'I don't understand why no one would help him. Let's find out what happened when he went to ask his friends.' It is important that discussion does not wear out the drama and that the role-play should begin as soon as there is enough of the situation to generate a play. The feeling that no one knows what is going to happen next is an exciting one and it is fatal to hold back the action too long. At the same time as the story seems to be emerging so the need for maximum involvement of the group arises. The teacher may be aware that one or two individuals are beginning to dominate the story and the danger sometimes arises of shy, quiet pupils becoming observers. It is the teacher's responsibility to help such individuals become involved and he can best do this by careful questioning during the discussion – 'How were the rest of the village people affected by this?' 'What did they do?' 'Did they meet together to discuss their action?' 'Did they come and demand more information?' – Such questioning builds, by pressing the pupils into decisions which raise problems that need to be solved. It also leads to the situation where the teacher can ask all individuals to define a role for themselves within the community.

Once all the pupils are enclosed within the situation, no matter how nominally to begin with, the teacher is in a better position to relate the elements of the drama as they begin to emerge. If some students are experiencing difficulty in establishing belief because they are shy or wary of the more extrovert students, the teacher can help in one of a number of ways. He may, for instance, adopt a role himself in order to relate in character to such pupils, thereby challenging them to respond in character and giving them confidence to do so. Or he may, as the teacher outside the situation, help individuals to build character by the kind of questioning suggested above: 'I suppose you are a bit fed up with this mess aren't you? I expect you have been wondering how it will affect you. Are you going to get together with your friends to do something about it or are you going to wait and see what happens?'

Sometimes it is appropriate to get pupils to try building by suggestion in this way, in pairs, suspending the development of the play whilst this is done. If it is done by one pair at a time in the centre of the circle with all the other pupils looking on, there can be amusement and interest in the technique.

Knowing when to stop a play in progress requires sensitivity and a clear understanding of what is being experienced by the students as they work – not simply what they are doing. For drama very quickly moves from the external situation – the play or improvisation – to the internal situation – the actual relationships between participants. Often the conflicts, rivalries and affections within the group are being explored at one remove, and the teacher needs to be aware of this. He needs to be able to move the play away from certain danger areas in good time and sometimes, when appropriate, to move the play closer to such areas. It is important, however, to help the group sustain belief in the role-play at such times. On one occasion a boy who had volunteered to play the role of an ostracised individual was being taunted by other characters in the play, and tears began to roll down his cheeks, noticed by the others. It was important to decide whether to continue the play and allow the boy to hide behind his character or to end it as too much of a strain for him. Only close knowledge of the pupils concerned and a close involvement with the play as it develops will enable the teacher to decide appropriately in such cases.

There is dynamite in drama at times. If the teacher is prepared to experiment with his own roles in relation to his students, he may be surprised to find how easily pupils accept a range of roles from him. So slipping from a character within the play to the role of group leader stopping the play for discussion, or to observer, or to confidant to a student who has a complaint about some bullying within the play, the teacher learns to handle the dynamite and to 'direct' the work productively. The great advantage of community drama is that it creates a one-remove community in which many different improvisations or situations can flourish at the same time whilst still allowing for all the work to be related, called together at times and creatively directed by the teacher. It can end when everyone is thoroughly tired with it or when it comes to an end in a story sense.

In addition to the 'object' starting point to drama there are many simple alternatives: photographs, films, a story, a poem or a legend, a news item, a title, a person's name. Suggestive questioning, as I have illustrated, will work on any of these stimuli.

Sometimes, a carefully prepared question to the group challenges them in such a way that drama will soon be suggested. For example, 'What is the most important quality in a friend?' 'What do friends most often quarrel about?' 'What do families argue about most?' 'What makes people strike?' 'Why do people steal?' Such questions may provide the opportunity to use drama as a means of exploration of problems and interests close to the hearts of the students and such work is sometimes referred to as Socio-drama.

Socio-drama

Drama that deals more directly with the lives of the participants still needs to be at one-remove. That is pupils need to be able to explore touchy relationships behind the shelter or mask of a character. And so the techniques of character building are extremely important. Often socio-drama arises naturally when the group want to make a play about a gang, or more often two rival gangs. This often brings out, particularly in adolescents, the fascination with violence. There is also a tendency for adolescents to enjoy a hunt situation when an individual is taunted and victimised by the rest of the group. If the teacher is able to encourage a strong development of role-play, such a situation may be faced without fear, the violence ritualised and controlled and discussion used to explore the forces at work and the consequences of violent action.

The role of the teacher in such explorations will again vary according to the needs of the situation but as with community drama it is imperative that the teacher is able to exercise his influence when it is needed and so he must remain within the work. One of the ways in which this may be done is by beginning the work with the pupils seated in a circle large enough for the drama situations to be played within it. The teacher can stop and start the work as it progresses, ask questions, get the other pupils to ask questions, change parts so that as many pupils as possible take an active part, change the scene to develop the story, ask for more detail and lead discussion. He may also suggest a change in technique, if appropriate, moving out of the circle situation into a more open physical setting where the place in which the drama occurs is more clearly defined and the special kind of control factor provided by the circle is removed.

Techniques and Games

Most techniques, games and exercises in drama can be used as an end in themselves, but they are often most appropriately and productively employed as part of more ambitious projects in improvisation of the kind described.

Building Techniques

Pupils new to drama benefit from practice in simple improvisations which are often amusing:

i) Group sits in a circle. Volunteer invited to come and sit, stand or squat in the middle. Second person invited to create a statement, or situation, or define the scene by adding himself to the first person, e.g., first person sits on chair, second person takes up hairdressing stance. This game can then be complicated in a variety of ways. The group can be challenged to add more and more individuals to the initial situation until it no longer makes sense. Or dialogue can be added, then movement, so that the scene 'lives'. The group may themselves find ways of developing disciplines to make the game more complex.

ii) Story-telling – the simple way of beginning the complex of story-telling games is to sit in a circle, begin a story with one word to each individual as the story goes round the circle. The need for rules may arise, such as time-limits, the need to make sense of some kind, or to prevent speaking out of turn. There are many variations. For instance, the first person begins the story and can say as much or as little as he likes before suddenly pointing to someone else in the circle who has to carry on immediately. Or the story may be mimed in the centre of the circle at the same time as it is being created. Or several stories may be told at the same time by individuals crossing to stand in front of others seated, telling the story so far and adding some more before exchanging places with the listener who then has to cross the circle and repeat

the performance, adding his own contribution. With six of these stories being told simultaneously, the effect can be amusing and stimulating.
iii) Contrapuntal dialogue, as it has been flamboyantly termed, is a means of creating a play, building characters, exploring background, by the use of voices only. Example: create a character's name, then anyone in the circle may begin by starting conversation spoken into the void of the centre of the circle; another person may join in the conversation and a scene has begun. This scene may then be interrupted or pushed aside by another conversation being started which takes place at another time or location in the 'life' of the created character. The first scene is suspended and may or may not be faded in later. The total effect once the play has taken off, is of a radio play in which impressions, dream sequences, conversations, simple statements, questions and exclamations, are the building blocks. Sensitivity is essential and the teacher's role may well be to conduct the group almost like an orchestra until the mechanisms are understood.

Trust Games

One of the main advantages of trust games is that they can be enjoyed and found useful by almost any group in age-range and ability. There are very many that are in common use and endless variations are possible if the basic idea of the game is understood:
i) *Blindness games* based on individual being led around by partner trying to keep his eyes closed and trusting his seeing partner to prevent collisions with obstacles. This can be more refined as confidence grows and volunteers required to walk around the room 'blind' being prevented from walking into obstacles by someone lightly touching his shoulder and facing him in a new direction.
ii) *Falling games:* a circle of about six to eight persons. A volunteer stands in the centre and closes his eyes. Individuals reach out to touch his shoulder without stretching to distance themselves properly. With his feet close together the centre man begins to fall, trusting those to whom he is falling, to gently ease him back to the centre where he will overbalance again in another direction. This game must be taken seriously and with concentration since if the individual in the middle is genuinely trusting his friends, he will hurt himself if allowed to fall.

Another falling game to be played with caution is rather more dramatic. An individual stands on the edge of a table and closes his eyes. The other members of the group, there must be eight or ten for this game, form two inward facing lines near the table and when ready, the individual falls or launches himself forward, trusting the group to catch him horizontally. When played with confidence, such games are very stimulating and help knit groups together.

It is impossible, in the available space, to go into greater detail about this particular aspect of education, but it is hoped that some of the suggestions will provide starting points and for those teachers who would like to know more in greater depth, then the L.E.A.'s adviser may be able to organise, or provide information on, courses.

B. PHOTOGRAPHY

Visual Communication for All

Many pupils are interested in photography. Unfortunately, it is too often only offered to the 'A' stream student. Photography offers the opportunity to communicate visually and is of great value, therefore, to those pupils who find difficulty in communicating through the more usual channel of words. Photography knows no age barriers and is equally suitable for junior school or secondary school age range.

Photography in the junior school: the pin-hole camera

It is not necessary to have elaborate equipment, as the following extract from a teacher's experience, when on teaching practice in a junior school, illustrates. (The two photographs were taken with a pin-hole camera as described.)

> 'My introduction to what was, for most of these bottom stream juniors, a completely new world, was by explaining and demonstrating the 'Camera Obscura', which, made from an old shoe box and greaseproof paper, helped the children to begin to understand the simple principle of how light-rays, entering through a pin-hole, could produce an image. The next step was to get some half-a-dozen children to make their own pin-hole cameras out of large cocoa tins. These were painted matt black inside and had a one-inch hole punched through the middle of the side. Over this hole was taped a thin piece of aluminium foil (of the kind used to hold fruit pies, etc.) in the centre of which I had made a *very* fine hole with a needle. The rough edges of the hole were rubbed away lightly by using the abrasive side of a matchbox. After making sure that the lids of the tins were light-tight, we went into our 'dark-room'. Before you say that most schools do not possess such a luxury, let me explain that ours was made from a storage cupboard which had been made light-proof with a sheet of black poly-

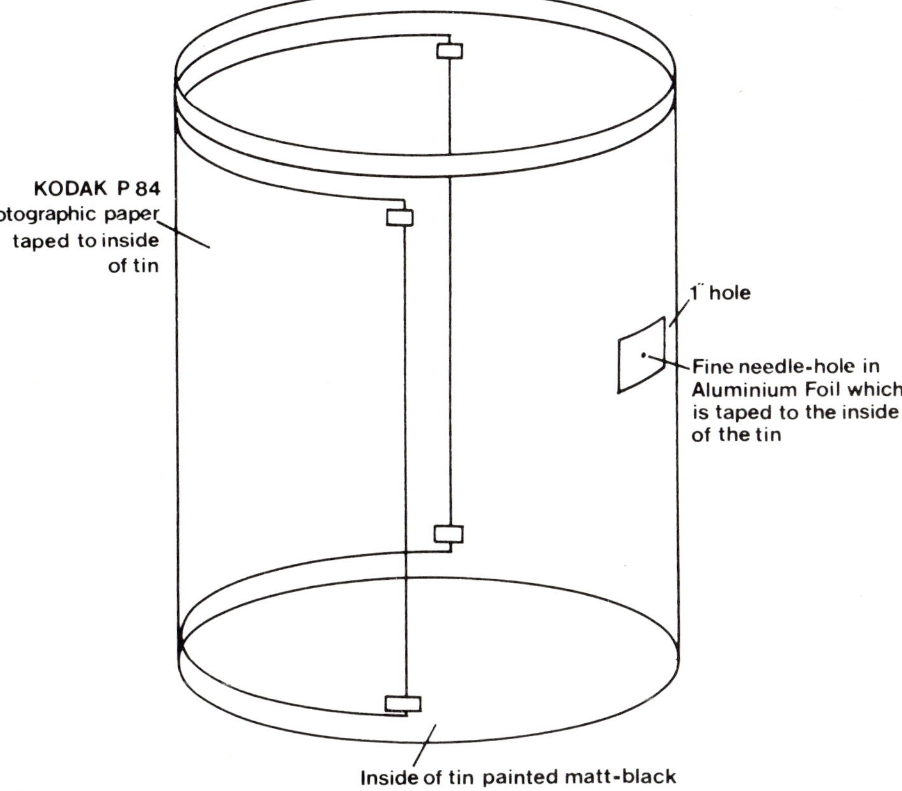

thene and tape. As a light, someone had made a red safelight out of a square biscuit tin by cutting a six-inch hole out of one side and covering this with red acetate. Inside the tin I used a sixty-watt light bulb in a holder screwed through the top of the tin. This light was quite good enough for our use providing it was not left on for long periods to get hot; if this was to have been the case, ventilation holes would have been necessary. Into the back of our camera/tins we taped a sheet of Kodak P.84 photographic paper, the light sensitive emulsion side facing the pin-hole. The lids were replaced and a piece of black tape was stuck over the pin-hole. Our cameras were now loaded and we were ready to take our first photographs. For our first experiments we decided to photograph the school and so, taking it in turns, the children positioned their cameras. As we didn't know how long each exposure should be we decided to choose different times ranging from one minute to four minutes. The black tape was taken from over the holes and the exposures were made. In no time at all we were back in the dark-room holding our pieces of photographic paper. Slowly the first child slid his paper into the developing dish and as if by magic an image of the school appeared. I don't think I've ever seen children so enthusiastic as, one by one, they developed their first photographs. They soon learned to master the four-step developing procedure of – (1) development of the image (develop until image is right density), (2) stopping the development by immersing the paper in 'Stop Bath Solution' (about one minute), (3) fixing the paper in 'Kodafix' (about 40 seconds, depending on mixture of fixer and water), (4) washing (in clean water for 20 minutes).

Much discussion followed our first experiments. Why were the photographs back to front? Why was the sky so dark? Of course the resulting photograph was in negative form. Why were some lighter and some darker? I re-explained the idea of 'exposure time' – the letting in of more light and the resultant effect of a darker photograph.

I showed the children how to turn their negative into a positive image by contact printing. One sheet of unexposed paper was placed emulsion-side up, on a table in the dark-room. Our pin-hole-produced negative was placed, image side down, on top of it. A sheet of glass was placed on top of the two sheets of paper to hold them in close contact and a light directly above was turned on (making sure all unexposed paper is safely packed away!), for five seconds. The exposed paper was developed in the same way as the original photo negative. After a few attempts we found out exactly how much time we needed to leave the light on in order to obtain a good photograph.

It didn't take long before the children were able to work for much of the time without my help. They produced many excellent photographs and these, in turn, proved to be a valuable stimulus for other areas of work. I found that many slow learners would willingly make brave attempts at writing captions and explanations to go with their pictures.

The children were using photography in its simplest form as a tool with which to explore and communicate their ideas. The emphasis of the project was for once not tied up with words but when the children realised that they could achieve success with their home-made cameras, their new-found confidence often led them into writing as an additional means of communication.

The energy and enthusiasm produced by the children continued for the whole term that I was at the school and I can see no reason why similar experiments elsewhere should not meet with the same success.'

Photography in the secondary school

In secondary schools photography is playing an increasingly important role in many areas of study. Many schools now have darkrooms with enlargers and good quality cameras. All students, regardless of academic ability, can master the skills of developing, printing and taking photographs. Some of the photographs reproduced here were taken by 14-year-old boys with severe learning difficulties who had mastered the techniques necessary to bring about a finished piece of work they are proud of. It is necessary to spend a lot of time, at the beginning, teaching and practising the basic skills until they are almost second-nature. It helps, to standardise the routine and always use the most simple and straightforward method. Once a student has grasped enough knowledge to ensure success, he can begin to experiment.

Many slow learners have shown a great interest in photography and it can play a valuable part in overcoming some of their difficulties. The very nature of photography's 'realness' of image appeals to them and each of their own photographs becomes a real piece of personal communication for them. John S – – – – aged 15, who has a serious speech defect, worked on a simple 8 mm. movie film for a whole term; his shyness and unwillingness to communicate decreased as his confidence grew with the film's final success. He is now working on another film 'A Study of a Farming Community' and I am sure there will be an even greater improvement as he is attacking his problem unconsciously whilst being totally involved in what he is doing. Reproduced in this book are some photographs taken by other 14-year-olds. They include one of a series of photographs illustrating 'The Changing Face of Leicester' (see Chapter 5 on Social Studies), one from a project on race and immigration, an illustration for a poem about bird-watching and one of a series on the 'Age of Steam'.

Photography provides a splendid starting point for many studies; it motivates those students who are often most difficult to motivate. It is an expensive medium; nevertheless it can play a large part in making lesson-time more exciting and relevant to the students' own interests.

A 'pin-hole camera' photograph of South Brent churchyard, taken by a ten-year-old pupil.

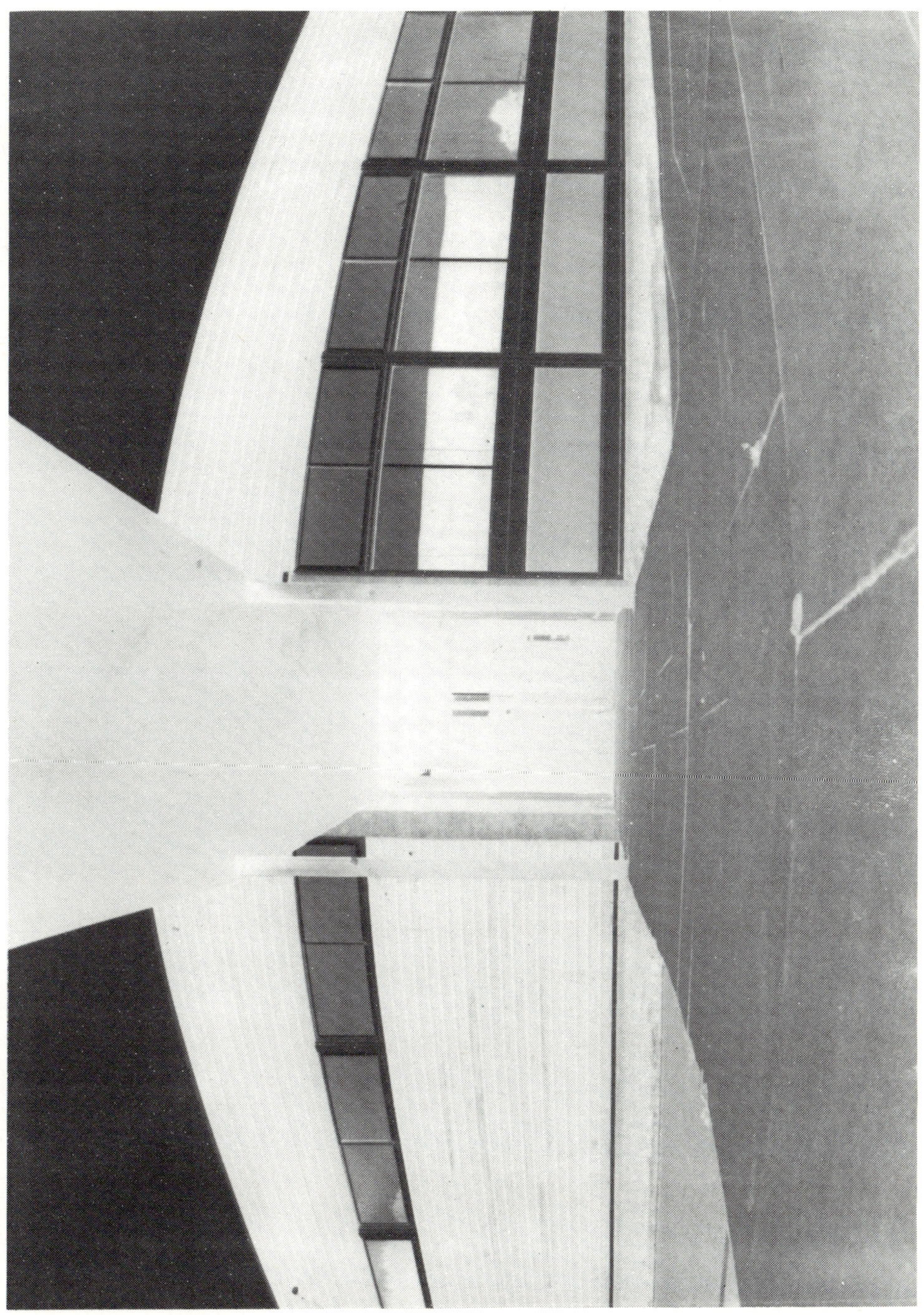

A 'pin-hole camera' view of a school

Canary Nesting in the Wild: photographed, developed and printed by a 14-year-old pupil for his project on bird-watching.

The Age of Steam: photographed, developed and printed by a 14-year-old pupil in connection with his project.

CHAPTER 8

RESOURCES AND MATERIALS

'School programmes devised for the early school leaver or for the slow learner . . . in the end will depend more on local initiative than on national projects, and national projects will depend for their effectiveness on their ability to stimulate local developments.' – Pamphlet. *Schools Council and the Young School Leaver.*

This is the essence of the message from a report by the Schools Council on the Early School Leaver. This report also claims that there is a lack of confidence and uncertainty of teachers about what to teach, the majority of teachers accepting that for slow learners the 'text' book is inadequate and out of place. Many authorities, realising that R.O.S.L.A. would keep many reluctant learners in school for the extra year and thereby pose many problems for the teachers, set up, as early as 1967, teachers' centres, working parties and development teams to create appropriate teaching materials. Some of these projects provide excellent starting points or supplementary materials and a list of available projects can be found in Appendix VI. However, these materials do not solve the problem for the majority of pupils for a great part of the time they spend in school.

Human resources are of primary value

The most successful resources are most often human contacts; teachers, nurses, social workers, youth leaders, postmen, shopkeepers, groundsmen, etc. It has been my experience that few people refuse to help when asked; most are glad to have young people with them, to provide anecdotes, to bring along treasures, to share experiences. The local pigeon-fancier in our area has proved invaluable. He not only teaches the skills of caring for the birds, of building lofts, of photographing the birds, but knowledge of people and places, laws and rules, excitement and heartache, the value of an absorbing leisure pursuit shared with others and a fund of stories that would fill several volumes. How much better is a judgment of 'Colditz' on T.V. when one has been in the company of someone who spent several years as a prisoner of war and can retell in detail the misery and sorrow, together with the humour and human dignity. What a better understanding of society pupils have, when the old lady they have visited regularly has to be taken into a home because she can't look after herself anymore and there is no alternative in the area open to her.

I am not suggesting that this kind of activity should form the total education of a pupil but I do believe it is greatly underrated and too many teachers allow themselves to be put off by imaginary difficulties. 'Our school is in a difficult locality', 'The parents would not like it', 'They can't be trusted out by themselves'. All these are poor excuses. People in the community at large are pleased to help. Parents, if they are properly informed of the objectives, will willingly co-operate, and teachers who feel they must accompany pupils everywhere greatly under-estimate their pupils and fail to understand that the only discipline worth having is self-discipline. Occasionally, some pupils will abuse the situation but then so will some adults and some teachers will undoubtedly abuse power! Using human resources is, in itself, an invaluable experience from which can come the opportunity for greater understanding of ourselves and society.

Paper resources

The majority of paper resources, if they are to be of real value, have to be made by the teachers concerned for the pupils they are working with at the time. That is not to say they cannot be used more than once, but initially they need to be created with a specific need in mind. There are some specific objectives which I feel should be borne in mind when a teacher sets about creating resources for slow learners. They should aim to:

a) improve reading skills
b) bring about problem-solving
c) help to organise thoughts, abilities, energies.

They need to:

a) use everyday language
b) make apparent that the problem is solved, thereby giving immediate sense of achievement
c) recognise that most students in this category have poor

Suggestions for other work.

Go to the
nearest primary
School.
Draw some of
the things in
the playground.
What changes
have there been?

Find someone old make a tape recording about their schooldays.

Collect photographs and pictures of different kinds of schools.

Draw and write about your idea of a perfect school.

Make up a play about school 100 years ago.

How the Lessons Have Changed

Lessons have changed a lot. These pictures show (a) A science lesson (b) a maths lesson (c) a P.E. lesson. In each space draw or write how lessons today are different. Do you think things have changed (A) for the better. Why or why not?

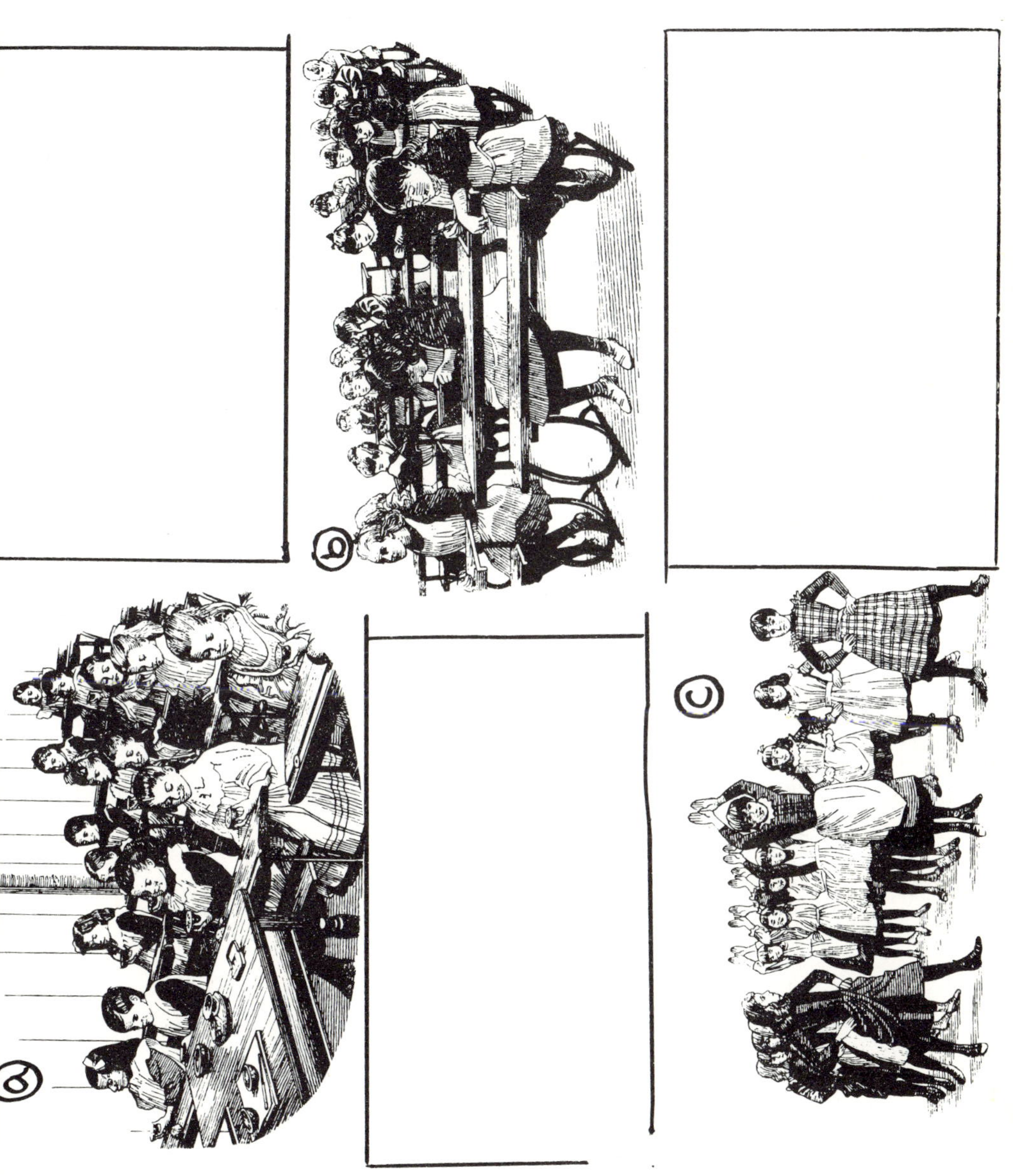

powers of concentration, therefore, provide short tasks with immediate end results. This can entail a lack of continuity if not used carefully, therefore long-term short, successful tasks should lead on to open-ended tasks which could lead to further exploration. They need to be visually stimulating.

The examples on pp. 160–63, taken from a booklet on 'Schools of Long Ago', illustrate some of these points. The language and graphics are simple. The instructions are clear and the spacing set out so that the student can immediately see where and what is expected.

Not fashion again!

It has been stated earlier that a pupil's own interest should form the basis of a learning programme and that the teacher should guide and direct where appropriate. When a pupil says that she would like to 'do fashion' many teachers' hearts sink, mine included, but I don't think it need be as depressing as it may at first seem. Through costume, many other things can come to light, if the 'costume' leads to further questions.

The material on p. 165, from a booklet made for a pupil interested in fashion from 1901 – 1914, illustrates this point.

Information cards

It is important to recognise that ploughing through a reference library to find relevant answers is not going to appeal to slow learners even if it is within their scope. With each booklet that is produced, then, it is necessary to provide reference cards which contain the information needed. These can be kept in a wallet which has the same title as the question booklets. Information on hand immediately simplifies the task and makes the likelihood of success much greater. The information cards must be well-illustrated – B.B.C. pamphlets are excellent for this – and the language must be simple. It must be accepted that on one card all the facts cannot be given, but sufficient information can be given to awaken interest and spark off discussion that can bring about, for pupils, a greater understanding of themselves and society.

Better future parents

> 'Education for parenthood is the most effective plan for putting into practice a programme of positive mental health.' – Professor Blatz.

More and more teachers are beginning to support the above statement. More and more youngsters are becoming aware of the importance of being 'good' parents. Many have a basic interest in the subject

1912 People were just becoming interested in the motor car.

They found motor cars very exciting

Only the most daring young people went about in motor cars.

The cars were beautiful, highly polished, brass headlamps and real leather seats.

Choose two or three cars from around these years. Draw or trace them and give some facts about them.

Find out all you can about Henry Ford and the start of mass production in the motor industry.

Henry Ford and the Development of MASS-PRODUCTION in the Motor-Car Industry.

Henry Ford in one of his cars.

When motor cars were first made, each workman built each car. This was a slow and expensive business. Then, big businessmen like William Morris and Henry Ford started a method of building cars, where workmen stood in a line and shared in the building of every car. One man fitted the wheels, another fixed the steering, another adjusted the brakes etc. This meant that building cars became very much easier and quicker. Cars became cheaper as a result.

2 Production lines

The effect on people's lives was very great. More and more people bought cars. People living in distant villages moved about much more. Lorries were used to carry goods. Thousands of people went on holiday to the country side or to the seaside. Not all the results were good, however. Look at the diagram below for a bad result of more motorcars. Think of other good and bad effects of great numbers of cars.

This diagram shows the number of cars on the roads in the last 60 years and a related table of road accidents.

			accidents	
			fatal	non-fatal
1910		53,196	1,241	28,950
1920		186,801	2,704	53,734
1930		1,056,214	7,305	177,895
1940		1,423,200	8,609	no figures available
1950		2,257,873	5,012	196,313
1960		5,525,828	6,970	340,581
1966		9,513,300	7,985	384,472
1969		11,227,900	7,383	345,811

and are anxious to learn as much as they can whilst still at school. This is especially true of girls, but more and more boys are admitting an interest too, as society changes its values and emphasis. Nothing can be as valuable in this field as practical experience. Working in nurseries, studying the teachers, children bringing their own siblings to school, taking part in holiday playschemes, acting, story-telling, regularly visiting infant schools, all are an important part of any programme looking at child development. All these experiences, however, can be backed up in schools. Very few books or published materials deal in simple enough terms with these subjects, certainly not in language that is easily understandable and identifiable with. It is a fairly simple matter for the teacher to find appropriate pictures and write a simple explanation. When preparing materials of this kind the same rules regarding language, graphics, relevance, etc. apply.

Below are two extracts from a booklet made at the request of two fourteen-year-old girls who had been working half a day a week in an inner city nursery class. They became interested in perception and intelligence. I have included them as, in my view, they are a good example of just how strong an interest in a complex subject can become, as a result of a meaningful practical experience.

Summary

No materials are of value without the necessary human contacts but I have found that pupils are very pleased when an information booklet is made to elaborate on something they have enquired about and in most cases it leads them to useful further enquiry. I believe most passionately that these materials should be relevant, well-presented, and stimulating visually. The Banda worksheet cannot be this and although there is the occasional use for a duplicated worksheet, I find the use made of them in some schools depressing. In my view a text book is infinitely preferable to yet another worksheet and I'm certain that many pupils' hearts sink when they see the teacher appearing with yet another clutch of duplicated papers. All the extracts here were originated at the request of individual pupils. They do mean a lot of work at the time, but they can then be fed into a resource system and used many times.

<u>The brain has almost finished growing by the end of the second year.</u>

If a child is not given the right amounts of the right foods between the 5th. and 10th. month following birth, he will not produce an adequate number of cells in the brain.

In order to learn we must be able to memorise. In order to memorise we must have an adequate number of cells to do the work. If a child does not get the right foods in its first year it will not be able to learn as well or as quickly as other children.

It will not matter how much extra protein a child eats later in its life. The damage is done in the womb and during the first year of life.

I.Q. gets its real start in the egg.

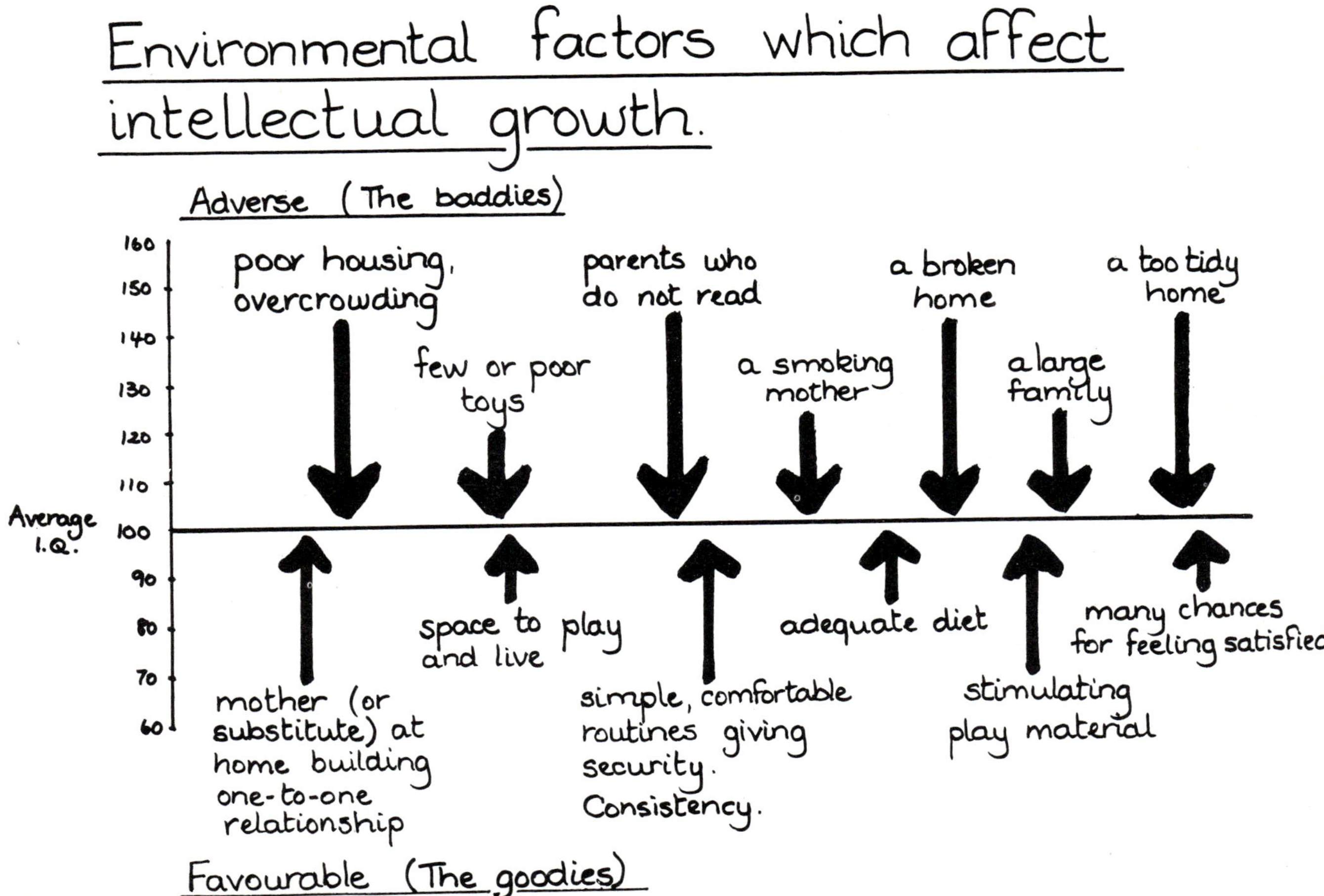
Environmental factors which affect intellectual growth.
Adverse (The baddies)
poor housing, overcrowding
few or poor toys
parents who do not read
a smoking mother
a broken home
a large family
a too tidy home
Average I.Q.
160
150
140
130
120
110
100
90
80
70
60
mother (or substitute) at home building one-to-one relationship
space to play and live
simple, comfortable routines giving security. Consistency.
adequate diet
stimulating play material
many chances for feeling satisfied.
Favourable (The goodies)

CHAPTER 9

SCHOOL ORGANISATION AND SLOW LEARNERS

> 'The farmer who puts his ten cows on good pasture and another ten cows on bad pasture and when the ten cows on bad pasture produce poor results he then blames it on the genes – that farmer is a bloody fool.' (Sir Alec Clegg.)

Alec Clegg, in the quotation above, puts the case for thinking, or in many cases, re-thinking the total environment and philosophy necessary to get good results from the least academic in our secondary schools. By good results I do not mean good 'O' levels or C.S.E. results but stable, confident, fully developed human beings. I believe that in order to do this it is necessary to work towards complete non-streaming in schools. To bring about, by care and encouragement, the conviction within each child that he is an individual that counts, we need to set up situations whereby he experiences success and knows that he matters. This cannot be done by streaming, setting, banding, or any other system which, however, it is wrapped up, sorts children out into groups of those who are expected to be successful and those who are not. Having said this, however, I recognise that teachers, however much they may believe in this philosophy, cannot go into an established school and put into effective action a system that will bring this about. Quite often they can only fit into whichever system is in operation and get the best possible out of that situation. Some teachers, too, have an equally strong belief in 'special classes' and a highly structured system for the learning of basic skills. Whichever system one favours it is important that those who play a leading part are committed to their system. For these reasons this section of the book deals with various types of organisation, all of them in practice at the present time, and, within the organisation of their schools, working well.

I have not attempted to compare the various systems or to offer any judgment. The reason for including them is so that the individual reader may make an evaluation himself and perhaps make use of whichever parts he feels will prove most useful in the situation in which he finds himself.

A completely unstreamed comprehensive school

The school is fully comprehensive, taking all children from 11 to 18 from a rural catchment area of two recently enlarged villages and a very large council estate on the edge of a city. There are no special schools within the area so children with special needs are catered for within the comprehensive school. These children include physically handicapped, partially hearing, E.S.N., and maladjusted. The two sections of the school – the High School (11–14 age group) and the Upper School (14–18 age group) – occupy separate buildings on the same campus. The schools are unstreamed, children being taught in mixed ability groups for all subjects. The two schools are separate, each having its own Head and staff. There is, however, considerable overlap between specialist departments, as facilities are shared between the two schools. The organisation operates in 'year' groups in the High School and 'teams' in the Upper School.

The High School

Although the school is completely unstreamed, the staff recognise the fact that some children need extra support. Therefore, each year group has one member of staff who is completely free-timetabled, i.e. they are not timetabled to teach classes or groups of children in the normal way. Their own individual timetable is determined by themselves with reference to the children's need and what is required of them by the teachers working within that particular year. These teachers were originally given a brief requiring them to spend one third of their time on remedial withdrawal work, one third to support work in the specialist subject areas and the remaining third in the preparation of resources. Although in practice it rarely works out precisely that way, these three categories provide a useful criterion to assess the impact of their work.

In order to carry out the specialist help needed for withdrawal work, two rooms are provided. They are pleasantly situated and adequately stocked with books, apparatus, A/V equipment and creative materials. The children themselves named the room 'reading room' and it has gradually become known as such to everyone in the school.

Withdrawal work

When the children come up from the junior schools they have

already been seen by their new teachers. They have met their personal tutors and the remedial specialist. The High School teachers have visited the junior schools and discussed with those teachers their assessment of a child's difficulties, both learning and emotional. All the children are screened on arrival (using the Daniels & Diack test). This is primarily to catch those with a reading level of below nine years, that might otherwise not have been apparent. This means, therefore, that not only children with obvious reading difficulties are seen, but also those still struggling or those who simply need encouragement to continue reading. These latter children would probably not receive extra help if the school was organised with a 'special class'.

As well as those with obvious problems, strugglers, or reluctant readers, there are approximately six children per year who could be classified as E.S.N. if the normal cut-off level of I.Q. 65–70 is accepted.

The actual number of times any given children are seen in a week depends entirely on the problems of the particular child. For example, a child with a reading age of under seven years would be withdrawn every day, whereas one with a reading age of nine years would be seen perhaps only once a week. The size of the group withdrawn at any one time depends on the timetable restrictions and the reading age levels at which the children are working, it being easier to work with larger groups of 10–12 for children with higher reading ages, whereas groups of 4–8 are more appropriate for those with more severe reading problems. Children are often withdrawn from Humanities, which are integrated and taught by individual methods, and therefore those withdrawn do not miss subjects in specialist areas which they might not be able to join in at another time.

What kind of work?

The type of work done with the children depends upon their specific or general difficulties. The primary aim is to find out as much as possible about the child and his background, to enable the primary stage of diagnosis to be as effective as possible, and to build up the child's confidence and trust in the teachers so that what is often a very delicate problem can be dealt with as sensitively as possible. To do this thoroughly, the first three weeks of the beginning of each academic year are spent just seeing the children individually.

Amount and type of help

Depending on the child's problems it may be decided that he needs help in one or more of the following areas: reading, sight or phonic analysis, language development, listening comprehension, perceptual or motor difficulties or handwriting problems. This wide approach to the child's problems requires a large quantity of the appropriate materials. This presupposes, therefore, that schools willing to organise on these lines are also willing to apportion a fair share of capitation towards meeting the cost of the materials. However, even allowing for a generous share of capitation with which to purchase suitable materials, there are often not enough to cope with the demands. Teachers in this situation, then, must be capable of creating and producing their own resources, and to do this they must be allowed time. They also need time and flexibility to take a child out of school. In the High School, a child needing free clothes could be taken by the teacher responsible for the slow learners in that particular year, to buy new clothes, to shop around and exercise some degree of self-choice. Project work that can also be done outside the immediate environment of school would be encouraged and again the specialist would take the children to the appropriate place.

All these activities are expensive in teacher-time, although, in the experience of those who work in this way, well worthwhile for the degree of trust it engenders. Before embarking on this kind of system – flexible time, generous allocation of capitation, small groups and at times a one-to-one relationship – very thorough and open discussion by all the staff is required so that everyone thoroughly understands the philosophy and method, and is agreeable to supporting it. In return they, too, get support in time, resources and individual attention for members of their classes who are giving concern and for whom, however willing they may be, they do not have the necessary time to concentrate their attention.

The Upper School

Before describing how slow learners are catered for in the 14 – 18 age range, it is necessary first to describe briefly how the school is organised, as this carries implications for remedial and slow learners and the relationship they have with their teacher/tutors.

The school is organised into teams. The teams comprise six teachers, making up an academic team which is responsible both for the greater part of its teaching throughout the week and for the overall supervision of the group's work at all times during the week. The objectives of these teams are to achieve both greater flexibility and greater stability in teaching and learning within the school: greater flexibility in order to pay more regard to the individuality of the student; greater stability in order to discover and foster that individuality. Each teacher in the team acts as teacher/tutor to approximately twenty-four students of mixed ability and background. Within team time, which takes up half the week, English, Social Studies and Mathematics are covered. Students leave the area for specialist subjects and facilities or courses which their own team cannot supply. Any problems which arise during these times are dealt with by the student and his personal tutor, in negotiation with the specialist teacher. By being organised in this way it has been found that the students' autonomy and individuality have been catered for in a personal way, avoiding many of the disciplinary problems and measures necessary to cope with them in this age group.

Support from an expert

Teaching a mixed ability group for up to half a week, however, calls for a vast number of resources and interests, both personal and material, and a support system to help with students who have learning difficulties. In the Upper School, therefore, there is one expert – a fully trained teacher with a degree in Psychology and a certificate in Remedial Education. This teacher is again untimetabled. He is in a specially equipped room to which both teachers and students with problems can come for expert help – to be provided with suggested programmes of work; to be helped with specific learning problems; to make or borrow resources or equipment; for students to have a change of environment, or enjoy a coffee, or a cooling off or just a chat. In effect, the room plays much the same role as a clinic, i.e. diagnostic, counselling, providing materials, or simple advice and suggestions. To facilitate the use of this service, each team has in it someone with special training or interest to liaise with the 'specialist' and coordinate the work and efforts of all the other tutors in the group team. Again, as in the High School, this type of organisation is made with the full support and cooperation of all the staff within the school and is supported not only by having an open attitude towards the needs of the slow learners but also being willing to show support with money, facilities and staff time. It is a commitment from all the staff to the importance of every student regardless of ability. Although, to a large extent, the system depends on personal contact between tutor and specialist, specially designed forms have proved to be helpful both in record-keeping of students' personal progress and also of resources which are requested, provided and available.

A banded comprehensive school

The structure of the Remedial Department within this school is very flexible. The groupings are altered as necessary and although the timetable is fixed it is flexible within the groups. For pastoral and administrative purposes all the children are in the care of an individual tutor, in a four-house system of a total of twenty-eight tutor groups. The groups contain about twenty-five children of all ages and abilities and it is the duty of each tutor to look after the welfare of each child in his or her group, both as regards personal problems and any difficulties the child may be having with staff around the school. This prevents the head of the Remedial Department from taking on the role of the 'Demon Discipline' and allows him to concentrate on the basic studies. The basic studies are very highly structured with the objectives of trying to restore confidence and to produce from the children spoken and written expressions of their own feelings and reflections. Although great emphasis is put on structured and programmed English, creative work is encouraged and efforts typed out for wall display and putting into a book. This all goes towards reinforcing the child's feelings of success. The example reproduced (see Appendix IV) illustrates how a piece can be descriptive, well thought-out and logical, and when typed out can give a real boost to a child's confidence. It can be seen from this example, which was not specially chosen in any way, that creative work is forthcoming however tight the structure. Indeed, in a banded school of this nature, unless a system is tightly structured, monitored and recorded, then there is a danger of slow learners and remedial children just drifting through the school system. It can be seen from the following information how carefully the remedial children are charted and organised and of how aware the staff are of the need to cooperate in keeping to the agreed procedures:

Sixth Year			
Fifth Year		5B(5)	5B(6)
Fourth Year		4B	4B
Third Year		3R	3P
Intake Year	2R	2P	2E

Children doing programmed English:

Class	*Girls*	*Boys*	*Total*
5B(6)	2	5	7
4B	0	5	5
3P	8	16	24
2P	10	15	25
2E	8	10	18
Totals	28	51	79

For the most part, these figures represent children who are in the last stages of learning to read, though some still have serious difficulties.

A number of children in the classes marked in the diagram above, 2R, 3R, still need a little specialist attention in both English and Mathematics and 5B(5) in Mathematics.

A. *The reading system*

Books are divided into two types: library books and 'text' books, from which the children work with printed or hand-written programmes devised by staff. All books are carefully graded into 'boxes' one to eleven, the first eight of which are on a half-yearly basis:

Box 1	5.0 to	5.5	years reading age
Box 2	5.6 to	6.0	years reading age
Box 3	6.1 to	6.5	years reading age
Box 4	6.6 to	7.0	years reading age
Box 5	7.1 to	7.5	years reading age
Box 6	7.6 to	8.0	years reading age
Box 7	8.1 to	8.5	years reading age
Box 8	8.6 to	9.0	years reading age
Box 9	9.1 to	10.0	years reading age
Box 10	10.1 to	11.0	years reading age
Box 11	over	11.0	years reading age

Each child is initially tested, usually with the 'Standard Test of Reading Skills' (Daniels & Diack) and is then 'fed' from a suitable box level, or slightly below. The child is thus given work he can do; this improves his confidence, and when ready, he goes on to the next box, being given individually suitable books. A good selection is available at each level.

B. *The spelling system*

This is a very simple linear programme, based on Tansley's work, of 150 steps, ranging from a spelling age of about 6.0 to 11.0. There are 150 (plus ten additional) word lists and the same number of tests. After initial testing on Schonell S1 and S2 and Daniels & Diack 11, word lists are issued at a suitable level and tests are issued five days later. As the children are all at different levels the system is (almost) cheatproof.

C. *Games and self-chosen activities*

These are usually given as a 'reward' towards the end of the work-session, and usually have a specific educational purpose, both mathematical and in terms of word-recognition. Small mammals are kept and these are a never-failing source of interest and activity.

D. *Summer Club*

This club was formed to take groups of 'remedial' children for Saturdays by the sea in groups of ten or so, either by train or in the school's mini-bus.

E. *Mathematics*

The children are, for the most part, relatively innumerate, and some, on admission, still need to work on the number bonds of ten. An attempt is made to move them from this level to at least a competence in the concept of 100, and an awareness of money-maths. For these purposes use is made of the sheets of a forty-eight page Maths Work Book designed for use with E.S.N. children, work cards made from the Beta book series and calculations from the Hesse 'Four Rules of Number' – most unfashionable, but a very valuable confidence builder. Activity Mathematics is minimal, apart from work with the animals, school plans and so on, and the various number games available.

This late in a child's school career, Mathematics must be sacrificed to literacy.

F. *Recording*

This is done with the following:

a) *Log book* for immediate notes of children's work and outbursts; general planning.

b) *Clients' book*: one page per child.

c) *Index card system*: any standardised test result is noted, with dates.

d) *Personal folder*: all exercise books in the basic subjects are retained, with dates.

e) *Printed programmes*: these are stapled into the exercise books, and are initialled and dated as the child works through.

f) *Transfer sheets*: staff working with these classes complete a form noting most of the above information, which is sent to the next basics teacher at the end of the school year or at such time as the child is moved to another group.

g) *Maths progress* is noted on squared paper grids, as is

h) *Spelling*

Except for (d) this material is not usually available to the children, although they are fully aware that records are kept. It is most important to know what any child is doing at any given moment, his rate of progress, and the nature of it. If he regresses in the general school situation, we must be able to trace the problem. In addition, if a child transfers to another school, a full and exact report to the Head of Remedial Education in that school is essential.

The growth of pastoral systems

Today, even the most traditional schools are trying to introduce some form of pastoral care. It is difficult to say why some schools are doing this. Is it because R.O.S.L.A. has forced them to do so, because it is the 'in' thing, or is it because of a genuine change in their attitude towards education? It is, no doubt, one of these in some schools, another in others and in some, a mixture of all three. Is the pastoral system within a school devised to bring about a more caring relationship, or to isolate and control the problem children or even, as I know of in some reorganised schools, the need to create jobs for those teachers who might otherwise find themselves redundant? It would be pleasant to think that it was for the reason first mentioned, but this, I fear, would be naive.

Infant and primary schools have the advantage over secondary schools as the majority of the children are in the care of one adult for at least a year. This adult has the opportunity to know each child well, both academically and pastorally. The adult can recognise the child with problems, can in some cases help to remedy them. In secondary schools, which, for economic reasons, grow bigger each year, no such security exists. In too many schools children are subjected to moving from one class to another for each lesson. They may see as many as fifteen teachers in a week and know none well. They do not have the security of one classroom or base and rarely have the opportunity to identify personally with any one area of the school. Little wonder then that many children have no sense of belonging, of being part of a community. Little wonder that vandalism, truanting and a sense of disillusionment with school are on the increase. To a large extent, pastoral systems have been forced on schools with greatly varying effects. Many schools, however, have organised pastoral systems because of the growing care and compassion of the teachers in them.

House and year pastoral systems

Some schools have moved to a direct copy of the Public Schools system. That is, they are being organised on a house system, the houses being vertically grouped and a conscious effort made to break down huge communities into acceptable units. Schools such as these often have a house or divisional head, a deputy house head and personal tutors for approximately one to twenty-five pupils. The houses hold meetings in the lunch hours or after school and all matters of welfare and discipline go through the house system before going to the head or deputy head. All administrative matters from a lost book to examination entries are dealt with through the house system. The advantage is that each student and his parents should be able to identify with a particular adult and feel free to consult this adult on any problems which may arise.

Some schools may be organised round a year system which, in tasks and role, is similar to a house system.

Where does the responsibility lie?

Both systems depend to some extent for success on the attitude of the head teacher. If he creates pastoral heads, pays them a scale 4 or 5 allowance, but still insists on playing a traditional hierarchical role of deciding which areas of responsibility he will allow the pastoral heads to have, then it will be a weak system indeed. Some people will say that no head is going to allocate points for pastoral heads and then keep from them relevant areas of responsibility, but this does happen. At a recent meeting of fifteen people from large schools, all of whom were on scale 5 allowances for pastoral responsibility for R.O.S.L.A. children, nine of them were not allowed by their headmasters to go to court, to see the social workers, or to talk with E.W.Os. This makes nonsense of pastoral care. It is also a nonsense to appoint people to this type of job and then fail to give them the time to do the job properly. They cannot carry out a full teaching role and at the same time properly care for up to two hundred children. In the more enlightened schools, pastoral teachers are on half timetable and are able to carry out their brief properly by knowing their students well and coordinating all the efforts being made on their behalf. Knowing and caring for each individual student cannot be achieved on the cheap either in time or money.

Although house, division, or year pastoral systems that are run well, do much to provide a more caring and considerate society within our schools, there can still be serious deficiencies. Who can say that a science specialist who only sees the people he has in his tutor group for registration, an occasional house meeting and perhaps two lessons a week, really knows the students in his group? It is an impossibility, and a natural development from the house system would seem to me to be the development of the mini-school.

Super-size organisations and institutions

All our organisations and institutions today grow bigger and bigger and more and more impersonal. Bureaucracy increases; more heads of department are appointed to be heads of department of the heads of departments. More forms are filled in, more money spent to check that the forms have been filled in properly. The argument for things getting bigger is that this is the only economically viable form for institutions including schools to take. Even accepting this, however, I would maintain that with more imagination and a group of teachers committed to providing a small, caring, independent community, economically viable alternatives can be found, and the mini-school is one.

What is the Mini-School?

The mini-school could be a group of approximately 120 students to seven teachers. This, providing everyone was prepared to teach and not administrate full time, would not be excessive compared with the pupil/teacher ratio at present in operation in large comprehensive schools. These teachers would include people with a specialism in one of the major disciplines but who had a desire to direct a student's learning from the student's own autonomy towards a very wide approach and variety. The students would be based in separate units built around a central complex of specialist resources, science labs, heavy crafts, central library and resources centres, sports facilities, etc. The students would work with their own teachers for a major part of the week. The teachers would interchange amongst themselves and go with the students to use the specialist facilities when the need arose. There would need to be, in building terms, no more spent than is spent at present (see plan). It would have the advantages of making manageable units with a definite sense of identity, keeping tutor groups small as all staff would be teaching, and making out-of-school activities, residential camps, courses, absences, etc. easier to manage as staff could cover for each other much more effectively. It would also break down the increasing barriers between specialists and pastoral staff and draw everyone into caring first for the student as an individual and then for their particular subject.

Mutually caring for each individual

In this kind of set-up there would be no need to stream, to set, to select, to try to get more money for individual departments, to acquire status for one subject over another, to be subjective. Everyone would be educators and all the students would know each other well and it is my belief that teachers and students would become mutually caring.

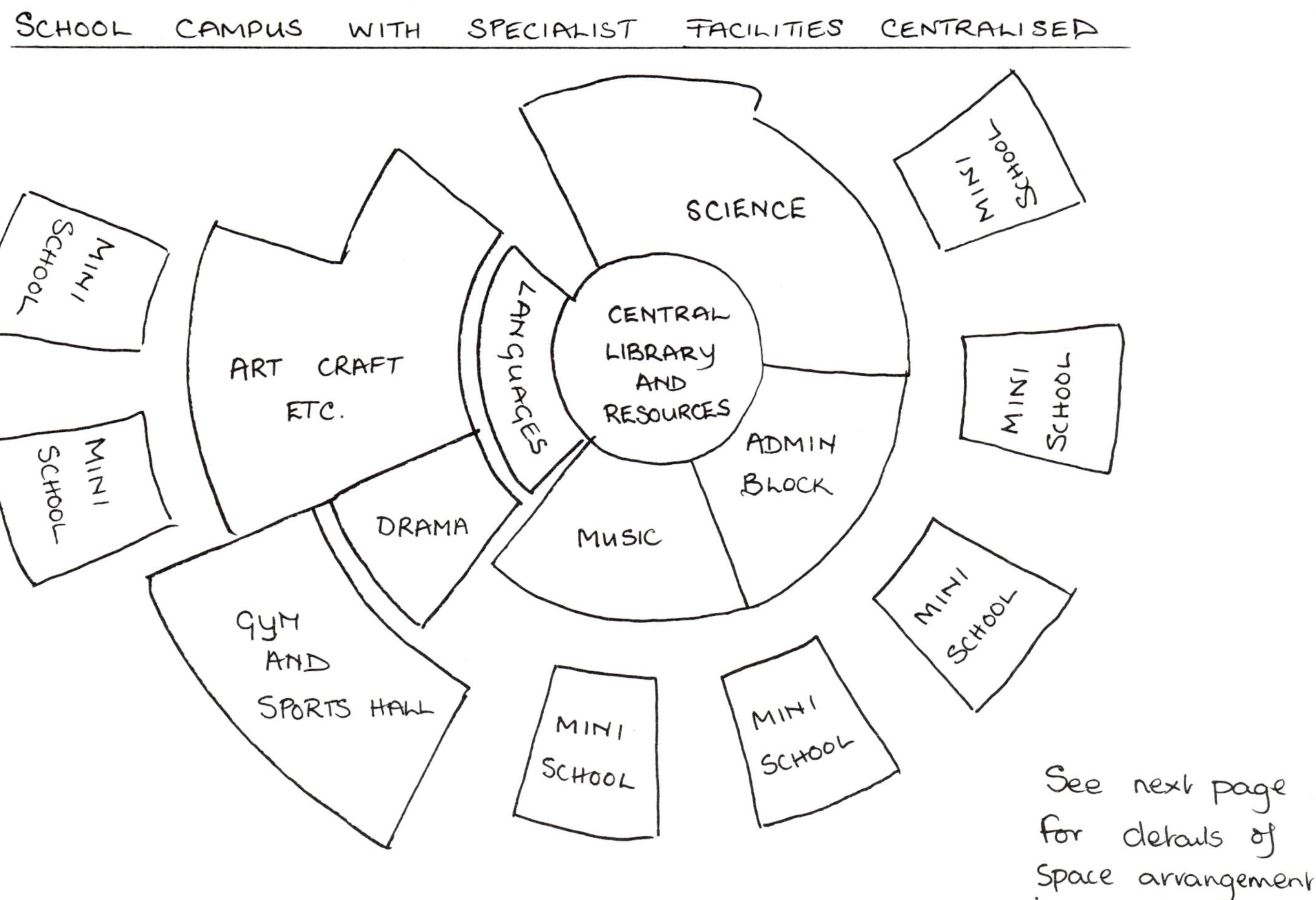
SCHOOL CAMPUS WITH SPECIALIST FACILITIES CENTRALISED
SCIENCE
CENTRAL LIBRARY AND RESOURCES
ADMIN BLOCK
MUSIC
LANGUAGES
ART CRAFT ETC.
DRAMA
GYM AND SPORTS HALL
MINI SCHOOL
MINI SCHOOL
MINI SCHOOL
MINI SCHOOL
MINI SCHOOL
MINI SCHOOL
MINI SCHOOL
See next page for details of space arrangement.

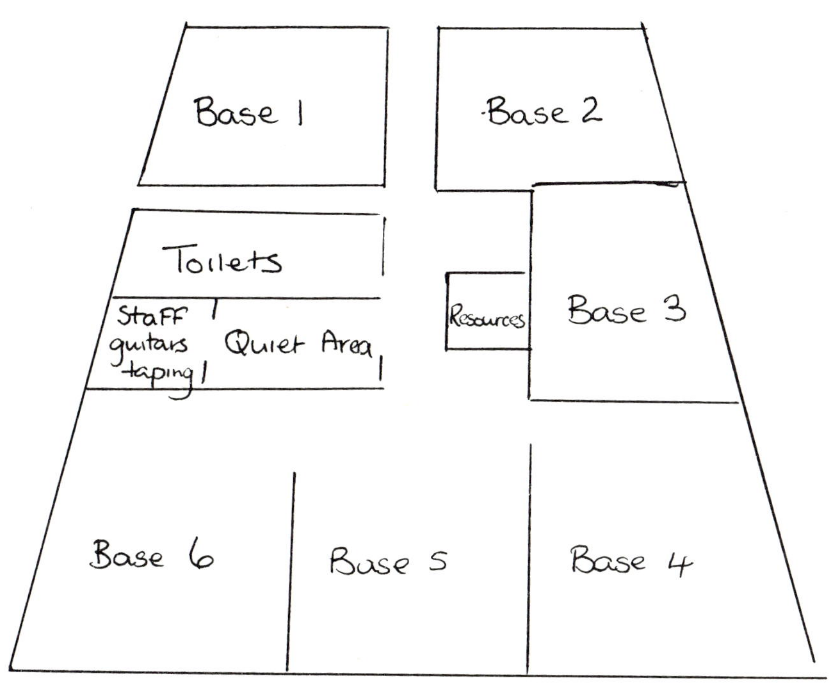

Space Utilization in Mini - School.

A school campus arranged with all specialist facilities grouped centrally and 'mini - schools' built around these facilities would be no more expensive in land or space or teachers than new schools which are now being built.

CHAPTER 10

HELP FROM SOCIAL AGENCIES

The responsibility for setting up further agencies to assist the pupil of school age who is having particular difficulties or showing obvious signs of maladjustment lies with the local education authority. Authorities vary widely in the kind of system they have devised and the method of referral they wish to use and of course in the effectiveness of their service. Every teacher, however, has not only a need but a right to know what services exist and can give help in cases of difficulty. The Heads of most schools will be issued with a circular setting this out, but if this is not so or it is not available, write to the l.e.a. and ask for the information. Having the information does not then guarantee prompt and efficient service. Like all other services of this nature, there is a grave shortage of personnel. Although in recent years there has been a notable expansion in the numbers of child guidance clinics, for example, there has not been a corresponding rise in the numbers of psychologists. It is essential, however, that in relevant cases referral is made as there certainly won't be the necessary improvement unless pressure is applied at the grass roots. There follows, therefore, a short breakdown of each kind of agency now available and the type of work they try to carry out.

School Psychological Service and Child Guidance Clinic

This is normally staffed by educational psychologists, child psychiatrists, psychiatric social workers, peripatetic remedial teachers. The kinds of problem they deal with vary enormously: a child with learning difficulties, general or specific, behaviour problems, suspected dyslexic children, maladjusted children, all should be referred with the parents' permission (verbal permission is usually regarded as sufficient). The clinic will need to know the name, address, date of birth, a short breakdown of the problem and any other relevant facts that are known. The person referred will then be interviewed and tested by an educational psychologist and the case discussed with the head teacher and, if it is to be of real use, the teacher who is most concerned with the child in question. A written report will follow and this may be backed up by a suggested learning programme in the case of specific difficulties, a visit or visits home by the psychiatric social worker if it is the home conditions which are giving concern, or, if thought advisable in the best interests of the pupil, transfer to a special school. Sometimes, it may be of help for a teacher just to discuss a child's problems with a psychologist, who can suggest reasons for certain behaviour and perhaps ways round it. Whatever the outcome, teachers should use this service when they are in real doubt about how to treat a particular pupil.

The Child Psychiatrist

Educational psychologists may often refer a client to the psychiatrist when they feel the trouble is deep-seated or when they fail to make any headway with a particular case. Assessment and treatment vary considerably, and although teachers in the past often mistrusted the work of child psychiatrists, there is no need for this mistrust to be present today. Very often they can offer what a busy teacher cannot, that is a one-to-one counselling situation, play, drama, or group therapy, or in extreme cases, residential treatment. Severely disturbed children need the help of a professional psychiatrist; often their families are unable to procure this. We, as teachers, can help them. The Underwood Report lists symptoms of maladjustment under the following headings and these may prove useful guidelines when making a decision regarding referrals.

1. *Nervous disorders*

   Fears and phobias, anxiety, timidity, over-sensitivity.
   Withdrawal, unsociability, solitariness.
   Depression, brooding, melancholy periods.
   Excitability, over-activity.
   Apathy, lethargy, lack of interest, unresponsiveness.
   Obsessions, rituals and compulsions.
   Hysterical fits, loss of memory.

2. *Habit disorders*

   Speech – speech defects, stammering.
   Sleep – night terrors, sleep-walking or talking.
   Movement – twitching, rocking, nail-biting.
   Feeding – Food fads, nervous vomiting, indiscriminate eating.

Excretion – incontinence of urine and faeces.
Nervous pains and paralysis – headaches, deafness, etc.
Physical symptoms – asthma and other allergic conditions.

3. *Behaviour disorders*

Unmanageableness – defiance, disobedience, refusal to go to school or work.
Temper.
Aggressiveness, bullying, destructiveness, cruelty.
Jealous behaviour, stealing and begging.
Demands for attention, lying and romancing.
Truancy, wandering, staying out late.
Sex difficulties – masturbation, sex play, homosexuality.

4. *Organic disorder*

Conditions following head injuries, encephalitis or cerebral tumours; epilepsy, chorea.

5. *Psychotic behaviour*

Hallucinations, delusions, extreme withdrawal, bizarre symptoms, violence.

6. *Educational difficulties*

Backwardness not accounted for by dullness.
Dislike connected with subjects and people.
Unusual response to school discipline.
Inability to concentrate.
Inability to keep jobs.

Education Welfare Officers

Although very recently the standing and training given to E.W.Os. has been upgraded considerably they are still among the most unappreciated and underused agencies available to a school. Too often their image is confined to 'the boardman' or 'the attendance lady'. A good E.W.O. is very much more and, properly used, can be invaluable. One who has been in the area for some time will know the background of individual pupils better than any teacher; they will know the family well, will often have provided clothing, taken the children to the doctor's, been present at case-conferences, liaised with courts, social services and probation services, had tea with grandma and found a pram for young Mary's offspring. My advice to any young teacher is to get to know your E.W.O. well and, together, the possibility of accomplishing real improvements with 'difficult' families will be so much greater. The diagram on

p. 188 shows all the agencies the E.W.O. has access to, and often they can short-circuit the red tape.

Social Workers and Probation Officers

The value of the work these people do will be greatly enhanced if they can have direct contact with the child's own teacher. They need to know the teacher and to discuss the pupil's problems, thereby gaining greater insight. The advantage is, of course, two-way; the teacher gains insight into the home situation and a better understanding results. Quite often probation officers only appear on the scene when a court case is directly pending but they quite rightly claim that they would like the emphasis of their work to be on the preventive side. In order for this to happen it is necessary, when teachers see signs of delinquent acts, to ask for help, before things become serious or habitual. Generally, whether a teacher suspects that a child is being ill-treated, neglected or abandoned, or that a child is in danger of committing an offence, his suspicions should be reported to the duty officer of the nearest Social Services Office. This officer will direct the need into the right channel.

Whatever the danger or need the critical thing is to make sure that close links are established by the school with all the social agencies. These relationships should be open and mutually trusting; the isolationist policies of the past must be broken down. Teachers play a part in helping to educate a member of a family and very often, if this is to be effective, the family, as a unit, must be helped too.

N.B. The work of the school nurse, the speech therapist and teachers of the partially hearing are referred to in the chapter on diagnosis.

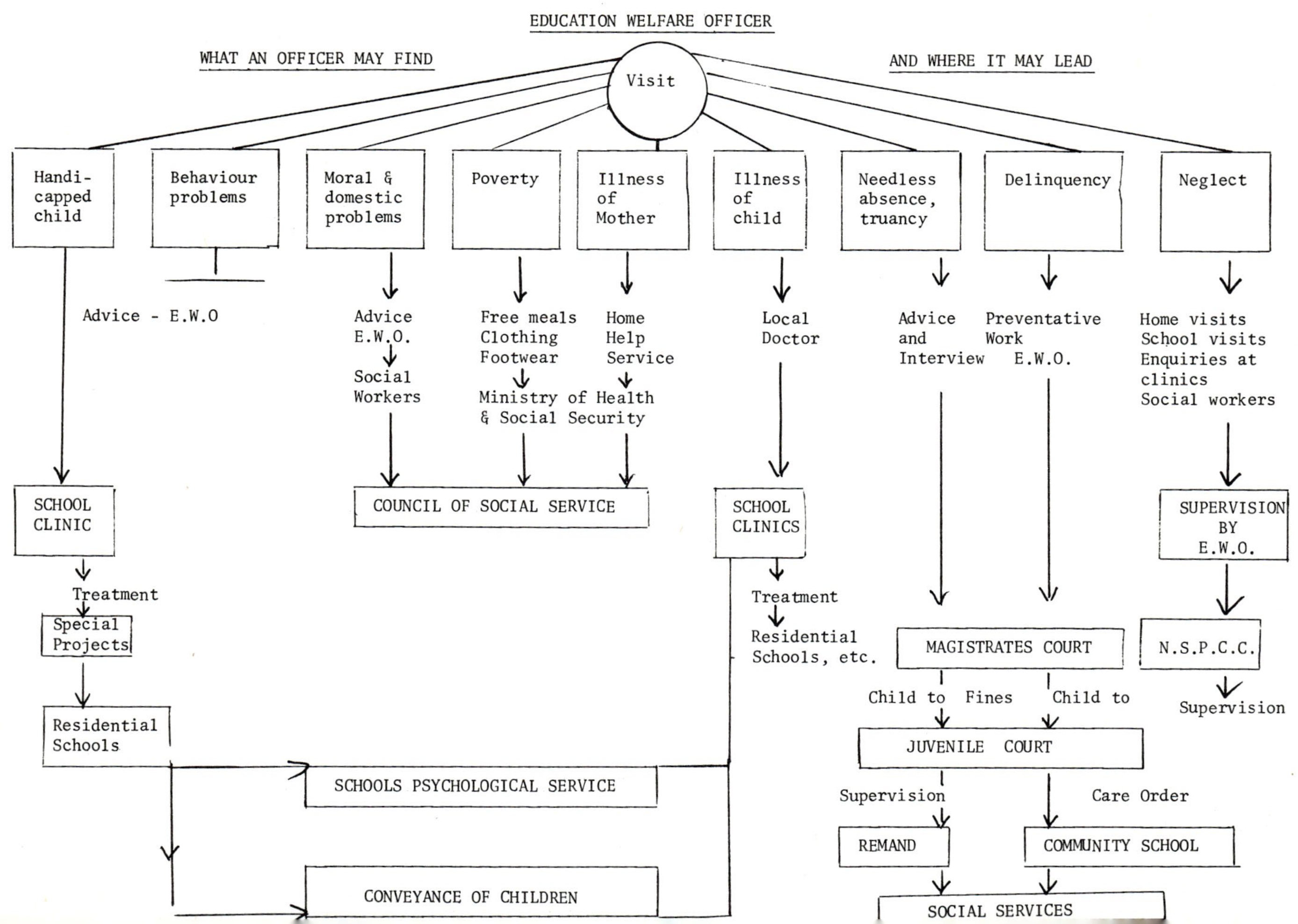
EDUCATION WELFARE OFFICER
WHAT AN OFFICER MAY FIND
AND WHERE IT MAY LEAD
Visit
Handi-capped child
Behaviour problems
Moral & domestic problems
Poverty
Illness of Mother
Illness of child
Needless absence, truancy
Delinquency
Neglect
Advice - E.W.O
Advice E.W.O.
Social Workers
Free meals Clothing Footwear
Home Help Service
Ministry of Health & Social Security
Local Doctor
Advice and Interview
Preventative Work E.W.O.
Home visits School visits Enquiries at clinics Social workers
SCHOOL CLINIC
COUNCIL OF SOCIAL SERVICE
SCHOOL CLINICS
SUPERVISION BY E.W.O.
Treatment
Special Projects
Treatment
Residential Schools, etc.
MAGISTRATES COURT
N.S.P.C.C.
Residential Schools
Child to
Fines
Child to
Supervision
JUVENILE COURT
SCHOOLS PSYCHOLOGICAL SERVICE
Supervision
Care Order
REMAND
COMMUNITY SCHOOL
CONVEYANCE OF CHILDREN
SOCIAL SERVICES

APPENDIX I

Useful Mathematical Materials for Slow Learners

Topic Booklets:

Mathematics in the Making: 1–10 – S. E. Bell; *11* – G. Long and K. A. Hides; *12* – I. Campbell. Longmans.
'Leapfrogs': Waves I to IV – books, slides, films. Hutchinson.
Topics from Mathematics: *Computers*; *Statistics*; *Towards Probability*. D. Fielker, *Circles*; *Number Lines*; *Rolling*; *Solid Models*; *Tessellations*; *Triangles*; *Counting Machines*; *Workshop Manual 1*. J. Mold. C.U.P.
Further Experiments in Mathematics: *The Ellipse*; *Paper Folding*; *Polyhedra*; *Mazes*. K. Lewis, Longmans.
Looking and Seeing, K. Rowland, Ginn & Co.

Workcards:

S.M.P. Workcards, C.U.P.
Fife Mathematics Project, Stirling University.

Teachers' guides – for ideas:

Mathematics in Art, M. Holt, Studio Vista.
Mathematics for the Majority, Peter Kaner *et al.*, Studio Vista.
Some Lessons in Mathematics, Association of Teachers of Mathematics, O.U.P.
Language of Mathematics, F. Land.
Numbers in Colours, Books I–VI, C. Gattegno, Cuisenaire Co.

Apparatus and games	*Supplier*
Soma Cube	Burdetts, Kibworth Beauchamp
Mastermind	Invicta
3-D O's and X's	Taskmaster
Towers of Hanoi	Burdetts
Formula 1	Waddington
Monopoly	Waddington
Hexagon Maze	E.S.A.
Logic blocks	E.S.A.
9-mens morris	E.S.A.
Shopping games	E. J. Arnold
Cuisenaire rods, prisms & cubes	Cuisenaire Co.

Materials for model-making should include a quick drying glue, toothpicks or cocktail sticks, panel pins, off-cuts of wood, thread, cardboard and appropriate tools.

Films

Square Shuffle
Moves
Mirrors
Let's take half
Leapfrogs, 6 King Edgar Close, Ely, Cambridgeshire

Slides, film strips, tapes, workcards

In Sight (an integrated approach) – P. Radley, R. Hirst, J. Bradley, S. Burns
Mathematical Projects – S. Burns
Visual Publications

Bibliography

Edith Biggs, *Freedom to Learn*, C.U.P.

Caleb Gattegno, *The Common Sense of Teaching Mathematics* (Cuisenaire Co. will supply).

Caleb Gattegno, *For the Teaching of Mathematics*, Educational Explorers, c/o Cuisenaire Co.

Madelaine Goutard, *Mathematics Teaching*, Educational Explorers, c/o Cuisenaire Co.

Moore & Williams, *Arithmetic at work*, O.U.P.

APPENDIX II

Example of C.S.E. Mathematics Syllabus

East Midlands Regional Examinations Board
North Leicestershire Local Group Committee
Mode III C.S.E. Mathematics Syllabus for Countesthorpe College from 1975

Aims

a) To produce a course which facilitates mixed ability teaching by being compatible both with the 'O' level syllabus requirements and with the needs of students who do not want to take any examination.
In order to satisfy these conflicting demands there is the option of doing an additional maths course (compatible with 'O' level) or of following individual interests in the form of mathematical topics. It is hoped that this will also allow some integration with other subject areas.

b) To lay stress on a high standard of achievement in basic mathematical ideas; numeracy, the ability to work with algebraic expressions and to recognise and calculate the properties of common figures. To test these basic mathematical ideas thoroughly and to remove (as far as possible) the selectivity of subject matter in examinations.
An attempt has been made to cover basic mathematical ideas in a compulsory section which will then be tested in two papers, each of $2\frac{1}{2}$ hours.

Pattern of Examination

Part I 60% of the total marks.
Two papers covering the work in the basic mathematics syllabus – all questions to be attempted. All topics in the syllabus will be covered as comprehensively as possible. The questions will be of the multiple choice type.

Part II 40% of the total marks.

Either One paper lasting 2 hours (there will be a choice of six questions from ten on the 'additional maths' syllabus).

Or Mathematics topics considered as projects. One or more projects, depending on the depth of study, up to a minimum of four.
This course work will then be considered as a whole, taking into account the fact that it should represent at least two terms' work. Usually some description is required, but the topics will mainly be marked on mathematical content.

Basic Mathematics Syllabus

1. Four rules applied to integers, decimals and fractions. Conversion from decimals to fractions and vice versa.
2. Number bases 2 to 10 and 12. Conversions and the four rules. Place value.
3. Percentages of money and other quantities. Simple and compound interest.
4. The ideas and notation of sets; union, intersection, complement, subset, empty and universal sets, Venn diagrams.
5. Metric measure – length, area, volume, mass.
6. Powers including square roots; multiplication and division by powers of ten. Expressions for large and small numbers. Negative powers.
7. Length, area and volume of plane and solid figures, rectangles, triangles, parallelograms, trapeziums, circles, prisms, cylinders, spheres.
8. Kinematics; distance, time, speed. Average speed, acceleration and average acceleration.

9. Approximations, the ability to give approximate answers in any of the above work.
10. Pictorial representation of data. Pie charts, barcharts, histograms. Travel graphs and conversion graphs.
11. Arithmetic mean, mode and modal class, median by inspection.
12. Simple probability, including success fraction.
13. Solution sets of linear equations in one and two variables. Cartesian graphs of the solution sets.
14. Graphs of simple inequalities.
15. Substitution in formulae, practical applications.
16. Solution of quadratic equations and simultaneous equations by substitution only.
17. Symmetry, transformation of reflections, rotation and translation. Congruence.
18. Angles as a measure of rotation: angles at a point, angles on a straight line, parellel lines and angle properties. Angles in a triangle.
19. Use of symmetry to determine properties of triangles, quadrilaterals and regular polygons.
20. Estimation of distances and angles by scaledrawing.
21. 3D models resulting from sets.

Additional Mathematics Syllabus

1. Closure, commutative, associative and distributive properties of operations. Identity and inverse elements.
2. Cartesian graphs of quadratic functions, determination of maxima and minima by graphical methods.
3. Algebraic identities, $x^2 + ax \div b$, difference of two squares. Distributive law.
4. Solutions of equations by graphical and algebraic methods.
5. The matrix as a store of information, stock records, describing networks and relationships. Combination of matrices to give further information.
6. Linear transformations in two dimension and their matrix representation. Combination of these transformations and the corresponding matrix operations. The identity matrix and inverse matrices.
7. Further statistics: mean of grouped data. Cumulative frequency curve, median and quadrils. Measures of spread, range and interquartile range.
8. Further probability: compound events. Treediagrams.
9. Calculations of distances and angles in right-angled triangles using sine, cosine, tangent functions and also the theorem of Pythagoras.
10. Simple linear programming.

Project Work

Some possible fields of study are listed below, but any topic with a large mathematical content would be considered satisfactory.

1. Astronomy. Astronomical distances, orbits, gravitation.
2. Surveying.
3. Geometry of circles.
4. Mathematics of patterns.
5. Probability (gambling).
6. Further graphs.
7. Statistics projects – surveys.
8. Statistics – correlation.
9. Mathematics and travel.
10. Design of switching circuits.
11. History of number-systems and measurement.
12. Computers and computing.

APPENDIX III

A C.S.E. Mode III Syllabus for Community Studies (Parenthood)

1st Year: Basic Course – Health & Sex Education

1. *Introduction*

   Reasons for studying:
   a) child development
   b) parentcraft

2. *How do we learn*:
   a) language (baby's few words – few words to baby)
   b) T.V.
   c) Teachers at school
   d) mixing – sharing with friends

3. *Love Pattern of Baby to Adults*
   a) baby as himself
   b) mother
   c) father
   d) other people
   e) things
   f) own sex
   g) opposite sex

   } Filmstrip Love Circle

Discussion – Is mother-love and father-love more important one than the other? Are babies capable of love? Does love come naturally to all parents?

4. *Preparation for a baby's arrival*

Introducing new event to family (importance of language again)

Room preparation Clothing for baby Use of correct size cot Safety precautions Hazards	Making of layette may come in here

5. *A day in the life of a baby*

a) bathing
b) talking (real 'talk' or baby 'talk')
c) sleep
d) baby's room
e) cot in mother's room
f) good chair
g) changing the baby
h) dressing the baby
i) handling the baby
j) leaving the baby
k) safety first

6. *Crying*

a) hunger b) thirst c) too hot or too cold d) lonely e) frightened f) uncomfortable	Refer to Newsomes (Nottingham). Get class to join in with reasons for crying and what they would do.

7. *Feeding*

a) breast & preparation b) artificial feeding c) times of feeding d) care of all baby's feeding equipment e) making of all feeding as close to breast feeding in technique as possible f) correct size of chair again	Blackboard work. Practical work of making up a feed. Use of doll to demonstrate. Refer to Winnicot & Mary McCarthy

8. *Weaning*

a) weaning and family foods
b) gradual routine changes
c) milestones
d) weight and size
e) protection of baby with immunisation

To include practical preparation of family meals. Safety in first year. Film strip.

9. *The Toddler ages 2 – 5*

a) changes & introduction to play
b) importance of talk (Britton & Piaget)
c) the young child's fantasies (sex, aggression, etc.)
d) use of toys (function in the child's development)
e) importance of play-groups and nursery schools

10. *Temper Tantrums*

a) nightmares
b) acceptance of destructive impulses
c) stories
d) comforting
e) sleep and fresh air
f) exercise

11. *Habit Training*

a) use of potty and toilet
b) punishments
c) are parents responsible for guilt feelings? Is this desirable? Can it be avoided or is it inevitable?
d) the question of masturbation
e) safety habits (kerb drill)
f) home accidents

12. *Child Ailments*

a) when to call the doctor
b) local authority nursing services
c) Psychiatric services
d) Child Guidance Clinic
e) Home Teaching services

13. *Healthy Living* – Introducing 7 rules of health

a) food
b) sleep
c) exercise
d) cleanliness
e) clothing
f) fresh air
g) leisure & recreation

14. *Growing Up*

a) physical changes
b) emotional changes
c) mental outlook

} Films – Girl to Woman – Boy to Man – Members of the Wedding – 15 – etc.

15. *Sexual Behaviour*

a) fears
b) fantasies
c) wrong or right
d) Homosexuality
e) Lesbianism
f) masturbation
g) V.D.

16. *Dependence & Addiction*

a) alcohol
b) smoking
c) drugs

17. *Relationships*

a) family quarrels
b) arguments
c) need for self-discipline

18. *Choice of Partners*

a) youth clubs
b) discos
c) the street
d) work
e) public transport
f) computers?

19. *Reproduction*

a) fertilisation
b) contraception
c) psychology of sex
d) development of the embryo
e) birth of the baby – film
f) different methods of childbirth

20. *Changed Roles*

a) responsibility of both parents
b) different roles
c) adjustments to new routine
d) deciding on priorities

21. *Budgeting*

a) essentials
b) desirables
c) luxuries

22. *Illness in the Home*

a) home nursing
b) use of medicine – temperature taking
c) useful games and toys for sick children

23. *Growing Older*

a) when children are adolescents
b) when they leave home
c) elderly citizens i) services
ii) Meals on Wheels
iii) loneliness

24. *Health Services for the Family* – local & governmental services available

25. *Starting Work*

Pupil's diary

The diary should be a record book with two kinds of entries: a short account of any film or talk you have had as part of the basic course; a record of any social work or visits you undertake (see the two examples given).

Examples from diaries:

'January 17th, 1973. Film – Birth of a Baby

This film was called "To Janet A Son". It was a colour film showing the birth of a baby. It started with the interview of the woman called Janet, at the beginning of her pregnancy and followed her through the remaining 6 months of her pregnancy, her admittance to hospital and the actual birth. The film though rather old, was quite good in showing the birth, with the use of gas and air during the 2nd stage of labour, still by far the commonest method of birth.

I felt it was useful because it did not over-glamourise or overdramatise and being a real film rather than diagrams, the points went home much more.

On the opposite page you can see a magazine cutting about "Natural Childbirth". This is just using control and deep breathing rather than gas and air during the second stage of labour. This method is becoming very popular in Britain.'

'January 19th, 1973. Visit to an infants' school

Throughout the Spring term we have arranged to go every Wednesday morning to the local Infants' School. Four of us are involved and today is the first morning.

When we got there Mrs. Hearn the Headmistress greeted us and showed us round the school. It is an old school built in 1867. It has been modernized but is too small for all of the children. Some are in an annexe the other side of the village.

Although old, the school is gaily decorated in bright colours. It is furnished with modern school furniture and is warm and comfortable.

The children I helped were the youngest 5-year-olds. I heard some of them read and helped with the paint. Before we go next time, we are preparing some templates for paper flowers and I am going to choose one of the children for a special study.'

2nd Year: Project Work

One depth study.

Any study of your own choice here. It can be a mainly written study or a practical study. It must be completed by the beginning of the March of your 5th year.

Below are a list of suggested studies or projects, but interests and ideas of your own would be very welcome.

A. *A Study of Childbirth:*

This could include the biological aspects from conception to birth; the facilities available to pregnant women; the social services available when the baby is born; local facilities here in Leicester; different methods of childbirth, e.g., natural childbirth, caesarean section, etc. Part of this could be making a layette for a new-born baby.

B. *Social Centre for Retired People:*

You could become involved with the 'Tuesday Club' – produce and print the newsletter; be involved in fund-raising; adopt a particular individual and make something especially needed by this person, e.g. a red-light warning system if the person is ill, a high armchair for someone unable, because of arthritis, to get up and down easily; study the services available to the elderly, both nationally and locally.

C. *Mental Health in Children under Five:*

You could study mental illness generally, or specific illnesses such as Mongolism. You could be involved in the Special Care Nursery on Wednesday morning; pay regular visits to Glenfrith Hospital or Birkett House; make a special piece of apparatus for an individual child, e.g. a climbing frame or a series of picture books or phonic books.

D. *The Two-Year-Old:*

This would be especially appropriate if you have a younger brother or sister of your own. You could study the physical and mental development of the toddler; the development language; make a set of story books or some constructive toys.

There are many things you can choose which will fit into the course. The important thing is to develop it steadily throughout the 4th and 5th year. If the project you choose involves making something, the 2D/3D staff have offered their help and you should discuss it with them and fix up a time when you go to their department to work on your project.

Social Involvement

This section can include any work which has involved, or is involving you with the community. Some of the things which students have done in previous years are noted below to give you some ideas, although fresh ideas would be very welcome.

1. Working on Tuesdays in the Old People's Club
2. Working in the Handicapped Children's Nursery

3. Regular projects with local Infant Schools
4. Running a Brownie Pack
5. Assisting at a school for the deaf
6. Working at a centre for the blind
7. Working at a mental hospital
8. Working at a handicapped village

Practical Project

1. Organising a party – including the cooking – for the handicapped nursery
2. Making a baby's layette; knitting pram coats; making soft toys; making musical chimes for infant schools, etc.
3. Planning and cooking meals for invalid old people
4. Designing toys for autistic children.

Community Studies (Parentcraft): Distribution of Marks

A course to incorporate all aspects of development – from the unborn child to parenthood.
The course will consist of:
1. A basic course of Health & Sex Education.
2. Throughout the course, a 'diary' to be kept of practical work, visits, special projects other than written projects, e.g. setting up a nursery/playgroup for handicapped children, running a social centre for old people, finding out about, and visiting, various types of infant schools, e.g. a hospital school, physically handicapped school, open-plan school, village school, etc. It is important that each week, you write your own opinion about the film or talk.
To carry 25%
3. One project of individual choice to be studied in depth, e.g. A Study of Childbirth, or The Plight of the Aged, or The Drug Problem, etc.
To carry 30%
4. In co-operation with the Design Department, specific items to fit in with study choice, e.g. doll's house, complete layette, soft toys, children's story books, tapes, etc., something specific for a handicapped person.
To carry 15%
5. A one-hour multi-choice written examination. To carry 20%
6. Social Involvement – some experience involving work with the community. To carry 10%

APPENDIX IV

Severely remedial children's creative writing

EXAMPLE 1

Lost on an island

The eairplaine Cras i got out and laned down on the sand for a wilden. i got up and i saw nobody i walk around to see were i was. it look to me as if i was on a island. i was very hunge. so as i look up i saw some frute trees i tray to sake the tree but i had no lack. so i had to go up the tree i got to the top. i puck some frute of and thoure it down to the floor. i got to the sand and i began to eat. i was very dry so i look for water i Could see a steram. i run to it and put my head in it was very nice and cold. the sun began to go down. so i had to get some shat for the night. i began to get some wood and make a fire. i saw a tree it look all right to sleep on, But if it roidone i mate full out. so i got some leaves what were strone and put it round the tree. i put more wood on the fire so it wound brun all of the night i got up the tree and with the leaves i put round the tree i tine myself with it so if i roundover i will not full out and no wild animans will get me. when i got up the fire was out and i was geting very hungry so i began to look for food i saw some brids so i new eggs would be there so i got up to the top of the Cave and got some eggs i counld not fry them so i had to eat them rore. and i had some frutes. i new i could not live of frutes and eggs so i had to got some meat i got some stack and some stons i got a shat ston and a long stack with the ston i hit the stack and the stack began to get shat. so it began to look like a spar it was very shat i look for some meat and i saw a goat so i thoun my spar it hit the goat the goat full to the graw i pick it up and put it on my shaun and took it back to the fire i got a stack and fifi it in the graw and i got a lond pice of stack and put a corss the frie i cut the goat up and put a pice on the stack to cook. i got some coconut down and put some water in to drink i eat the meat. and i put the fire out. and when and look for a cave i fiund one and i put in the cave some food and fruts. i got some leaves to make a bed to lade on. i put water in the cave, with coconut shats. i had a cup made of coconut what to drunk out of i made a fire at the cave door, so no amians could get in in the night.

Did you follow the story? Here it is:

The aeroplane crashed. I got out and lay down on the sand for a while. I got up and I saw nobody. I walked round to see where I was. It looked to me as if I was on an island. I was very hungry, so I looked up. I saw some fruit trees. I tried to shake the tree but I had no luck, so I had to go up the tree. I got to the top. I picked some fruit off and threw it down to the floor. I got to the sand and began to eat. I was very dry so I looked for water. I could see a stream. I ran to it and put my head in. It was nice and cold. The sun began to go down, so I had to get some shelter for the night. I began to get some wood and make a fire. I saw a tree – it looked alright to sleep on, but if it moved I might fall out, so I got some leaves which were strong and put them round the tree. I put more wood on the fire, so it would burn all night. I got up the tree and with the leaves I put round the tree, I tied myself with it, so if I rolled over I would not fall out and no wild animals will get me.

When I got up the fire was out and I was getting very hungry so I began to look for food. I saw some birds so I knew eggs would be there, so I got up to the top of the cave and got some eggs. I could not fry them so I had to eat them raw. I had some fruit. I knew I could not live on fruit and eggs, so I had to get some meat. I got some sticks and some stones. I got a sharp stone and a long stick. With the stone I hit the stick and the stick began to get sharp. So it began to look like a spear. It was very sharp. I looked for some meat and I saw a goat, so I threw my spear. It hit the goat. The goat fell to the ground. I picked it up and put it on my shoulder and took it back to the fire. I got a stick and stuck it in the ground, and I got a long piece of stick and put it across the fire. I cut the goat up and put a piece on the stick to cook. I got some coconuts down and put some water in to drink. I ate the meat and I put the fire out, and I went and looked for a cave. I found one and I put in the cave some food and fruit. I got some leaves to make a bed to lay on. I put water in the cave with coconut shells. I had a cup made of coconut shell to drink out of. I made a fire at the cave door, so no animals could get in, in the night.

EXAMPLE 2

Lost on an island

When I was on a island I was very fritend at first But then I went firther on the sand I saw some goets, at first I got a coconut and I opened it with a sharp stone then I took the milk out of it and

I put the coconut shells on the sand and I was waiting for it to rain while I was waiting for it to Rain I found some Bambo shoots and thort to make a trap then I started to make a hole with my hands and after I done that I put some Banana leaves over the hole and I wated and wated until some thing came But nothing at all. I was very hungry so I went and got some Bananas iT was getting Darh now and I thort I felt some rain come. Down on my face. then all of a sudden it Becone to pore Down then I had to get under a tree Because I had not Bult a house yet so I got under this tree But I still got wet in the mornig when I woke up I was very wet But I said to myself They will get Dry In the sun. they I thort to my self I wander iF the coconut shells are full with water they wore then I went to the Trape and there was a Baby wild pig I left it in the Trap and went to Build a house or some kinde of a shelter. I put Bambo shoots and Banana leaves on Top and put them Round the side then I went to Find some vegterBles and I found a old pot and put some vedterBles and I got 4 stink's and put two gett gether and the other two Together and I put the pot on the fire and then I went and made a spare to hill the wild pig with. I made The spare out of Bambo shoots and and a very sharpe starve. and went over to the wild Big and Just chunked the spare Down the hole and Draged it out.

Here it is again

When I was on an island I was very frightened at first, but then I went further on the sand. I saw some goats. At first I got a coconut, and I opened it with a sharp stone, then I took the milk out of it and I put the coconut shells on the sand and I was waiting for it to rain. While I was waiting for it to rain I found some bamboo shoots and thought to make a trap. Then I started to make a hole with my hands, and after I'd done that, I put some banana leaves over the hole, and I waited and waited until something came but nothing came at all. I was very hungry, so I went and got some bananas. It was getting dark now, and I felt some rain come down on my face. All of a sudden it began to pour down, then I had to get under a tree because I had not built a house yet. So I got under a tree, but I still got wet. In the morning when I woke up I was very wet, but I said to myself 'They will dry in the sun.' Then I thought to myself 'I wonder if the coconut shells are full with water?' – They were. Then I went to the trap and there was a baby wild pig. I left it in the trap and went to build a house or some kind of shelter. I put bamboo shoots and banana leaves on top and put them round the side. Then I went to find some vegetables and I found an old pot, and put some vegetables in, and I got four sticks, and put two together, and I put the pot on the fire, and then I went and made a spear to kill the wild pig with. I made the spear out of bamboo shoots and a very sharp stone, and went over to the wild pig, and just chucked the spear down the hole and dragged it out.

APPENDIX V

British Publishers' Addresses

Allman and Son Ltd., 17–19 Foley St., London W1A 1DR
Arnold, E.J. and Son Ltd., Butterley Street, Leeds LS10 1AX
Arnold, Edward (Publishers) Ltd., Woodlands Park Ave., Maidenhead, Berks.
Athena Reproductions, Bishops Stortford, Herts.
Baker (John) Ltd., 35 Bedford Row, WC1R 4JH
Bell and Howell, Alperton House, Bridgewater Road, Wembley, Middlesex
Benn, Ernest, Ltd., Sovereign Way, Tonbridge, Kent TN9 1RW
Black, A. and C., 35 Bedford Row, London WC1R 4JH
Blackie and Son Ltd., Book Centre Ltd., Southport, Lancs.
Blackwell, Basil, Ltd., 5 Alfred Street, Oxford OX1 4HB
Blandford Press Ltd., Link House, West St., Poole, Dorset
Blond, 12 Caroline Place, London W2
Bodley Head, 9 Bow St., London WC2E 7AL
Brockhampton Press Ltd. (*now* Hodder and Stoughton Children's Books), Arlen House, Salisbury Rd., Leicester LE1 7QS
Burke Publishing Co. Ltd., 14 John St., London WC1N 2EJ
Butterworth and Co., 88 Kingsway, London WC2B 6AB
Cape, Jonathan, Ltd., 30 Bedford Sq., London WC1B 3EL
Cassell and Co. Ltd., 35 Red Lion Sq.,London WC1R 4SG
Chambers, W. and R., Ltd., 11 Thistle St., Edinburgh EH2 1DG
Chapman, Geoffrey Ltd., 35 Red Lion Sq.,London WC1R 4SG
Charles and Son Ltd., 55 West Regent St., Glasgow G2 2DU
Chatto and Windus, The Hogarth Press, Ltd., 40–42 William IV St., London WC2N 4DF
Collins, 14 St James's Pl., London SW1A 1PS
Common Ground (1951) Ltd., 44 Fulham Rd., London SW3
Crosby Lockwood Staples Ltd. *see* Granada Publishing Ltd.
Cuisenaire Co. Ltd., 40 Silver St., Reading, Berks. RG1 2SU
Davis and Moughton Ltd., Ludgate House, 23 Waterloo Place, Leamington Spa, Warks.
Dent, J.M. and Sons, Ltd., 26 Albemarle Street, London W1X 4QY

Educational Evaluation Enterprises, 1st Floor, 5 Marsh St., Bristol BS1 4AE
Educational Productions Ltd., Bradford Rd., East Ardsley, Wakefield, W. Yorks. WF3 2JN
Educational Supply Association (now ESA Creative Learning Ltd.), Pinnacles, Harlow, Essex CM19 5AY
Evans Bros Ltd., Montague House, Russell Sq.,London WC1B 5BX
Faber and Faber Ltd., 3 Queen Sq., London WC1N 3AW
Galt, James and Co. Ltd., 30/31 Gt Marlborough St., London W1
George's, 89 Park St., Bristol, BS1 5PW
Gibson, Robert and Sons Ltd., 17 Fitzroy Pl., Glasgow G3
Ginn and Co. Ltd., Elsinore Hse, Buckingham St., Aylesbury, Bucks.
Granada Publishing Ltd., 29 Frogmore, St Albans, Herts.
Grant Educational Co. Ltd., 91 Union St., Glasgow
Hamilton (Hamish) Ltd., 90 Gt Russell Street, London WC1B 3PT
Hamlyn Group, Astronaut Hse, Hounslow Rd., Feltham, Middlesex
Harrap, George G. and Co. Ltd., 182–4 High Holborn, London WC1V 7AX
Hart-Davis Educational *see* Granada Publishing Ltd.
Heinemann Educational, 48 Charles St., London W1X 8AH
Hodder & Stoughton, St Paul's House, Warwick Lane, London EC4P 4AH
Hodder & Stoughton Educational, P.O. Box 702, Mill Rd., Dunton Green, Sevenoaks, Kent
Holmes McDougall, 137–141 Leith Walk, Edinburgh EH6 8NS
Hope (Thomas) & Sankey Hudson Ltd., St Philip's Drive, Royton, Oldham OL2 6AG
Hulton Educational Publications Ltd., Raans Rd., Amersham, Bucks.
Hutchinson, 3 Fitzroy Sq.,London W1P 6JD
Initial Teaching Alphabet Foundation, 39 Parker St., London WC2B 5PB
Initial Teaching Publishing Co., 39 Parker St., London WC2B 5PB
Invicta Plastics Ltd., New St., Oadby, Leics.
Johnston & Bacon, 35 Red Lion Sq., London WC1R 4SG
Kaye & Ward Ltd., 21 New St., London EC2M 4NT
Ladybird Books Ltd., Loughborough, Leics.
Learning Development Aids, Park Works, Norwich Rd., Wisbech, Cambs.
Lewis (H.K.) & Co. Ltd., 136 Gower St., London WC1E 6BS
Longman Group Ltd., Pinnacles, Harlow, Essex
Lutterworth Press, Luke House, Barnham Rd., Guildford, Surrey
Macdonald & Co. Ltd., B.P.C. Publishers Service Centre, Paulton, Bristol BS18 5LQ

McGraw-Hill Co. Ltd., Shoppenhangers Rd., Maidenhead, Berks.
Macmillan Publishers Ltd., Houndmills, Basingstoke, Hants.
Matthews, Drew & Shelbourne Ltd., 78 High Holborn, London WC1
3M Company Ltd., 3M House, Wigmore St., London W1
Methuen, 11 New Fetter Lane, London EC4P 4EE
Mills & Boon Ltd., 17–19 Foley St., London W1A 1DR
Moor Platt Press, 294 Chorley New Road, Horwich, Lancs.
Muller, Frederick, Ltd., Victoria Works, Edgware Rd., London NW2 6LE
Nelson, Thomas & Sons, Lincoln Way, Windmill Rd., Sunbury-on-Thames, Middx.
Newnes *see* Butterworth
N.F.E.R., The Mere, Upton Park, Slough, Bucks. (Test Division: 2 Jennings Buildings, Thames Ave., Windsor, Berks.)
Nisbet, James & Co. Ltd., Digswell Place, Welwyn Garden City, Herts.
Oliver & Boyd Ltd., 23 Ravelston Terrace, Edinburgh EH4 3TJ
Oxford University Press, Walton St., Oxford
Panther *see* Granada Publishing Ltd.
Parrish, 2 Portman St., London W1
Penguin Education, Harmondsworth, Middlesex
Pergamon Press Ltd., Headington Hill Hall, Oxford OX3 0BW
Philip & Tacey Ltd., North Way, Andover, Hants.
Philip, George & Son Ltd., 12–14 Long Acre, London WC2E 9LP
Philograph – Philip & Tacey Ltd.
Pitman Publishing Ltd., 39 Parker St., London WC2B 5PB
Purnell-Bancroft, B.P.C. Publishers Service Centre, Paulton, Bristol BS18 5LQ
Reader's Digest, 25 Berkeley Sq., London W1X 6AB
Remedial Supply Co., Dixon St., Wolverhampton, Staffs.
Schofield & Sims Ltd., 35 St John's Rd., Huddersfield, Yorks.
Scholastic Publications, 161 Fulham Road, London, SW3 6SW
Science Research Associates, Newtown Rd., Henley-on-Thames, Oxon.
Scott Foresman & Co., 32 West Street, Brighton BN1 2RT
Special Ed. Publications, Street Cottage, North Waltham, Basingstoke, Hants.
Stillit Books Ltd., 72 New Bond St., London W1Y OQY
Studio Vista, 35 Red Lion Sq., London WC1R 4SG
Transworld Publishers Ltd., Century House, 61–63 Uxbridge Rd., London W5
Tull Graphic Ltd., 84 Teesdale St., London E2
Ulverscroft Foundation, The Green, Bradgate Rd., Anstey, Leics.

University of London Press Ltd., *now* Hodder & Stoughton Educational
Visual Publications, 197 Kensington High Street, W8 6BB
Ward, Edmund, *now* Kaye & Ward
Ward Lock Educational, 116 Baker St., London W1M 2BB
Warne (Frederick) & Co. Ltd., 40 Bedford Sq., London WC1B 3HE
Watts (Franklin) Ltd., 1 Vere St., London W1M OAD
Wayland (Publishers) Ltd., 49 Lansdowne Place, Hove, E. Sussex
Weidenfeld & Nicolson, 11 St Johns Hill, London SW11 1 XA
Weston Woods Studios Ltd., P.O. Box 2, Henley-on-Thames, Oxon.
Wheaton, Customer Service Dept., Pergamon Press Ltd., Headington Hill Hall, Oxford OX3 OBW
Wills & Hepworth Ltd. *see* Ladybird Books
World's Work, The Windmill Press, Kingswood, Tadworth, Surrey

Useful Addresses

National Association for Remedial Education, The Editor, 20, Hanbury Cresent, Penn, Wolverhampton. (Membership – Quarterly, *Remedial Education.)*

Association for Special Education, L.J. Macdonald, Secretary, 19, Hamilton Road, Wallasey, Cheshire. (Membership – Quarterly, *Special Education,* & Newsletter.)

National Foundation for Educational Research (N.F.E.R.), Test Agency, The Mere, Upton Park, Slough, Bucks. (Mainly tests.)

College of Special Education, 85, Newman Street, London, W1P 3LD. (Set up by Guild No. 5. Advice to teachers, cheap notes on various aspects of remedial teaching, maladjustment, etc. Catalogue free).

Guild of Teachers of Backward Children, Minster Chambers, Southwell, Nottingham. (Quarterly Journal *Forward Trends.)*

Centre for the Teaching of Reading, c/o Betty Roots, 29, Eastern Avenue, Reading, Berks. RG1 5 RU. (Exhibitions of materials, courses, in-service, etc., cheap pamphlets on teaching reading, catalogue.)

West Sussex County Psychological Service, Education Department, County Hall, Chichester, Sussex. (*Assessment of Intelligence, Gifted Children, Teaching Non-Readers, Phonics, Reading Schemes, Assessment of Reading.*)

United Kingdom Reading Association, 63, Laurel Grove, Sunderland, Co. Durham, SR2 9EE. (Membership – Journal, *Reading* – three a year.)

APPENDIX VI

List of Schools Council Research and Development Projects for use with ROSLA children

Humanities Curriculum Project

War and Society Education The Family Relations between the Sexes People and Work Poverty Law and Order Living in Cities Race Relations	Author: L.A. Stenhouse Published by Heinemann Educational Books

Integrated Studies Project

Exploration Man Living Together Communicating with Others Development in West Africa Groups in Society Man-made Man	Author: D. W. Bolam Published by Oxford University Press

Mathematics for the Majority

Mathematical Experience Machines Mechanisms and Mathematics Assignment Systems	Author: P. Floyd Published by Chatto & Windus

Moral Education	Author: P. McPhail, published by Longman, Green & Co.
Nuffield Secondary Science	Author: Mrs. H. Misselbrook Published by Longman, Green & Co.
Project Technology	Published by Project Technology Handbooks, Project Briefs – Heinemann Educational Books
Technology & Man	Published by Blackie & University of London Press

A-level Course Elements	Published by English Universities Press
The Next Two Years (A Progress Report)	Author: G. B. Harrison Published by The Schools Council

Religious Education in Secondary Schools (Working Paper 36) Published by Eyre-Methuen

APPENDIX VII

American Books and Materials for and about Slow Learners

A. ENGLISH AND GENERAL READING

Interest Level Grades 5–8; Instructional Level Grades 4–5–6

Author	Title	Publisher	Reading Level	Interest Level
Beauchamp et al	*Discovering My World(I)*	Scott, Foresman	4–5	5–6–7
Bunce, ed.	*O. Henry's Best Stories*	Globe	4–5	6–7–8
Cass	*How We Live* (Adult Educ. Series)	Noble and Noble	4–5	7–8–9
Commager, H.S.	*1st Book of Amer. Rev.*	Watts	4–5	6–7–8
Dale	*Stories for Today*	Govt. Printing Office	4–5	6–7–8
Heavey & Stuart	*Teen Age Tales*	Heath	4–5–6	6–7–8
Kottmeyer (ed.)	*Greek & Roman Myths*	Webster, McGraw-Hill	4–5	6–7–8
Kottmeyer (ed.)	*Old Testament Stories*	Webster, McGraw-Hill	5	5–6–7
Clark	*First Men in Space*	Follett	5	5–6
Dalgliesh	*The Davenports are at Dinner*	Scribner	5	5–6
Dressell & Hirsch-Zeno	*Strange Paper Glue*	Row, Peterson	5	6–7
Dressell & Hirsch-Zeno	*Find Formula X-48*	Row, Peterson	5	6–7
Gelman	*Football Fury*	Doubleday	5	5–6
George, Jean	*Julie of the Wolves* *My Side of the Mountain*	G. K. Hall	6	5–9
Guthridge	*Tom Edison*	Merrill	5	6–7
Ketcham	*Dennis the Menace*	Holt Rinehart	5	5–6–7
Orbaan	*Civil War Soldier*	Doubleday	5	6–7

Parker	*Carol Heiss Olympic Queen*	Doubleday	5	5–6
Rambeau	*Mystery Series*	Harr Wagner Div. Field Enterprises	4–5	5–6–7
Stevenson	*Booker T. Washington*	Merrill	5	5–6–7
Stevenson	*Clara Barton*	Merrill	5	5–6–7
Stevenson	*George Washington Carver*	Merrill	5	5–6–7
Stevenson, R. L.	*Treasure Island* (adapted)	Scott, Foresman	5	6–7
Van Riper	*Lou Gehrig*	Merrill	5	5–6
Weil	*Franklin Roosevelt*	Merrill	5	6–7
Wilson	*Ernie Pyle*	Merrill	5	6–7

List of Simplified Classics: Instructional Level 5–8; Interest Level 5–11

Author	Title	Publisher	Reading Level	Interest Level
Defoe	*Robinson Crusoe*	Random House	5	5–6–7
Dickens	*A Tale of Two Cities*	McGraw-Hill	6	6–7–8
Dumas	*The Count of Monte Cristo*	Webster-McGraw-Hill	5–6	6–7–8
Dumas	*The Three Musketeers* (adapted)	Webster-McGraw-Hill	5–6	6–7–8
Hugo	*Les Miserables*	Globe Books	5–6	7–8–9
Ed. Kottmeyer	*Robin Hood*	Webster-McGraw-Hill	4–5	5–6–7
Melville	*Moby Dick* (adapt.)	Sanborn	5–6	6–7–8
Poe	*Stories*	Webster-McGraw-Hill	6–7	7–8–9–10–11
Scott	*Ivanhoe*	Webster-McGraw-Hill	6	7–8–9–10
Swift	*Gulliver Stories*	Garrard	5	5–6–7
Twain	*Tom Sawyer*	Scott, Foresman	5	5–6–7
Verne	*Around the World in 80 Days*	Scott, Foresman	5	6–7–8
Wallace	*Ben Hur*	Wallace	6	7–8–9–10

More advanced reading level

Author	Title	Publisher	Reading Level	Interest Level
Austen	*Pride and Prejudice*	Globe Books	8	8–9–10–11
Coolidge	*Hercules*	Scholastic Press	7	7–8–9–10
Cooper	*The Last of the Mohicans*	Scott, Foresman	7	7–8–9–10–11
Dickens	*David Copperfield*	Scott, Foresman	7	8–9–10
Dickens	*A Tale of Two Cities*	Laidlaw	8	8–9–10–11
Eliot	*Silas Marner*	Scott, Foresman	7	8–9–10

Eliot	*Silas Marner*	Globe	8	8–9–10
Eliot	*The Mill on the Floss*	Globe	8	8–9–10
Hawthorne	*The Scarlet Letter*	Globe	8	8–9–10–11
Hugo	*Les Miserables*	Laidlaw	8	8–9–10
Kipling	*Captains Courageous*	Scott, Foresman	7	8–9–10
Melville	*Moby Dick*	Scott, Foresman	7	7–8–9–10
Shakespeare	*Julius Caesar*	Globe	7	8–9–10–11

For Severely Impaired Readers

Willis and His Friends, by Turner, Low, and Jacob: Fearon Lear–Siegler, Belmont, Calif.
Cartoon stories, interesting to grades 5–8, reading level grades 3–5.

Hip Readers, by Pollack: Book Lab Inc., 1449 37th Street, Brooklyn, N.Y.
Cartoon type reading interesting to grades 5–8, reading level grades 1–2–3.

Sullivan Reading Program, Webster-McGraw-Hill, N.Y.
Interesting to young adults, reading level graduating from grade 2 up.

Checkered Flag Series, Field Enterprises, 396 Springfield Ave., Berkely Hts., N.Y.
Interest level grades 4–8, reading level grades 2–5.

Phonetic Readers

Educators Publishing Service, 75 Moulton St., Cambridge, Mass.
Reading Level 3–9, Interest Level 4–7

Pacemaker Grades 4–7 $1.50 each
True Adventure Series
Fearon/Lear-Siegler, Belmont, Calif.

Pacemaker Story Books $1.50
Many titles
Fearon/Lear-Siegler, Belmont, Calif.

For Severely Impaired Spellers

Typing Program
Ring – n – Key, Play – – Talk: International Hdqtrs., Oklahoma City, Okla.

Johnny Right to Read Program by Ray Laurita & Philip Trembley:
Academic Therapy, 1539 Fourth St., San Rafael, Calif.

A total program of sound symbol association skills to develop word attack and discrimination skills.

Auxiliary Workbook Materials for Junior High School & Grades 9–10

Specific Skill Mastery – Reading Skills
Specific Skill Series: Levels D-E-R
by Richard A. Boning: Barnell Loft, Rockville Center, N. Y.

a. *Locating the Answer*:
b. *Following Directions*:
c. *Getting the Main Idea*:
d. *Drawing Conclusions*:
e. *Getting the Facts*:
f. *Using the Context*:

Standard Test Lessons in Reading by Wm. McCall and Lelah M. Crabbs
Levels A, B, C, D, E
Bureau of Publications, Columbia University, N. Y.
Reading Exercises by Arthur I. Gates and C. C. Pearson:
Teachers College Press, Teachers College, Columbia University, New York
What is the Story About? (Elementary 3–6, Intermediate & Advanced, Gr. 6–12)
Can You Follow Directions? (Elementary 3–6, Intermediate & Advanced, Gr. 6–12)
Reading for Meaning by Guiler and Coleman:
J.B. Lippincott Co., New York, various levels
Scope Reading Skills Series
Dimensions
Trackdown
Countdown
Scholastic Books, Englewood, New Jersey

Books for Use Grades 3–10 to develop Word Attack

Conquests in Reading – Word Attack & Reading Skills, by Kottmeyer & Ware, Webster Div., McGraw-Hill Co., N. Y. (pp. 96-end of book)
Mott Language Skills Program "*Word Attack*", Book 160, 600A-B, 900A-B
Allied Educational Distribution Center
P. O. Box 78, Galien, Michigan

B. SOCIAL STUDIES READING

American History

American Adventures, a new American History Program for Slow Readers
School Social Studies Center
904 Sylvan Avenue, Englewood Cliffs, New Jersey 07632
Paperbacks, reading level grades 5–7, interest level 6–12

M Numbers	*Title*	*New Price*
8969	*A Nation Conceived and Dedicated, Vol. I*	$1.65
8970	*Teaching Guide*	1.00
8971	*Record*	4.15
8972	*History Lab Program*	6.50
8973	*Poster Set*	3.95
8974	*Old Hate – New Hope, Vol. II*	1.65
8975	*Teaching Guide*	1.00
8976	*Record*	4.15
8977	*History Lab Program*	6.50
8978	*Poster Set*	3.95
8979	*Between Two Wars, Vol. III*	1.65
8980	*Teaching Guide*	1.00
8981	*Record*	4.15
8982	*History Lab Program*	6.50
8983	*Poster Set*	3.95
8984	*Yesterday, Today, Tomorrow, Vol. IV*	1.65
8985	*Teaching Guide*	1.00
8986	*Record*	4.15
8987	*History Lab Program*	6.50
8988	*Poster Set*	3.95

Skill text on the U.S. Constitution: Charles E. Merrill Co.
Reading level 5–7, interest level 5–10.
The Free and the Brave, Graff, Rand McNally Co.
Diamond Edition at level 6 reading.
Regular Edition at level 8–10 reading.
Study Lessons in Our Nations History, by Abramowitz, Jack:
Follett Educational Corp., Chicago.
Reading level 5–7, interest level 6–10.

General Topics

A.E.P. Booklets: American Education Publications
(400) Education Center, Columbus, Ohio, 43216
Interest level ranges from grade 5–12
These are small booklets including interesting case study materials, having high interest level.

A.E.P. Series grades 5–9

The American Revolution
Crisis of Law & Change

The Railroad Era
Business Competition & the Public Interest

Religious Freedom
Minority Faiths & Majority Rule

The Rise of Organized Labor
Worker Security & Employer Rights

The Immigrant's Experience
Cultural Variety & the "Melting Pot"
Negro Views of America
The Legacy of Oppression
Municipal Politics
Interest Groups & the Government
Taking a Stand
A Guide to Clear Discussion of Public Issues

Community Change
Law, Politics & Social Attitudes

Rights of the Accused
Criminal Procedure & Public Security

The Lawsuit
Legal Reasoning & Civil Procedure

Colonial Kenya
Exploitation or Progress?

Communist China
Communal Progress & Individual Freedom

Nazi Germany
Social Forces & Personal Responsibility

20th Century Russia
Agents of the Revolution

Status
Achievement & Social Values

The Civil War
Crisis in Federalism
Race and Education
Integration & Community Control
The New Deal
Free Enterprise & Public Planning
The Limits of War
National Policy & World Conscience

Organizations Among Nations
The Search for World Order

Science and Public Policy
Uses and Control of Knowledge

Diplomacy and International Law
Alternatives to War

Revolution and World Politics
The Search for National Independence

World Affairs

These pamphlets are short, interesting materials involving case studies and role playing activities.

		Grade Level
(301)	Current Events Yearbooks, 1970–71	7–12
(302)	Our Presidents and Their Times	7–9
(306)	Map Skills for Today's Geography	7–9
(310)	Liberty under Law	7–12
(311)	Today's Economics	9–12
(312)	Anthropology in Today's World	7–12
(313)	Africa: Emerging Nations	7–12
(314)	Changing Latin America	7–12
(315)	Southeast Asia	7–12
(316)	China: Troubled Asian Giant	7–12
(317)	India and Pakistan	7–12
(318)	The Middle East	7–12
(319)	Japan	7–12
(340)	Know About Drugs	7–12
(362)	Our Polluted World	7–12
(364)	Physical Geography	7–12
(367)	Political Parties in the U.S.	7–12
(370)	The Conservation Story	7–12
(372)	Civilizations of Africa	7–12
(373)	Dissent and Protest	7–12
(374)	American Indians Today	7–12
(375)	The Soviet Union	7–12
(376)	The British Isles	7–12

New Public Issues Series: Harvard Social Studies Project

National Geographic $6.95 each
  Explorer Series Grades 4–10
  National Geographic Society, Washington, D. C. 20036

National Geographic World Traveller Magazine, 12 issues, $2.50 per year subscription, Grades 3–4 reading level, grades 5–7 interest level

Contemporary Affairs and Current Events

New York Times, Large Print Edition New York Times, 229 W. 43, N.Y.

Communique
  The Miami Herald, 1 Herald Plaza, Miami, Florida

This free publication helps teach students how to use the daily newspaper in the classroom and gain information.

Teaching Reading Skills Through the Newspaper, IRA Service Bulletin

Paul S. Amidon & Association
5408 Chicago Avenue South
Minneapolis, Minnesota
  Communications: The Problems Approach
  Personal Money Management

Dell Publications Company
750 Third Avenue
New York, N.Y. 10017
Narcotics: Nature's Dangerous Gift

Educational Activities, Inc.
P. O. Box 392
Freeport, New York
Capstone Lessons in American History
This is My Country (13 cassettes)

Follett Publishing Co.
Study Lessons in Our Nation's History
American History Study Lessons
Study Lessons on Documents of Freedom
World History Study Lessons

Globe Book Company, Inc.
175 Fifth Avenue
New York, N.Y. 10017
Exploring World History

Grolier Educational Corp.
Modern Consumer Education Kit

Western Publishing Company, Inc.
School and Library Dept.
160 Parish Drive
Waync, New Jersey 07470
Simulation Games
Ghetto
Consumer
Democracy
Economic System
Community Disaster
Life Career
Generation Gap

C. SCIENCE READING MATERIAL

		Interest Level	Reading Level
The How & Why Wonder Books:		6–9	5–6
Ecology			
Basic Inventions			
Weather			
Beginning Science			
The Human Body			
Rocks & Minerals			
Science Experiments			
Caves to Skyscrapers			
Atomic Energy			
Deserts			
Prices $1.00 to $3.59			
Wonder Books, Grosset & Dunlop, New York			
Basic Science Education Series: Unitext		5–8	4
Insect Parade			
Pebbles & Sea Shells			
The Aquarium			
Leaves			
Row Peterson & Co., Elmsford, N.Y.			
All About Books			
All About the Arctic & Antarctic		6–8	5–6
All About the Changing Rocks			
(Write for other titles)			
Random House, New York			
Life Nature Library			
Young Readers Edition, Life-Time			
Evolution	($1.50)	7–10	6–7
The Fishes			
The Earth			
Early Man			
The Sea			
The Reptiles			
The Desert			
The Primates			
The Universe			
The Mammals			
The Birds			
Animal Behavior			
A Short History of the Universe, by Gregor, A. S.			
Macmillan Co., New York		7–10	7
Prehistoric America, by White			
Random House, New York		7–10	6
The First Men in the World, by White			
Scholastic, New York		7–10	6
Xerox Education Division, Curriculum Programs			
600 Madison Ave. New York, N.Y.			
Science: A Process Approach			

D. SOURCES OF FURTHER READING MATERIALS

The Allied Education Council
P.O. Box 78
Galien, Michigan 49113
The Fitzhugh Plus Program elementary level
Spatial Organization Series
Language and Number Series
The Mott Basic Language Skills Program
Semi-Program Series – grades 1–8
Comprehension Series – grades 4–12
Series 900A, 900B
Sound and Structure

Allyn and Bacon
Piermont Road
Rockleigh, New Jersey 07647
Breakthrough Series:
Winners' Circle
Beyond the Block

American Education Publication
Education Center
Columbus, Ohio 43216
The English Language
Your English Skills
How to Study Workshop
20 Steps to Better Composition
The Magic of Words
How Words Use You
Levels of Meaning

Continental Press, Inc.
Elizabethtown, Pa. 17022
Crossword Puzzles for Reading – Thinking Skills
It's Your World (program)
Phonics and Word Analysis Skills (Grade 5)
Reading – Thinking Skills (Grade 6) Level 2
Language and Study Skills Program

EDL New Jersey, Inc.
3145 Bordentown Ave.
Parlin, New Jersey 08859
Learning 100, Levels BA to FA

Educators Publishing Service
75 Moulton St., Cambridge Mass.
Materials for Specific Language Disability according to linguistic approach
Spelling Workbooks (elementary, advanced) by Mildred Plumkett
The Spell of Words, by Elsie T. Rake (Grades 6–8)
Improving Word Skills, by Smith (Word Attack Skills, Gr. 6–10)
Solving Language Difficulties, by Steere, Peck and Kahn, (syllable analysis & rules of language, exceptions to the rules are taught as well).

The Structure of Words, by Rule (Linguistic approach to word analysis)
Basic English Sentence Patterns, by Helson (Sentence structure & composition)
Wordly Wise, by Hodkinson & Ornato, (Books 1–9, Gr. 4–12, vocabulary building with interesting exercises).
Vocabulary Builders (Books 1–9, vocabulary building with a literary contextual format for the youngster with academically stronger verbal skills but poorer recognition and vocabulary skills.)

Follett Publishing Co.
1010 W. Washington Blvd.
Chicago, Illinois 60607
Turner-Livingston Communication Series
The Television You Watch
The Phone Calls You Make
The Newspaper You Read
The Movies You See
The Letters You Write
The Language You Speak
Learning Your Language – One
Booklets (6 to a set)
Success in Language – A
Booklets (8 to a set)
Individualized English – Set J & H

Grolier Educational Corp.
575 Lexington Avenue
New York, N.Y. 10022
Modern English
TT 101 – Spelling
TT 102 – Punctuation

Harcourt, Brace and World
757 Third Avenue
New York, N.Y. 10022
English 2100: A Programmed Course in Grammar and Usage

Holt Rinehart and Winston, Inc.
383 Madison Ave.
New York, N.Y. 10017
Reading Skills

McGraw-Hill Book Company
330 West 42nd Street
New York, N.Y. 10036
Programmed Reading for Adults by Sullivan Associates

Prentice Hall, Inc.
U.S. Highway 9W
Englewood Cliffs, New Jersey 07632
Be a Better Reader, 2nd Ed. by Nila, Banton, Smith

Garrard Books,
Garrard Publishing Co.
Champaign, Ill., 61820
Reluctant Reader Series for Junior and Senior High School Reading, and good Social Studies books

Scholastic Magazines, Inc.
902 Sylvan Avenue
Englewood Cliffs, New Jersey 07632
30 Days to Better English
Scholastic Dictionary of Synonyms, Antonyms
20 Days to Better Spelling
Across and Down
Word Puzzles and Mysteries
Sprint
Reluctant Reader Library (50 books)

Science Research Associates, Inc.
259 East Erie Street
Chicago, Illinois 60611
Reading in High Gear
Reading Laboratory
How to Become a Better Reader
How to Improve Your Reading

Scott, Foresman
1900 East Lake Ave.
Glenview, Illinois 60025
Activity Concept English

J. Weston Walch
Portland, Maine 04104
Today's Words
Communications
Adventures in Practical English

E. GENERAL

Benefic Press
10300 West Roosevelt Road
Westchester, Ill. 60153
Success Oriented Learning Programmes

Field Educational Publications, Inc.
396 Springfield Ave.
Berkeley Heights, New Jersey 07922
Cyclo-Teacher Learning Aid

Opportunities for Learning
5024 Lankerskim Boulevard, Dept T5
North Hollywood, Calif. 91601
Selected Materials for Special Learners – basically learning games, kits, A.V. materials, mostly Primary level but also some Junior High

Frank E. Richards Publishing Co. Inc.
330 First Street, Box 370
Liverpool, New York 13088
Educational Materials for Special Education, Disadvantaged, Slow Learners and Basic Adult Education. Many things on Career Education.

Special Child Publications
4535 Union Bay Place N. E.
Seattle, Washington
Education as Therapy, by Elinor Mallinson
Other fine programs

Taplinger Publishing Co.
29 East Tenth St.
New York, N. Y. 10003
Wordless Workshop

John Wiley & Sons, Inc.
605 Third Ave.
New York, N. Y. 10016
Springboards Series
World History
American History
Human Rights: The American Scene
Biography
Programmed Instruction Materials
Study Skills
Thinking Metric
Spelling for Adults, Grades 10–11–12–P.G.

Books for the Blind
Large type editions of standard favorites are available at libraries

Talking Books
Cassette versions of many classics and contemporary books are available to the perceptually handicapped.

BIBLIOGRAPHY

A. AMERICAN

Baker, Bruce L. *et al., Steps to Independence. A Skills Training Series for Children with Special Needs*. Incl. *Early Self Help Skills*; *Intermediate Self Help Skills*; *Advanced Self Help Skills*; *Behavior Problems*; *Training Guide*. Research Press, 1976.

Bell, Peter, *Basic Teaching for Slow Learners,* Transatlantic, 1971.

Bruton, Milton *et al., Something's Wrong with my Child – A Parents Book about Children with Learning Disabilities,* HarBrace, 1973.

Cawley, John F. *et al., The Slow Learner and the Reading Problem,* C. C. Thomas, 1972.

Cushenberry, Donald C. and Gilreath, Kenneth J., *Effective Reading Instruction for Slow Learners,* C. C. Thomas, 1972.

Dobbs, Jack P., *Slow Learner and Music: A Handbook for Teachers,* O.U.P., 1966.

Ebersole, James *et al., Steps to Achievement for the Slow Learner,* Merrill, 1968.

Eden, D. J., *Mental Handicap,* Intl Pubns Service, 1975.

Educable Mentally Retarded Student in the Secondary School, NEA, 1975.

Gaddis, Edwin A., *Teaching the Slow Learner in the Regular Classroom,* Fearon, 1971.

Hayes, Marnell, *Oh Dear Someone Said 'Learning Disability',* Academic Therapy Pubns., 1975.

——*The Tuned-In, Turned-On Book,* Academic Therapy Pubns., 1974.

Heidemann, Mary A., *The Slow Learner in the Primary Grades,* Merrill, 1973.

Howitt, Lillian C., *Creative Techniques for Teaching the Slow Learner,* Lieber-Atherton, 1964.

Humphrey, J. H. and Sullivan, Dorothy D., *Teaching Slow Learners Through Active Games,* C. C. Thomas, 1973.

Ingram, Christine P., *Education of the Slow Learning Child,* Ronald, 1960.

Johnson, George O., *Education for the Slow Learners,* Prentice Hall, 1963.

Kahn, Charles H. *et al., Measure Up* (Illus. Special Education Set for slow learners, incl. Teachers' Manual), Fearon, 1968.

Kauffman, James M. and Hallahan, Daniel P., *Teaching Children with Learning Disabilities: Personal Perspectives,* Merrill, 1976.

Kephard, Newell, *Slow Learner in the Classroom,* Merrill, 1971.

Kronick, Doreen, *What About Me? The L. D. Adolescent,* Academic Therapy Pubns., 1975.

Long, Kate, *'Johnny's Such a Bright Boy, What a Shame He's Retarded',* Houghton Mifflin, 1977.

Lowell, Stephen S., *Coping with the Slow Learner,* J. Weston Walch, Publisher, Portland, Maine 04104, 1975.

Markoff, Annabell N., *Teaching Low Achieving Children Reading, Spelling and Handwriting. Developing Perceptual Skills with the Graphic Symbols of the Language,* C. C. Thomas, 1976.

Owen, J., *Classroom Activities for Motivating Understanding Children,* Ctr Appl Res., 1974.

Roswell, Florence and Natchez, Gladys, *Reading Disability, Diagnosis and Treatment,* Basic Books, 1965.

Shelton, Baker O., *Teaching and Guiding the Slow Learner,* Prentice Hall, 1971.

The Slow Learner in Mathematics 1972, National Council of Teachers of Mathematics, 1201 Sixteenth St. NW, Washington D. C. 20036.

Smith, Bert K., *Your Nonlearning Child,* Beacon Press.

Stevenson, Nancy, *The Natural Way to Reading. A How to Method for Parents of Slow Learners, Dyslexic and Learning Disabled Children,* Little, 1974.

Wallace, Gerald and Kauffman, James, *Teaching Children with Learning Problems,* Merrill, 1973.

Weiss, Helen T. and Martin S., *A Survival Manual: Case Studies and Suggestions for the Learning Disabled Teenager,* Treehouse Associates, Box 568, Great Barrington, Mass. 01230, 1974.

Younie, William J., *Instructional Approaches to Slow Learning,* Tchrs Coll., 1967.

B. BRITISH

Anastasie, A., *Psychological Testing,* Macmillan, 1968.

Bell, Peter, *Basic Teaching for Slow Learners,* Muller.

Berg, Leila, *Look at Kids,* Penguin.

Biggs, Edith, *Freedom to Learn,* C.U.P.

Brierly and Dufton, *An Equal Chance,* Routledge & Kegan Paul.

Buckman, Peter, ed., *Education without Schools,* Souvenir Press.

Butcher, H.J., *Human Intelligence,* Methuen, 1968.

Cave, Ronald G., *Partnership for Change,* Ward Lock.

Clegg, Alec and Megson, Barbara, *Children in Distress,* Penguin.

Craft, Raynor and Cohen, *Linking Home and School,* Longmans.

Ellis, James, *The Slow to Learn,* Priory Press.

Goodacre, Elizabeth, *School and Home,* N.F.E.R.

Hall, Julian, ed., *Children's Rights,* Panther.

Hannam, Charles, *Young Teachers and Reluctant Learners,* Penguin.

Holt, John, *How Children Fail,* Penguin.

The Underachieving School, Penguin.

Hoyle, Eric, *The Role of the Teacher,* Routledge & Kegan Paul.
Jones, Ann, *School Counselling in Practice,* Ward Lock.
Klein, *Working with Groups,* Heinemann.
McGeeney, Patrick, *Parents Are Welcome,* Longmans.
Miller, Derek, *The Age Between,* Hutchinson.
Reisman, David, *The Lonely Crowd,* Yale University Press.
Rowe, Albert, *The School as a Guidance Community,* Pearson Press.
Schaffer, M.R., *The Growth of Sociability,* Penguin.
Sharp, John, *Open School,* Dent.
Shields, Robert W., *A Cure for Delinquents,* Heinemann.
Sprott, W.J.H. *Human Groups,* Penguin.
Stoneman, Colin, and Rubenstein, David, Eds., *Education for Democracy,* Penguin.
Storr, Anthony, *The Integrity of the Personality,* Penguin.
Tansley, A.E. *Reading and Remedial Reading,* Routledge & Kegan Paul.
Weber, Kenneth, *Yes They Can,* Methuen.
Williams, Francis, *Children with Specific Learning Difficulties,* Pergamon.

NOTES